Microsoft®
Windows® XP
Illustrated Introductory

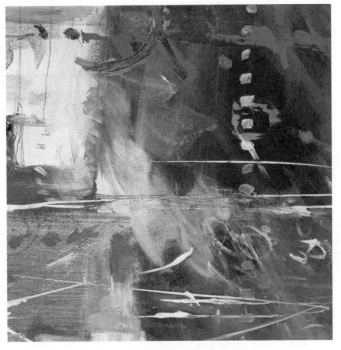

Steven M. Johnson

**COURSE
TECHNOLOGY**
™
THOMSON LEARNING

Australia • Canada • Mexico • Singapore • Spain • United Kingdom • United States

Microsoft ® Windows ® XP—Illustrated Introductory
Steven M. Johnson

Managing Editor:	**Editorial Assistant:**	**Composition House:**
Nicole Jones Pinard	Elizabeth M. Harris	GEX Publishing Services
Senior Product Manager:	**Production Editor:**	**QA Manuscript Reviewers:**
Emily Heberlein	Karen Jacot	Christian Kunciw, Harris Bierhoff
Associate Product Manager:	**Developmental Editor:**	**Text Designer:**
Christina Kling Garrett	Jennifer T. Campbell	Joseph Lee, Black Fish Design

The Illustrated Series Vision

Teaching and writing about computer applications can be extremely rewarding and challenging. How do we engage students and keep their interest? How do we teach them skills that they can easily apply on the job? As we set out to write this book, our goals were to develop a textbook that:

- works for a beginning student

- provides varied, flexible and meaningful exercises and projects to reinforce the skills

- serves as a reference tool

- makes your job as an educator easier, by providing resources above and beyond the textbook to help you teach your course

Our popular, streamlined format is based on advice from instructional designers and customers. This flexible design presents each lesson on a two-page spread, with step-by-step instructions on the left, and screen illustrations on the right. This signature style, coupled with high-caliber content, provides a comprehensive yet manageable introduction to Microsoft Windows XP — it is a teaching package for the instructor and a learning experience for the student.

ACKNOWLEDGMENTS

Once again, it has been a wonderful experience working with the talented and professional people at Course Technology. I would like to especially thank Jennifer Campbell for making this book easier to read, understand, and follow. I would also like to thank the manuscript reviewers, Rebekah May and Tracy Miller, for their helpful feedback during the writing process. And, most importantly, I would like to thank my wife, Holly, and three children JP, Brett, and Hannah for their support and encouragement during the project.

Steven Johnson

Preface

Welcome to *Microsoft Windows XP—Illustrated Introductory*. This highly visual text offers users an introduction to Windows XP, covering both the Home and Professional versions. It also serves as an excellent reference for future use.

► Organization and Coverage

This text contains eight units, which cover basic through intermediate Windows XP software skills. Students learn how to work with Windows programs, manage files and folders, customize Windows using the Control Panel, maintain their computers, explore the Internet with Microsoft Internet Explorer, and exchange mail and news using Outlook Express. A comprehensive appendix covers the new features of Windows XP and differences between the Home and Professional versions, as well as how to install Windows XP.

► About this Approach

What makes the Illustrated approach so effective at teaching software skills? It's quite simple. Each skill is presented on two facing pages, with the step-by-step instructions on the left page, and large screen illustrations on the right. Students can focus on a single skill without having to turn the page. This unique design makes information extremely accessible and easy to absorb, and provides a great reference for after the course is over. This hands-on approach also makes it ideal for both self-paced and instructor-led classes.

Each lesson, or "information display," contains the following elements shown in the sample two-page spread to the right.

Easy-to-follow introductions to every lesson focus on a single concept to help students get the point quickly.

Each 2-page spread focuses on a single skill or concept.

Paintbrush icons introduce the real-world case study used throughout the book.

Windows XP

Using Personal Folders

Windows makes it easy to manage the personal and business files and folders you work with everyday with a set of *personal folders*. My Documents is a personal folder, which contains additional personal folders, such as My Pictures, My Music, and My Videos. Depending on previous installation, devices installed or other users, your personal folders might differ. The contents of your personal folders are private, unless you decide to share the contents with others who use your computer. Windows creates personal folders for everyone on your computer to make sure the contents of personal folders remain private. Each personal folder is identified by the user's name. For example, if John Casey and an associate Shawn Brooks use the same computer, there are two sets of personal folders, one named John Casey's Documents and another named Shawn Brooks' Documents. When John logs on to the computer, his personal folders appear as My Documents and Shawn's appear as Shawn Brooks' Documents, but John cannot access them. John wants to open his personal folders and find out more about their functionality.

Steps

1. Click the **Start button** on the taskbar, then click **My Documents**
   The My Documents window opens, as shown in Figure D-17.

QuickTip
To open the My Pictures folder from the Start Menu, click the Start button, then click My Pictures.

2. Double-click the **My Pictures folder**
   The My Pictures window opens, displaying the contents of the folder as thumbnails. A thumbnail is a miniature image of the contents of a file; thumbnails are often used to quickly browse through multiple images. If the folder doesn't contain images, Windows inserts icons instead of thumbnails.

3. Double-click the **Sample Pictures folder**
   The Sample Pictures window opens, displaying the contents of the picture folder as a filmstrip, as shown in Figure D-18. Filmstrip is a special view, located on the Views button or View menu, available only for folders with many pictures.

QuickTip
To rotate pictures in Filmstrip view, click the Rotate Clockwise button or the Rotate Counterclockwise button.

4. Click the **Next Image (Right Arrow) button** until the last image in the Sample Pictures folder appears in the filmstrip

5. Click the **Back button** on the Standard Buttons toolbar twice to display the My Documents folder

6. Double-click the **My Videos folder**
   The My Videos folder opens, displaying the contents of the folder as thumbnails. For videos, the first frame appears in the thumbnail.

TABLE D-1: Picture tasks in the My Pictures folder

picture task	description
View as a slide show	Displays a full screen version of each picture in the folder for five seconds; click buttons on the Slide Show toolbar to start, pause, and stop the show
Order prints online	Opens the Online Print Ordering Wizard, which helps you order prints of your digital photographs over the Internet
Print this picture or Print the selected pictures	Opens the Photo Printing Wizard, which helps you format and print photographs from a digital camera or scanner
Set as desktop background	Sets the selected picture as the desktop background
Show for pictures online	Opens the Windows XP Pictures Online Web site in your Web browser, where you can find and download pictures over the Internet

► WINDOWS XP D-14 **CUSTOMIZING FILE AND FOLDER MANAGEMENT**

Hints as well as troubleshooting advice, right where you need them — next to the step itself.

Tables provide quickly accessible summaries of key terms, toolbar buttons, or keyboard alternatives connected with the lesson material. Students can refer easily to this information when working on their own projects at a later time.

Clear step-by-step directions explain how to complete the specific task. What students will type is in green.

Every lesson features large-size, full-color illustrations, bringing the lesson concepts to life.

FIGURE D-17: My Documents folder

General file and folder task links

Personal folders; yours might differ

FIGURE D-18: Sample Pictures folder

Picture specific task links

Buttons to display and modify pictures

Filmstrip view

Pictures in filmstrip

CLUES TO USE

Using the Shared Documents folder

Shared folders are related to your personal folders on a shared computer. They provide a place for you to make files, pictures, and music available to everyone who uses your computer. Your personal folders: My Documents, My Pictures, My Music, and My Videos each have a shared counterpart: Shared Documents, Shared Pictures, etc., in which you can copy files and folders to share with others. To share files and folders on your computer, click the Start button on the taskbar, click My Documents, click the file or folder you want to share, then drag the file or folder to Shared Documents in the left pane under Other Places. To share pictures and music on your computer, open My Documents, double-click the My Pictures or My Music folder, click the file or folder you want to share, click Move this file or Move this folder to open the Move Items dialog box, click the Shared Documents folder, click Shared Pictures or Shared Music, then click Move.

Clues to Use boxes provide concise information that either expands on one component of the major lesson skill or describes an independent task that is in some way related to the major lesson skill.

▶ What kinds of assignments are included in the book? At what level of difficulty?

The lesson assignments use Wired Coffee, a fictional coffee company, as the case study. The assignments on the blue pages at the end of each unit increase in difficulty. Project files and case studies, with international examples, provide a great variety of interesting and relevant business applications for skills. Assignments include:

- **Concepts Reviews** include multiple choice, matching, and screen identification questions.

- **Skills Reviews** provide additional hands-on, step-by-step reinforcement.

- **Independent Challenges** are case projects requiring critical thinking and application of the skills learned in the unit. The Independent Challenges increase in difficulty, with the first Independent Challenge in each unit being the easiest (most step-by-step with detailed instructions). Independent Challenges 2-4 become increasingly open-ended, requiring more independent thinking and problem solving.

- **Visual Workshops** show a completed file and require that the file be created without any step-by-step guidance, involving problem solving and an independent application of the unit skills.

▶ What online learning options are available to accompany this book?

Options for this title include a testbank in WebCT and Blackboard ready formats to make assessment using one of these platforms easy to manage. Visit www.course.com for more information on our online learning materials.

Instructor Resources

The Instructor's Resource Kit (IRK) CD is Course Technology's way of putting the resources and information needed to teach and learn effectively into your hands. All the components are available on the IRK, (pictured below), and many of the resources can be downloaded from www.course.com.

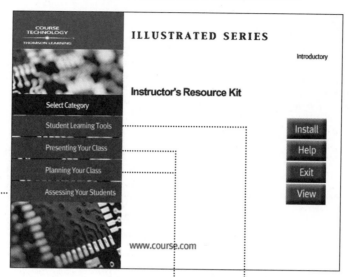

ASSESSING YOUR STUDENTS

Solution Files
Solution Files are Project Files completed with comprehensive sample answers. Use these files to evaluate your students' work. Or, distribute them electronically or in hard copy so students can verify their own work.

ExamView
ExamView is a powerful testing software package that allows you to create and administer printed, computer (LAN-based), and Internet exams. ExamView includes hundreds of questions that correspond to the topics covered in this text, enabling students to generate detailed study guides that include page references for further review. The computer-based and Internet testing components allow students to take exams at their computers, and also save you time by grading each exam automatically.

PRESENTING YOUR CLASS

Figure Files
Figure Files contain all the figures from the book in .bmp format. Use the figure files to create transparency masters or in a PowerPoint presentation.

STUDENT TOOLS

Project Files and Project Files List
To complete some of the units in this book, your students will need **Project Files**. Put them on a file server for students to copy. The Project Files are available on the Instructor's Resource Kit CD-ROM, the Review Pack, and can also be downloaded from www.course.com.

Instruct students to use the **Project Files List** at the end of the book. This list gives instructions on copying and organizing files.

PLANNING YOUR CLASS

Instructor's Manual
Available as an electronic file, the Instructor's Manual is quality-assurance tested and includes unit overviews, detailed lecture topics for each unit with teaching tips, comprehensive sample solutions to all lessons and end-of-unit material, and extra Independent Challenges. The Instructor's Manual is available on the Instructor's Resource Kit CD-ROM, or you can download it from www.course.com.

Sample Syllabus
Prepare and customize your course easily using this sample course outline (available on the Instructor's Resource Kit CD-ROM).

Brief Contents

Contents

⌐ Windows XP ⌐

Contents

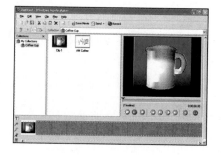

Managing Files and Folders   C-1

Contents

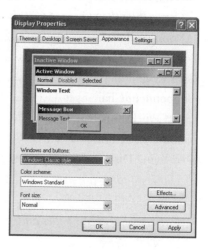

Maintaining Your Computer   F-1

Exploring the Internet with Microsoft Internet Explorer
G-1

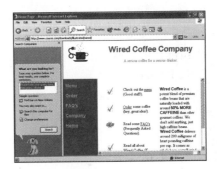

Contents

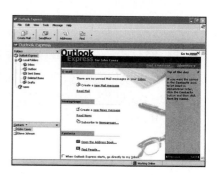

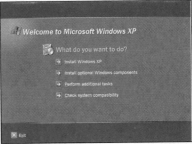

Read This Before You Begin

Differences between Microsoft® Windows® XP Home and Professional

This book is written for Microsoft Windows XP Home and Professional Editions. The Home Edition is a subset of the Professional Edition. In other words, the Home Edition contains all the same features contained in the Professional Edition. However, the Professional Edition contains additional features geared toward the business world that are not included in the Home Edition. When there are differences between the two versions of the software, steps or features written for a specific Windows XP edition are indicated with the name of the edition, either Home or Professional. See the appendix topic "Identify Differences between Windows XP Home and Professional" for a list of differences in the two software versions.

Windows XP Software

Windows XP ships in three editions, including Home Edition for consumers, Professional Edition for business and power users, and a 64-bit version for Intel Itanium processor-based systems, called Windows XP 64-bit Edition.

Installing/Upgrading: Windows 98, 98 SE, and Me users can upgrade to Windows XP Home Edition or Professional. Windows 2000 Professional and Windows NT 4.0 Workstation users can upgrade to Windows Professional, but not to Home Edition. Windows 95 and Windows NT 3.51, or earlier, are not supported for upgrading, so you will need to buy a full version of Windows XP if you wish to upgrade your system.

Uninstalling: Windows 98, 98 SE, and Me users can uninstall Windows XP if the upgrade doesn't work out for some reason. This capability is not available to Windows NT 4.0 and Windows 2000 upgraders.

Windows XP Settings

Each time you start Windows XP, the operating system remembers previous settings, such as the Control Panel options. When you start Windows XP, your initial screen might look different than the ones in this book. For the purposes of this book, make sure the following settings in Windows XP are in place before you start each unit.

- To change folder option settings to match the steps and screens in the book: Click the Start button on the taskbar, click My Documents, click View on the menu bar, then click Folder Options. In the Folder Options dialog box, set the following settings:
  - On the General tab, click the Open each folder in the same window option button.
  - On the General tab, click the Double-click to open an item (single-click to select) option button.
  - On the View tab, click Restore Defaults, then click the Hide file extensions for known file types check box to deselect it in the Advanced settings list box to make sure you can see the three letter DOS filename extensions on your computer.
- In addition to the programs installed during the typical Windows installation, the following Windows programs should also be installed: Clipboard Viewer, Character Map, Paint, and Backup. If a program is not available, use the Add or Remove Programs icon in the Control Panel to install the program. (See "Adding a Program" in Unit F for more information and specific instructions.)
- Turn Status Bar Off for Control Panel. Click the Start button on the taskbar, click Control Panel, click View on the menu bar, then click Status Bar to uncheck the option.
- Turn off AutoArrange icons on desktop. Right-click a blank area on the desktop, point to Arrange Icons By, then click Auto Arrange to uncheck the option.
- Reset toolbars. Click the Start button on the taskbar, click My Computer, click View on the menu bar, point to Toolbars, click Customize, click Reset, then click Close.

Project Files

To complete the lessons and end-of-unit material in this book, you need to obtain the necessary project files. Please refer to the instructions on the back inside cover for various methods of getting these files. Once obtained, the user selects where to store the files, such as to the hard disk drive, network server, floppy disk, or Zip disk. See the Project Files List in the back of the book for more information. Depending on where you store the files, you might need to relink any external files, such as a video clip, associated with a project file when prompted as you open it. If you use a 1.44 MB floppy disk, you might not have enough space to store all the solutions files on the disk. If so, use additional floppy disks as necessary.

Using Copies: For Units C and D, in which you work with managing folders and files using My Computer and Windows Explorer, make sure to use a *copy* of the Project Files instead of the originals. Using a copy of the Project Files will allow you to work through the lessons again in the future.

Restore Settings: In order to work through the lessons in this book, you need to change operating system and program settings. The lessons make every attempt to restore the operating system and program settings, but please be aware that your initial settings might be different than the ones in this book.

To Use Print Screen

To complete many of the lessons and end-of-unit material in this book, you need to take a snap shot of the screen and print it out.

To take a snap shot of the screen and print it, complete the following instructions: Press [Print Screen] (also appears as [PrtScrn] or [Print Scrn]) to place the entire screen on the Clipboard or press [Alt][Print Screen] to place the active window on the Clipboard. Click the Start button on the task bar, point to All Programs, point to Accessories, then click Paint to open Microsoft Paint, a graphics capable program. In Paint, click Edit on the menu bar, click Paste to paste the screen into Paint, then click Yes to paste the large image, if necessary. Click the Text button (contains the letter A) on the Toolbox, click a blank area in the Paint work area, then type your name to identify your print out. Click File on the menu bar, click Page Setup, change 100 % normal size to 50% in the Scaling area, then click OK. Click File on the menu bar, click Print, then click Print in the Print dialog box.

Getting
Started with Windows XP

Objectives

▶ **Start Windows and view the desktop**

▶ **Use the mouse**

▶ **Get started with the Windows desktop**

▶ **Manage windows**

▶ **Use menus, toolbars, and panes**

▶ **Use scroll bars**

▶ **Use dialog boxes**

▶ **Use Windows Help and Support**

▶ **Turn off the computer**

Microsoft Windows XP Home and Professional is an **operating system**, a computer program that controls the basic operation of your computer and the programs you run on it. **Programs**, also known as **applications**, are task-oriented software you use to accomplish specific tasks, such as word processing, managing files on your computer, and performing calculations. When you work with Windows XP, you will notice **icons**, which are small pictures on your screen intended to be meaningful symbols of the items they represent. You will also notice **windows** (thus the name of the operating system), rectangular frames on your screen that can contain several icons, the contents of a file, or other usable data. A **file** is a collection of information (such as a letter or list of addresses) that has a unique name, distinguishing it from other files. This use of icons and windows is called a **graphical user interface** (**GUI**, pronounced "gooey"), meaning that you interact ("interface") with the computer through the use of graphics: icons and other meaningful words, symbols, and windows. ✐ In this unit, you will be introduced to basic Windows skills.

Windows XP

Starting Windows and Viewing the Desktop

When you first start Windows XP, you see the Windows desktop, as shown in Figure A-1, or a logon screen (a way to identify yourself on the computer) depending on your installation. See Table A-1 for a description of your computer start-up type. The **desktop** is an on-screen version of an actual desk, containing windows, icons, files, and programs, which you can use to access, store, organize, modify, share, and explore information, such as a letter, a list of addresses, or the news, whether it resides on your computer, a network, or the Internet. The **Internet** is a worldwide collection of computers linked together to share information, while a **network** is a local area one. The desktop is sometimes called **active** because it allows you to access the Internet and view Internet content directly from it. The bar at the bottom of your screen is called the **taskbar**; it allows you to start programs and switch among currently running programs. (At the moment, none are running; the computer is idle.) At the left end of the taskbar is the **Start button**, which you use to start programs, find and open files, access the Windows Help and Support Center, and much more. At the right end of the taskbar is the **notification area**, which displays the time, date, and program related icons. If icons in the notification area are not used for awhile, an arrow appears to hide the icons and reduce clutter. You can click the arrow to display and hide the icons. When you use a hidden icon, it reappears in the notification area. If you upgraded your computer to Windows XP from a previous version of Windows, your desktop might contain additional desktop icons and toolbars, such as the **Quick Launch toolbar**, which contains buttons you use to quickly start your Internet browser and media player and show the desktop. ➤ Windows XP automatically starts when you turn on your computer. If Windows is not currently running, follow the steps below to start it now.

Steps

1. Turn on your computer

Windows automatically starts and displays the desktop, as shown in Figure A-1, or a logon screen (either the Welcome screen or Network dialog box) asking you to select or enter a user name and password to identify yourself on the computer, before showing the desktop. If the desktop appears (meaning you are using a nonshared computer), continue to Step 3, otherwise, continue to Step 2 to log on.

Trouble?

If you are new to using the mouse, read through the next topic "Using the Mouse."

2. In the Welcome screen (on a shared computer), click your user name, type your password, then press [Enter], or in the Network dialog box (on a networked computer), press and hold [Ctrl] and [Alt] with one hand, then press [Del] with the other to display the Windows Security dialog box, in the User name text box type your username if necessary, type your password in the Password text box, then click OK

Only bullets appear as you type the password. This helps to prevent other people from learning your password. Once the password is accepted, the Windows desktop appears on your screen, as shown in Figure A-1.

QuickTip

To run the Windows XP tour, click the Start button ◢ start on the taskbar, point to All Programs, point to Accessories, then click Tour Windows XP.

3. If a ScreenTip appears, click the Close button in the ScreenTip

A **ScreenTip** is informational help that appears when you need it. When you start Windows XP for the first time, a ScreenTip pointing to the Windows XP Tour icon on the taskbar appears, asking if you want to take a tour of Windows XP. The ScreenTip closes, and the Windows XP Tour icon is removed from the notification area on the taskbar.

FIGURE A-1: **Windows XP desktop**

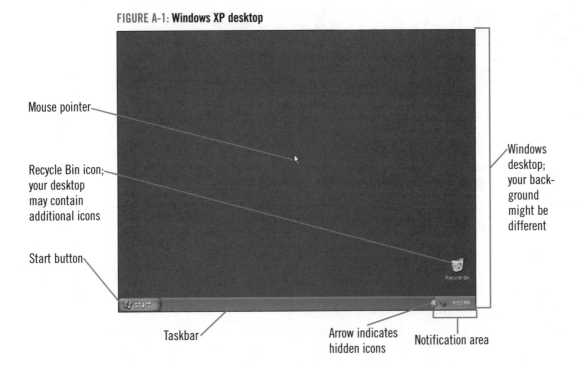

Mouse pointer—

Recycle Bin icon;
your desktop
may contain
additional icons

Start button—

Windows
desktop;
your back-
ground
might be
different

Recycle Bin

start

9:53 PM

Taskbar

Arrow indicates
hidden icons

Notification area

TABLE A-1: **Starting a computer with Windows XP**

what you see at start up	means you have a
desktop	nonshared (single user) computer; no user name and password required
Welcome screen	shared (multiple users) computer; user name and password required
Network dialog box	networked (connected to a computer on a network) computer; user name and password required

CLUES TO USE

Using and changing a password

Passwords are used to maintain security on a shared or networked computer. Windows uses encryption, which is the process of logically scrambling data, to keep your password secure on your computer. When choosing a password, remember that the Windows password program is case-sensitive, which means the program makes a distinction between uppercase and lowercase letters. Your password should be at least seven characters long, which is optimal for encryption. It should include, if possible, combinations of capital letters, lowercase letters, and non-alphabetic characters (numbers and symbols). Never write down your password on paper or let someone look over your shoulder as you log on to the computer. Always be sure to log off or shut down when you walk away from your computer. You specify a user name and password when you install Windows XP or open User Accounts in the Control Panel on a shared computer, or an instructor or technical support person (the person in charge of your network) assigns you a user name and password on a networked computer. To change your password on a networked computer with Windows XP Professional, press [Ctrl][Alt][Del] after you start Windows to open the Windows Security dialog box, click Change Password, type the old password in the Old Password text box, type the new password in the New Password and Confirm New Password text boxes, then click OK. If you have forgotten your password, the Forgotten Password Wizard allows you to create a password reset disk that you can use to recover user account information (user name and password) and personalized computer settings. To create a reset disk, click Change Password in the Windows Security dialog box, click Backup, click Next, then follow the wizard instructions. To change your password or create a password reset disk on a shared computer, click User Accounts in the Control Panel, then follow the instructions provided.

Windows XP

Using the Mouse

A **mouse** is a handheld input device you roll across a flat surface (such as a desk or a mouse pad) to position the **mouse pointer**, the small symbol that indicates the pointer's relative position on the desktop. When you move the mouse, the mouse pointer on the screen moves in the same direction. The shape of the mouse pointer changes to indicate different activities. Table A-2 shows some common mouse pointer shapes. Once you move the mouse pointer to a desired position on the screen, you use the **mouse buttons**, shown in Figure A-2, to "tell" your computer what you want it to do. Table A-3 describes the basic mouse techniques you use frequently when working in Windows. Now you will try using the mouse to become familiar with these navigational skills.

1. Place your hand on the mouse, locate the mouse pointer ⏳ on the desktop, then move the mouse back and forth across your desk

As you move the mouse, the mouse pointer moves correspondingly.

Trouble?

Your icon may differ.

2. Move the mouse to position the mouse pointer over the **Recycle Bin icon** 🗑 in the lower-right corner of the desktop

Positioning the mouse pointer over an icon or over any specific item on the screen is called **pointing**. If pointing to the icon highlights it, you are not using default Windows XP settings. Consult your instructor or technical support person. This book assumes you are using Windows default double-click mouse settings.

3. Press and release the **left mouse button**

The act of pressing a mouse button once and releasing it is called **clicking**. The icon is now highlighted, or shaded differently than the other icons on the desktop. The act of clicking an item, such as an icon, indicates that you have **selected** it to perform some future operation on it. To perform any type of operation on an icon, such as moving it, you must first select it.

4. Point to 🗑, press and hold down the **left mouse button**, move the mouse to the center of the desktop, then release the mouse button

The icon moves with the mouse pointer. This is called **dragging**, which you use to move Windows elements. If the icon jumps a little when you release the mouse, the desktop is set to automatically align icons with an invisible grid. To turn off the automatic alignment with the grid, right-click a blank area of the desktop, point to Arrange Icons By, then click Align to Grid to deselect it. If you are still having trouble, right-click the desktop again, point to Arrange Icons By, then click AutoArrange to deselect it.

QuickTip

When a step tells you to "click," it means, by default, to left-click. The step says "right-click" if you are to click with the right mouse button.

5. Point to 🗑, then press and release the **right mouse button**

Clicking the right mouse button is known as **right-clicking**. Right-clicking an item on the desktop displays a **shortcut menu**, shown in Figure A-3. This menu displays the commands most commonly used for the item you clicked; the available commands differ for every item.

6. Click anywhere outside the menu to close the shortcut menu

Clicking outside the menu in a blank area, or pressing [Esc], closes the shortcut menu without performing a command.

QuickTip

To quickly rearrange icons on the desktop, right-click a blank area of the desktop, point to Arrange Icons By, then click the appropriate option.

7. Move 🗑 back to its original position in the lower-right corner of the desktop using the pointing and dragging skills you just learned

8. Point to 🗑, then click the **left mouse button** twice quickly

The Recycle Bin window opens, containing file icons, which you want to delete. Clicking the mouse button twice is known as **double-clicking**, and it allows you to open the window, program, or file that an icon represents. Leave the desktop as it is and move on to the next lesson.

FIGURE A-2: Typical mouse

Right mouse button

Left mouse button

Mouse; your mouse may be different

FIGURE A-3: Shortcut menu

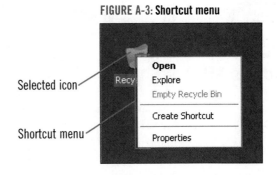

Selected icon

Shortcut menu

TABLE A-2: Common mouse pointer shapes

shape	used to
↖	Select items, choose commands, start programs, and work with programs
I	Position the mouse pointer for editing or inserting text; called the insertion point or cursor
↖⧖	Indicate Windows is busy processing a command
↔ or ↕	Position the mouse pointer on the edge of a window to change its size
↡	Position the mouse pointer to select and open Web-based content

TABLE A-3: Basic mouse techniques

task	what to do
Pointing	Move the mouse to position it over an item on the desktop
Clicking	Press and release the left mouse button
Double-clicking	Press and release the left mouse button twice quickly
Dragging	Point to an item, press and hold the left mouse button, move the mouse to a new location, then release the mouse button
Right-clicking	Point to an item, then press and release the right mouse button

CLUES TO USE

Using the mouse with the Web style

When you use the standard Windows operating system, you click an item to select it, then double-click the item to open it. However, when using the Internet, you point to an item to select it and single-click the item to open it. Because Windows XP integrates use of the Internet with its other functions, it allows you to choose whether you want to extend the way you click on the Internet to the rest of your computer work by single-clicking (known as the Internet or Web style) icons to open them, or by double-clicking (known as the Classic style). To change from one style to the other, click the Start button on the taskbar, click Control Panel, click Switch to Classic View (if necessary), double-click Folder Options, click the Single-click to open an item (point to select), or Double-click to open an item (single-click to select) option button, then click OK. Windows XP is set by default to double-click, and the steps in this book assume you are using Windows Classic style.

Getting Started with the Windows Desktop

The key to getting started with the Windows desktop is learning how to use the Start button on the taskbar. Clicking the Start button on the taskbar displays the **Start menu**, a list of commands that allows you to start a program, open a document, change a Windows setting, find a file, or display support information. Table A-4 describes the available commands on this menu that are installed with Windows XP. As you become more familiar with Windows, you might want to customize the Start menu to include additional items that you use most often and change Windows settings in the Control Panel to customize your Windows desktop. ➤ You will begin by viewing the Start menu and opening the **Control Panel**, a window containing various programs that allow you to specify how your computer looks and performs.

Steps 1 2 3 4

QuickTip

To remove a program from the pinned items list, right-click the program on the Start menu, then click Unpin from Start menu, or Remove from This List.

1. Click the **Start button** on the taskbar

The Start menu opens, as shown in Figure A-4. You use commands on the Start menu to start programs or change Windows system settings. The top of the Start menu indicates who is currently using the computer. The left column of the Start menu is separated into two lists: pinned items above the separator line and most frequently used items below. The **pinned** items remain on the Start menu, like a push pin holds paper on a bulletin board. The most frequently used items change as you use programs: Windows keeps track of which programs you use and displays them on the Start menu for easy access. The right column of the Start menu provides easy access to folders, Windows settings, help information, and search functionality. An arrow next to a menu item indicates a **cascading menu**, or **submenu**, which is a list of commands for that menu item. Pointing at the arrow displays a submenu from which you can choose additional commands.

QuickTip

To move an item on the Start menu, click the Start button, then drag it to a new location. A black horizontal bar indicates the new location.

2. Click **Control Panel** on the Start menu

The Control Panel opens, containing categories or icons for various programs that allow you to specify how your computer looks and performs. The Control Panel appears in Category view, which groups program items together to reduce the clutter, or in Classic View, which displays program items individually. Leave the Control Panel open for now, and continue to the next lesson.

CLUES TO USE

Changing the display to Windows classic settings

The Windows XP enhanced user interface provides a new look for the desktop. If you prefer the desktop display of Windows 98 or Windows Me, you can change the display to Windows Classic. With the Windows Classic display, you can take advantage of the new Windows XP functionality, yet work in an environment with which you are more familiar. To change the desktop display, right-click a blank area of the desktop, then click Properties on the shortcut menu. The Display Properties dialog box opens, displaying the Themes tab. A theme is a desktop background and a set of sounds, icons, and other Windows elements. On the Themes tab, click the Theme list arrow, click Windows Classic, then click

OK. To add desktop Windows Classic icons (My Documents, My Computer, My Network Places, and Internet Explorer) to the desktop, click the Desktop tab in the Display Properties dialog box, click Customize Desktop, click the check boxes with the icons you want to display, then click OK twice. To change the Start menu to Windows Classic, right-click the Start button on the taskbar, click Properties, click the Classic Start menu option button, then click OK. To show folders in Windows Classic View without the left pane of Common tasks, open My Computer, click Tools on the menu bar, click Folder Options, click the General tab if necessary, click the Use Windows classic folders option button, then click OK.

FIGURE A-4: **Start menu**

Open Recycle Bin window

Current user

Pinned items

Most frequently used items; your list might be different

Arrow indicates submenu

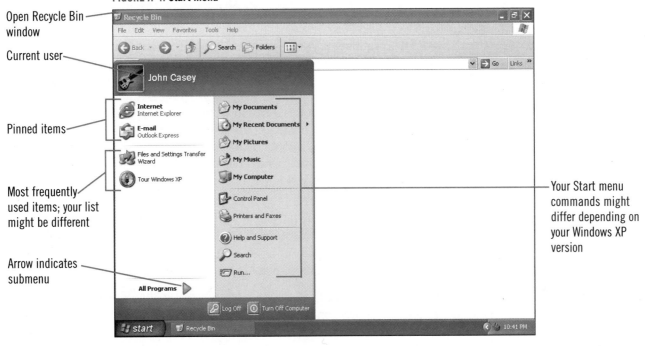

Your Start menu commands might differ depending on your Windows XP version

TABLE A-4: **Start menu commands**

Icon	command	description
	Internet	Starts your Internet browser; by default, Internet Explorer
	E-mail	Starts your e-mail program; by default, Outlook Express
	All Programs	Opens all the programs included on the Start menu
	My Documents	Opens the My Documents folder, where you store and manage files
	My Recent Documents	Opens a list of the most recently opened and saved documents
	My Pictures	Opens the My Pictures folder, where you store and manage photos, images, and graphic files
	My Music	Opens the My Music folder, where you store and manage sound and audio files
	My Computer	Opens the My Computer window, where you access information about disk drives, and other hardware devices
	Control Panel	Provides options to customize the appearance and functionality of the computer
	Printers and Faxes	Displays installed printers and fax printers and a wizard to help you install additional devices; available only with Windows XP Professional
	Printers and Other Hardware	Displays installed printers and other hardware and a wizard to help you install other devices; available only with Windows XP Home
	Help and Support	Displays Windows Help topics, tutorials, troubleshooting, support options, and tools
	Search	Allows you to locate programs, files, folders, or computers on your computer network, or find information or people on the Internet
	Run	Opens a program or file based on a location and filename that you type or select
	Log Off	Allows you to log off the system and log on as a different user
	Turn Off Computer	Provides options to turn off the computer, restart the computer, or set the computer in hibernate mode

Windows XP

Managing Windows

One of the powerful things about the Windows operating system is that you can open more than one window or program at once. This means, however, that the desktop can get cluttered with many open windows for the various programs you are using. You can identify a window by its name on the **title bar** at the top of the window. To organize your desktop, you must sometimes change the size of a window or move it to a different location. Each window, no matter what it contains, is surrounded by a border that you can use to move or resize the window. Each window has three buttons in the upper-right corner that allow you to resize it. Table A-5 shows the different mouse pointer shapes that appear when resizing windows. Now you will try moving and resizing the Control Panel window.

Steps

1. **Click the Recycle Bin button on the taskbar or click anywhere in the Recycle Bin window**
   The Recycle Bin window moves in front of the Control Panel window. The Recycle Bin window is now **active**, which means that any actions you perform take place in this window. At times, you might want to hide a window so that it isn't visible on the desktop but is still open.

QuickTip

You can press [D] or click the Show Desktop button on the Quick Launch toolbar to minimize all open windows and programs and see the desktop.

2. **Click the Minimize button** in the upper-right corner of the Recycle Bin window
   The window no longer appears on the desktop, but you can still see a button named Recycle Bin on the taskbar. When you **minimize** a window, you do not close it but merely reduce it to a button on the taskbar so that you can work more easily in other windows. The button on the taskbar reminds you that the program is still running.

3. **Position the mouse pointer on the lower-right corner of the Control Panel window until the pointer changes to ↘, then drag the corner up and to the left until your screen resembles Figure A-5**
   The window is now resized. You can resize windows by dragging any corner, not just the lower-left. You can also drag any border to make the window taller, shorter, wider, or narrower.

4. **Point to the title bar on the Control Panel**
   When a window is active, the title bar color changes from gray to blue. You can move any window to a new location on the desktop by dragging the window's title bar.

QuickTip

To arrange all open windows, right-click a blank area on the taskbar, then click the appropriate option.

5. **With the mouse pointer over any spot on the title bar, click the left mouse button, then drag the window to center it on the desktop**
   The window is relocated. This action is similar to dragging an icon to a new location.

6. **Click the Maximize button** in the upper-right corner of the Control Panel
   When you **maximize** a window, it fills the entire screen.

QuickTip

You can double-click the title bar of a window to switch between maximizing and restoring the size of a window.

7. **Click the Restore Down button** in the upper-right corner of the Control Panel
   The **Restore Down button** returns a window to its previous size. The Restore button appears only when a window is maximized.

8. **Click the Recycle Bin button on the taskbar**
   The Recycle Bin window is now the size it was before you minimized it and is now active. When you finish using a window, you can close it with the Close button.

9. **Click the Close button** in the upper-right corner of the Recycle Bin window
   The Recycle Bin window closes. You will learn more about the Recycle Bin in later lessons.

FIGURE A-5: Resized Control Panel window

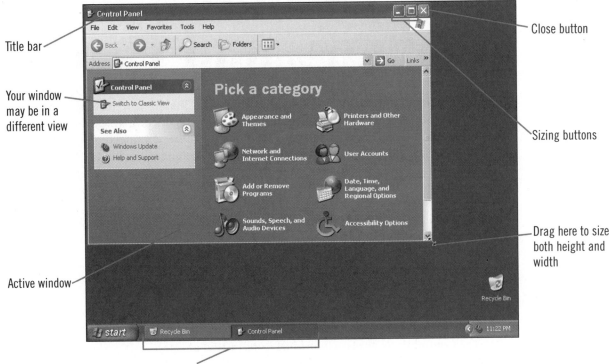

Title bar

Your window may be in a different view

Active window

Close button

Sizing buttons

Drag here to size both height and width

Taskbar buttons

TABLE A-5: Mouse pointer shapes that appear when resizing windows

mouse pointer shape	use to
↔	Drag the right or left edge of a window to change its width
↕	Drag the top or bottom edge of a window to change its height
↘ or ↗	Drag any corner of a window to change its size proportionally

CLUES TO USE

Moving and resizing the taskbar

In addition to windows, you can also resize and move other elements on the desktop, such as the taskbar, using the methods in this lesson. With Windows XP, the taskbar is locked by default, so it cannot be accidentally resized or moved. Before you can resize or move the taskbar, you need to unlock it. To unlock the taskbar, right-click a blank area on the taskbar, then click Lock the Taskbar on the shortcut menu to deselect the option. You can move the taskbar by dragging it to any edge (right, left, top, or bottom) of the desktop. You can also change the size of the taskbar by dragging its edge with the pointer ↕.

Using Menus, Toolbars, and Panes

A **menu** is a list of commands that you use to accomplish certain tasks, such as when you used the Start menu to open the Control Panel. A **command** is a directive that provides access to a program's features. Each Windows program has its own set of menus, which are on the menu bar along the top of the program window. The **menu bar** organizes commands into groups of related operations. Each group is listed under the name of the menu, such as File or Help. To access the commands in a menu, you click the name of the menu. If a command on a menu includes a keyboard reference, known as a **keyboard shortcut**, you can perform the action by pressing the first key, then pressing the second key to perform the command quickly. See Table A-6 for examples of items on a typical menu. You can also carry out some of the most frequently used commands on a menu by clicking a button on a toolbar. A **toolbar** contains buttons that are convenient shortcuts for menu commands. A **pane** is a frame within a window where you can quickly access commands and navigation controls. You can use menus, toolbar buttons, and commands in a pane to change how the Control Panel window's contents appear.

1. Click **Switch to Classic View** in the left pane of the Control Panel, if necessary
The Control Panel displays individual icons instead of categories.

2. Click **View** on the menu bar
On a menu, a **check mark** identifies a currently selected feature, meaning that the feature is **enabled**, or turned on. To **disable**, or turn off the feature, you click the command again to remove the check mark. A **bullet mark** also indicates that an option is enabled. To disable a command with a bullet mark next to it, however, you must select another command (within the menu section, separated by gray lines) in its place. In the next step, you select a command.

3. Click **Status Bar** to enable it, if necessary, then click **View** on the menu bar
The View menu appears, displaying the View commands, as shown in Figure A-6. The status bar appears at the bottom of the Control Panel window.

4. Click **List** on the View menu
When you click a menu name, a general description of the commands available on that menu appears in the status bar. The icons are now smaller than they were before, taking less room in the window.

5. Position the pointer over the **Views button** 🔲▾ on the Control Panel toolbar
When you position the mouse pointer over a button, the name of the button appears as a ScreenTip. Use the ScreenTip feature to explore a button on the toolbar. The toolbar at the top of the window includes buttons for the commands that you use most frequently while you work with the Control Panel. Some toolbar buttons appear with an arrow, which indicates the button contains several choices. You click the button arrow to display the choices.

6. Click 🔲▾ on the Control Panel toolbar, then click **Details**
The Details view includes a description of each Control Panel program. In the next lesson, you will use scroll bars in the Control Panel to view and read the description of each Control Panel program.

FIGURE A-6: View menu in the Control Panel

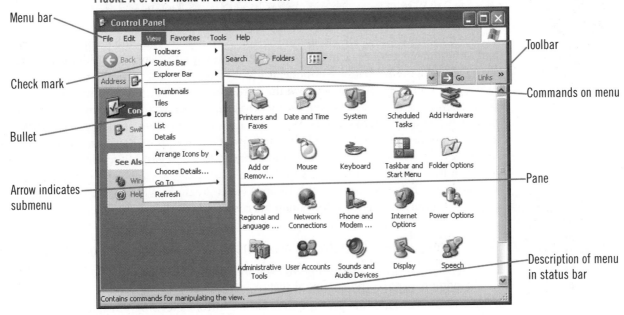

Menu bar

Check mark

Bullet

Arrow indicates submenu

Toolbar

Commands on menu

Pane

Description of menu in status bar

TABLE A-6: Typical items on a menu

item	description	example
Dimmed command	A menu command that is not currently available	Object
Ellipsis	Indicates that a dialog box will open that allows you to select from several options	Find...
Triangle	Indicates that a cascading menu will open containing an additional list of commands	▶
Keyboard shortcut	An alternative to using the mouse for executing a command	Ctrl+Z
Underlined letter	Indicates the letter to press while holding down the [Alt] key for a keyboard shortcut; underline only appears on menu when you press and hold [Alt]	Clear

Unlocking and customizing toolbars

Most toolbars in Windows XP are locked, so they cannot be accidentally moved. If you want to move the toolbars around, click View on the menu bar, point to Toolbars, click Lock the Toolbars to remove the check mark and unlock the toolbars, then drag the dotted left toolbar edge. You can also change the buttons on a toolbar to customize it to the way you work by clicking View on the menu bar, pointing to Toolbars, then clicking Customize. In the Customize Toolbar dialog box, select buttons in the left pane, then click Add to add buttons to the current toolbar. Select buttons in the right pane, then click Remove to delete buttons. At the bottom of the dialog box, you can select options to change the button size or include button text.

Windows XP

Using Scroll Bars

When you cannot see all of the items available in a window, scroll bars appear on the right and/or bottom edges of the window. **Scroll bars** allow you to display the additional contents of the window. Figure A-7 shows components of the scroll bars. The vertical scroll bar moves your view up and down through a window; the horizontal scroll bar moves your view from left to right. There are several ways you can use the scroll bars. When you need to scroll only a short distance, you can use the scroll arrows. When you need to scroll more quickly, you can click in the scroll bar above or below the **scroll box** to move the view up or down one window's height. Dragging the scroll box moves you even more quickly to a new part of the window. See Table A-7 for a summary of the different ways to use scroll bars. ✎ You can use the scroll bars to view and read the description of each Control Panel program. When no scroll bars appear in a window, it means that all the information fits completely in the window.

QuickTip

You can also drag ✛ to resize a column.

1. **If ellipses (…) appear at the end of comments in the Control Panel, position the pointer to the right edge of the Comments header until it changes to ✛, then double-click the edge to expand the comment text**
   The column expands the description of each Control Panel program and a horizontal scroll bar appears.

2. **In the Control Panel, click the down scroll arrow in the vertical scroll bar**
   See Figure A-7. Clicking the down scroll arrow moves the view down one line. Clicking the up arrow moves the view up one line at a time.

3. **Click the up scroll arrow in the vertical scroll bar**
   The view moves up one line.

4. **Click anywhere in the area below the scroll box in the vertical scroll bar**
   The contents of the window scroll down in a larger increment.

QuickTip

If you have a mouse with a wheel button between the left and right buttons, you can roll the wheel button to scroll up and down quickly, or click the wheel button and move the mouse in any direction.

5. **Click the area above the scroll box in the vertical scroll bar**
   The contents of the window scroll back up. To move in even greater increments, you can drag the scroll box to a new position.

6. **Drag the scroll box in the horizontal scroll bar to the middle of the bar**
   The scroll box indicates your relative position within the window, in this case, the halfway point. The size of the scroll bar indicates the amount of information available to scroll. A small scroll box indicates a lot of information, while a large scroll box indicates a small amount. After reading the Control Panel program descriptions, you restore the Control Panel to its original display.

7. **Click the Views button ⊞ ▾ on the Control Panel toolbar, then click Icons**

8. **Click View on the menu bar, then click Status Bar to deselect it, if necessary**
   The status bar is removed from the bottom of the Control Panel. In the next lesson, you will open a Control Panel program to learn how to work with dialog boxes.

FIGURE A-7: Scroll bars in Control Panel

Up scroll arrow

Horizontal scroll bar

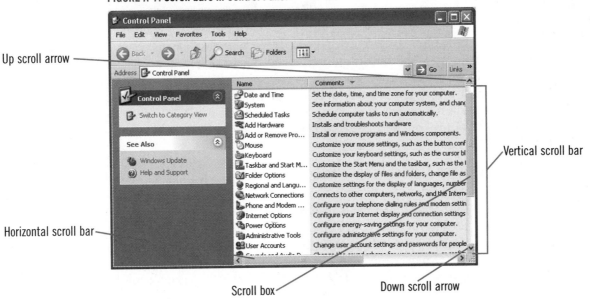

Vertical scroll bar

Scroll box

Down scroll arrow

TABLE A-7: Using scroll bars in a window

to	do this
Move down one line	Click the down arrow at the bottom of the vertical scroll bar
Move up one line	Click the up arrow at the top of the vertical scroll bar
Move down one window's height	Click in the area below the scroll box in the vertical scroll bar
Move up one window's height	Click in the area above the scroll box in the vertical scroll bar
Move up or down a greater distance in the window	Drag the scroll box in the vertical scroll bar
Move a short distance side to side in a window	Click the left or right arrows in the horizontal scroll bar
Move to the right one window's width	Click in the area to the right of the scroll box in the horizontal scroll bar
Move to the left one window's width	Click in the area to the left of the scroll box in the horizontal scroll bar
Move left or right a greater distance in the window	Drag the scroll box in the horizontal scroll bar

CLUES TO USE

Accessibility for special needs

If you have difficulty using a mouse or typing, have slightly impaired vision, or are deaf or hard of hearing, you can adjust the appearance and behavior of Windows XP to make your computer easier for you to use. The Accessibility Wizard helps you configure Windows for your vision, hearing, and mobility needs. The Accessibility Wizard also enables you to save your settings in a file that you can use on another computer. To open the Accessibility Wizard, click the Start button on the taskbar, point to All Programs, point to Accessories, point to Accessibility, click Accessibility Wizard, then follow the steps in the wizard. You can also double-click the Accessibility

Options icon in the Control Panel to adjust the way your keyboard, display, and mouse function to suit various vision and motor abilities. Some of the accessibility tools available include StickyKeys, which enables simultaneous keystrokes while pressing one key at a time; FilterKeys, which adjusts the response of your keyboard; ToggleKeys, which emits sounds when you press certain locking keys; SoundSentry, which provides visual warnings for system sounds; ShowSounds, which instructs programs to provide captions; High Contrast, which improves screen contrast; and MouseKeys, which enables the keyboard to perform mouse functions.

Windows XP

Using Dialog Boxes

A **dialog box** is a window that opens when you choose a menu command that is followed by an ellipsis (. . .). The **ellipsis** indicates that you must supply more information before the program can carry out the command you selected. Dialog boxes open in other situations as well, such as when you open a program in the Control Panel. In a dialog box, you specify the options you want using a variety of elements. See Figure A-8 and Table A-8 for some of the typical elements of a dialog box. Practice using a dialog box to control your mouse settings.

Steps

Trouble?

If your dialog box differs from Figure A-9, read through Steps 2-4 and do not perform any actions, then continue with Step 5.

1. In the Control Panel, scroll if necessary to locate the Mouse icon, then double-click
The Mouse Properties dialog box opens, as shown in Figure A-9. The options in this dialog box allow you to control the configuration of the mouse buttons, select the types of pointers that appear, choose the speed of the mouse movement on the screen, and specify what type of mouse you are using. Tabs at the top of the dialog box separate these options into related categories. The tabs in the dialog box vary depending on the mouse installed on the computer.

2. Click the **Buttons tab**, if necessary
This tab has two or more sections. The first section, Button configuration, has options you can select to make the mouse easier to use for a right-handed or left-handed person. The second section, Double-click speed, has a slider for you to set how fast the mouse pointer responds to double-clicking. The slider lets you specify the degree to which the option is in effect. The other sections vary depending on the Windows version and mouse installed on the computer. Next, you experiment with the double-click speed options.

3. In the Double-click speed section, drag the **slider** halfway to the right
You set the mouse pointer to respond to a fast double-click. You can test the double-click speed in the Test area to make sure it is comfortable for you to use on a regular basis.

4. Double-click the **Test area** to the right of the slider until the graphical icon moves
As you double-click the test area, the folder icon opens or closes.

5. Click the other tabs in the Mouse Properties dialog box, and examine the available options in each category
Now you need to select a command button to carry out the options you selected. The two most common command buttons are OK and Cancel. Clicking OK accepts your changes and closes the dialog box; clicking Cancel leaves the original settings intact and closes the dialog box. The third command button in this dialog box is Apply. Clicking the Apply button verifies the changes you've made and keeps the dialog box open so that you can select additional options. Because you might share this computer with others, it's important to restore the dialog box options to their original settings.

6. Click **Cancel** to leave the original settings intact and close the dialog box

7. Click **Switch to Category View** in the left pane of the Control Panel, then click the **Close button** in the Control Panel to close the window

FIGURE A-8: **Dialog box elements**

Check box

Option button

Text box

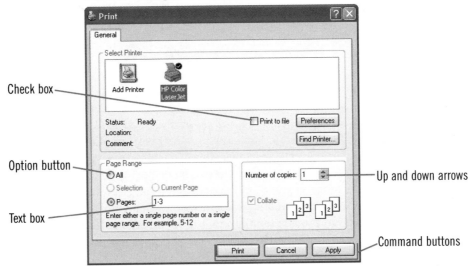

Up and down arrows

Command buttons

FIGURE A-9: **Mouse Properties dialog box**

Tabs; yours might
be different

Slider

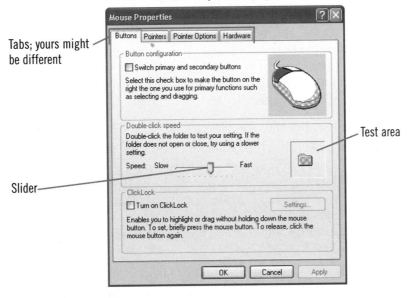

Test area

TABLE A-8: **Typical items in a dialog box**

item	description
Check box	A square box that turns an option on when the box is checked and off when the box is blank
Command button	A rectangular button with the name of the command on it; it carries out a command in a dialog box
List box	A box containing a list of items; to choose an item, click the list arrow, then click the desired item
Option button	A small circle that selects a single dialog box option (you cannot check more than one option button in a list)
Up and down arrows	A box with two arrows and a text box; allows you to scroll through and choose from numerical increments or type a number
Slider	A shape that you drag to set the degree to which an option is in effect
Tab	A place where related options are organized
Text box	A box in which you type text

Windows XP

Using Windows Help and Support

When you have a question about how to do something in Windows XP, you can usually find the answer with a few clicks of your mouse. The Microsoft Help and Support Center is a complete resource of information, training, and support to help you learn and use Windows XP. **Help and Support** is like a book stored on your computer with additional links to the Internet, complete with a search feature, an index, and a table of contents to make finding information easier. If you have an Internet connection, you can get online help from a support professional at Microsoft or from other users on the Windows newsgroup (an electronic form where people share information), or invite a friend with Windows XP to chat with you, view your screen, and work on your computer to provide remote support. If you are new to Windows XP, you can also take a multimedia tour from the Help and Support Center. Now you will use the Help and Support Center to learn more about Windows XP.

QuickTip

To get help on a specific program, you can click Help on the program's menu bar.

1. Click the **Start button** on the taskbar, then click **Help and Support**
   The Help and Support Center window opens with a list of help and support categories, as shown in Figure A-10.

2. In the Search text box, type **using windows**, then press **[Enter]**
   A search pane opens, displaying results from the search in three areas: Suggested Topics, Full-text Search Matches, and Microsoft Knowledge Base (available only when connected to the Internet). A list of tasks, overviews, articles and tutorials appear under Suggested Topics. To switch between result areas, click the gray title with the area name.

QuickTip

To print a help topic, click the Print button on the Help Topic toolbar.

3. In the results area under Overviews, Articles, and Tutorials, click **What's new for Help and Support**, then click the **Expand indicator** ⊞ next to **Online Help** in the right pane
   The Help topic appears in the right pane, as shown in Figure A-11. **Panes** divide a window into two or more sections. When you point to a Help category, the mouse changes to the hand pointer 🖑, and the Help category text becomes underlined or bolded to indicate that more information is available by clicking. A single click opens the Help category or topic. This is similar to the way selecting on the Internet works. Read the help information on Windows online help.

4. Click the **Home button** 🏠 on the Help toolbar
   The main Help and Support window appears. Now you will display a search pane with more topics.

QuickTip

To find topics from a list of subjects, click the Index button on the Help toolbar, type a keyword in the text box, then press [Enter], or scroll down the list, then double-click a topic.

5. Under Pick a Help topic, click **Windows basics**, click **Tips for using Help** under Windows basics, then click **Get more out of Help and Support Center** in the right pane
   The help topic appears. You can move back and forth between Help topics you have already visited by clicking the Back button ◀ Back ▾ and the Forward button ▶ ▾ on the Help toolbar.

6. Click the **Add to Favorites button** ⭐ on the Help Topic toolbar, then click **OK** if you get a warning box
   The Help topic appears in the right pane.

7. Click the **Favorites button** ⭐ on the Help toolbar to display a list of favorites, double-click **Get more out of Help and Support Center** in the list, then click **Remove** below the list to remove the topic

8. Click the **Close button** in the Help and Support Center window
   The Help and Support window closes.

FIGURE A-10: Microsoft Help and Support Center window

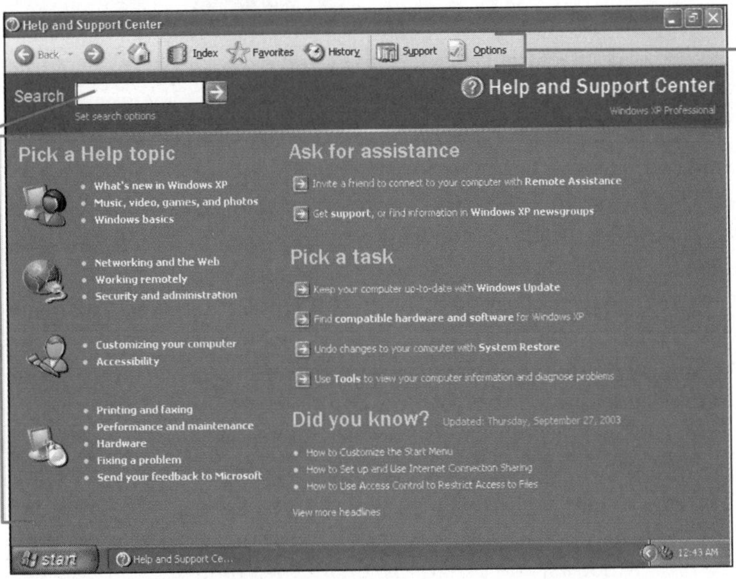
Help toolbar
Search box
Help and Support categories and topics

FIGURE A-11: Help topic

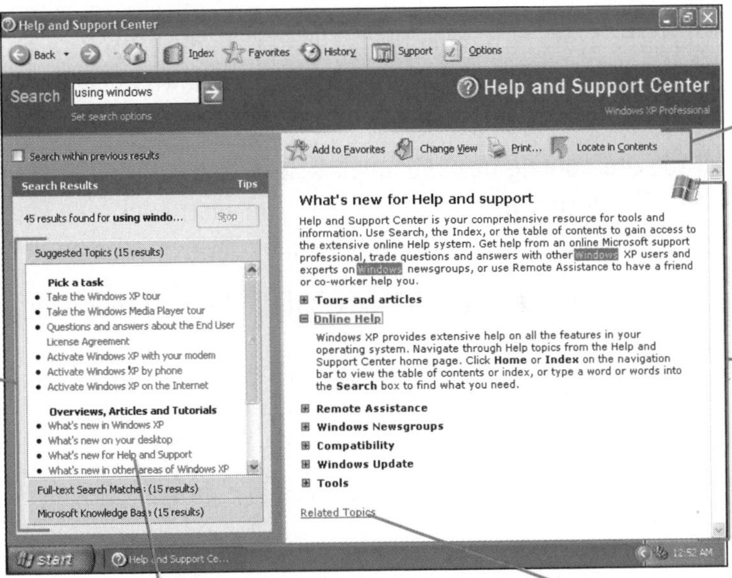
Help Topic toolbar
Search results
Right pane displays help on the topic you select
Help topic
Click to access related information

CLUES TO USE

Getting Help while you work

You can also access **context-sensitive help**, help specifically related to what you are doing, using a variety of methods, such as pointing to or right-clicking an object. To receive help in a dialog box, click the Help button ? in the upper-right corner of the dialog box. The mouse pointer changes to ?. Click on the item in the dialog box for which you need additional information. A shortcut window opens, providing a brief explanation of the selected feature. You can also right-click an item in a dialog box, then click What's This? to display the explanation. In addition, when you click the right mouse button in a Help topic window, you can choose commands to copy and print the contents of the topic. Help windows always appear on top of the currently active window, so you can see Help topics while you work.

Turning Off the Computer

When you finish working on your computer, you need to make sure to turn off, or shut down, your computer properly. This involves several steps: saving and closing all open files, closing all open windows, exiting all running programs, shutting down Windows itself, and, finally, turning off the computer. Shutting down your computer makes sure Windows and all its related programs are properly closed; this avoids potential problems starting and working with Windows in the future. If you turn off the computer by pushing the power switch while Windows or other programs are running, you could lose important data. Once you close all files, windows, and programs, you choose the Turn off computer command from the Start menu. If a program is still open, it will prompt you to save the file and close the program before continuing the shutting down process. The Turn off computer dialog box opens offering several options, as shown in Figure A-12. See Table A-9 for a description of each option. Depending on your Windows settings, your shut down options might be different. To shut down, you will close all your open files, windows, and programs, then exit Windows.

1. If you have any open windows or programs, click the **Close button** in the upper-right corner of each window

2. Click the **Start button** on the taskbar, then click **Turn off computer** ⏻
   The Turn Off Computer dialog box opens as shown in Figure A-12. In this dialog box, you have several options for turning off your computer.

3. If you are working in a lab, click **Cancel** to return to the Windows desktop; if you are working on your own machine or if your instructor tells you to shut down Windows, click **Turn Off** to exit Windows and shut down your computer

4. If you see the message "It's now safe to turn off your computer," turn off your computer and monitor
   Some computers power off automatically, so you may not see this message.

TABLE A-9: Shut down options

shut down option	function	when to use it
Turn Off	Prepares the computer to be turned off	When you finish working with Windows and you want to shut off your computer
Restart	Restarts the computer and reloads Windows	When you want to restart the computer and begin working with Windows again (when your programs may have frozen or stopped working)
Hibernate	Saves your session to disk so that you can safely turn off power; restores your session the next time you start Windows	When you want to stop working with Windows for a while and start working again later; available when the Power Options setting (in the Control Panel) is turned on
Stand By	Maintains your session, keeping the computer running on low power	When you want to stop working with Windows for a few moments and conserve power (ideal for a laptop or portable computer); available when a power scheme is selected in Power Options (in the Control Panel)

FIGURE A-12: Turn off computer dialog box

 Working on a computer for multiple users

Many users may use the same computer, in which case each user has his or her own Windows identity, allowing them to keep their files completely private, and customize the operating system with their own preferences. Windows manages these separate identities by giving each user a unique user name and password. You set up user accounts during Windows XP installation or by using User Accounts 🖳 in the Control Panel, as shown in Figure A-13. When Windows starts, a Welcome screen appears, displaying user accounts. When a user selects an account and types a password (if necessary), Windows starts with that user's configuration settings and network permissions. To quickly change users on the same computer, you choose the Log Off command from the Start menu. On a shared computer, click Log Off to save your current settings and log off, or click Switch

User to quickly switch between users without having to save your current settings. On a network computer, press [Ctrl][Alt][Del], type your user name and password, then click OK.

FIGURE A-13

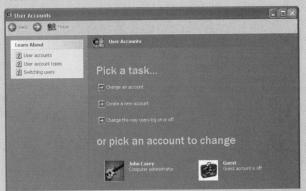

Practice

► Concepts Review

Label each of the elements of the screen shown in Figure A-14.

FIGURE A-14

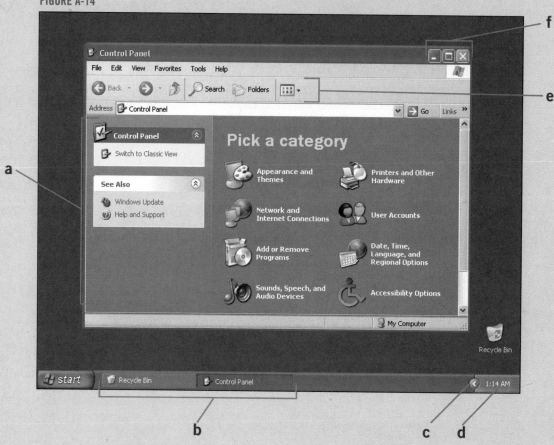

1. Which element do you click to display hidden icons on the taskbar?
2. Which element(s) do you click to resize and close windows?
3. Which element points to the window's pane?
4. Which element points to the notification area?
5. Which element(s) do you click to open and activate a program that is running?
6. Which element points to a toolbar?

Match each term with the statement that describes its function.

7. **Recycle Bin**	a. Where the name of the program and file appear
8. **Sizing buttons**	b. Where deleted files are placed
9. **Start button**	c. Displays the Start button and buttons for currently open programs and windows
10. **Taskbar**	d. Allows you to minimize, maximize, and restore windows
11. **Title bar**	e. The item you click first to start a program
12. **Mouse**	f. Used to point at screen elements and make selections

Select the best answers from the following lists of choices.

13. **Moving an item to a new location on the desktop is called:**
    a. Dragging.
    b. Restoring.
    c. Pointing.
    d. Clicking.

14. **The Maximize button is used to:**
    a. Scroll slowly through a window.
    b. Reduce a window to a button on the taskbar.
    c. Return a window to its original size.
    d. Expand a window to fill the entire screen.

15. **The Minimize button is used to:**
    a. Scroll slowly through a window.
    b. Reduce a window to a button on the taskbar.
    c. Return a window to its original size.
    d. Expand a window to fill the entire screen.

16. **The Menu bar provides access to a program's functions through:**
    a. Commands.
    b. Dialog box elements.
    c. Toolbar buttons.
    d. Scroll buttons.

17. **An ellipsis after a menu command indicates:**
    a. Another menu will display.
    b. A keyboard shortcut to that command.
    c. The menu command is not currently available.
    d. A dialog box will open.

18. **Which is not a method for getting Help?**
    a. Clicking Help on a program's menu bar
    b. Right-clicking in a dialog box, then using the Help pointer to point to what you need help with
    c. Clicking the Start button on the taskbar, then clicking Help and Support
    d. Clicking the question mark button in a dialog box

▶ **Skills Review**

1. **Start Windows and view the Windows desktop.**
   a. Start Windows and log on, if necessary.
   b. Identify and write down as many desktop items as you can, without referring to the lesson.
   c. Compare your results with Figure A-1.
2. **Use the mouse.**
   a. Move the mouse on your desk, and watch how the mouse pointer moves across the screen.
   b. Point at an icon on the desktop.
   c. Click the icon once. Notice the icon's highlighted title.
   d. Press and hold down the mouse button, then drag the icon to the opposite side of the desktop. (*Hint:* release the mouse button when you finish dragging.)
   e. Drag the icon back to the original location.
   f. Double-click the Recycle Bin icon.
3. **Get started with the Windows XP desktop.**
   a. Click the Start menu on the taskbar.
   b. Click Control Panel.
4. **Manage windows.**
   a. Click the Recycle Bin button on the taskbar.
   b. Click the Minimize button.

    c. Position the mouse pointer on any corner of the Control Panel window and drag to make the window smaller.

    d. Point to the title bar on the Control Panel window, then drag the window to the center of the desktop.

    e. Click the Maximize button.

    f. Click the Restore button.

    g. Click the Recycle Bin button on the taskbar.

    h. Click the Close button on the Recycle Bin window.

5. Use menus, toolbars, and panes.

    a. In the Control Panel, click Switch to Classic View if necessary.

    b. Click View on the menu bar, then click Thumbnails.

    c. Click View on the menu bar, then click Tiles.

    d. Click the Views button on the toolbar, then click Details.

6. Use scroll bars.

    a. In the Control Panel, click the vertical scroll box.

    b. Click the vertical up scroll arrow.

    c. Drag the horizontal scroll box to the right-side of the scroll bar (if visible).

    d. Click the Views button on the toolbar, then click Icons.

    e. Click Switch to Category View.

7. Use dialog boxes.

    a. In the Control Panel, click Appearance and Themes.

    b. Click Change the computer's theme.

    c. Click the Theme list arrow, then click Windows Classic.

    d. Click Apply (but don't click OK yet).

    e. Click the Theme list arrow, then click Windows XP to restore the former theme.

    f. Click OK, then click the Control Panel Close button.

8. Get Windows Help and Support.

    a. Click the Start button on the taskbar, then click Help and Support.

    b. In the Search text box, type **dialog boxes**, then press [Enter].

    c. In the Search Results pane, click Get Help in a dialog box, then read the Help topic in the right pane.

    d. Click Related Topics, click Change views in Help and Support Center, then read the Help topic.

    e. Click the Help window Close button.

9. Turn off the computer.

    a. Click the Start button on the taskbar, then click Turn Off Computer.

    b. If you are not working in a lab or if your lab manager approves of shutting down the computer, click Turn Off. Otherwise, click Cancel.

► Independent Challenge 1

Windows XP provides extensive online help and support. At anytime, you can select Help and Support from the Start menu and get the assistance you need. Use the Help and Support options to learn about the topics listed below.

    a. Start the Help and Support Center, then locate and read the help information on the following topics: What's new in Windows XP, Windows keyboard shortcuts overview, Accessibility options overview, and Support overview.

    b. If you have a printer connected to your computer, print one or more Help topics.

    c. Close the Help and Support window.

▶ Independent Challenge 2

You are a student in a Windows XP course and want to review basic Windows XP skills. Use the Help and Support Center to find information on Windows XP tour, then take the tour from the Help and Support Center.

a. Start the Help and Support Center, then locate and read the help information on the Windows XP tour.

b. If you have a printer connected to your computer, print one or more Help topics.

c. Start the Windows XP tour from within the Help and Support Center.

d. Take the Windows XP tour, then click the Exit Tour button on the lower-right corner of the tour window to return to the Help and Support Center.

e. Close the Help and Support window.

▶ Independent Challenge 3

You can customize many Windows features to suit your needs and preferences. One way you do this is to change the appearance of the taskbar on the desktop.

a. Position the mouse pointer over the top border of the taskbar. When the pointer changes shape, drag up to increase the size of the taskbar. (*Hint*: If the pointer does not change, right-click the task bar, then deselect Lock the Taskbar.)

b. Position the mouse pointer over a blank area of the taskbar, then drag to the top of the screen to move the taskbar.

c. Open the Control Panel, click Switch to Classic View if necessary, then double-click Taskbar and Start Menu. On the Taskbar tab, click the Show the clock check box to deselect the option, click Apply, then observe the effect on the taskbar.

d. Print the screen. (Press [Print Screen] to make a copy of the screen, open Paint, click Edit on the menu bar, click Paste to paste the screen into Paint, then click Yes to paste the large image, if necessary. Click the Text button on the Toolbox, click a blank area in the Paint work area, then type your name. Click File on the menu bar, click Page Setup, change 100% normal size to 50% in the scaling area, then click OK. Click File on the Menu bar, click Print, then click Print in the Print dialog box.)

e. Restore the taskbar to its original setting, size, and location on the screen.

f. Switch the Control Panel back to Category view and close the Control Panel window.

Independent Challenge 4

You accepted a new job in London, England. After moving into your new home and unpacking your boxes, you decide to set up your computer. Once you set up and turn on the computer, you decide to change the date and time settings to reflect London's time zone.

a. Open the Control Panel, click Switch to Classic View if necessary, then double-click the Date and Time icon.

b. Click the Time Zone tab, then click the Time Zone list arrow.

c. Select Greenwich Mean Time: Dublin, Edinburgh, Lisbon, London from the list (scroll if necessary).

d. Click the Date & Time tab, change the month and year to September 2003, then click Apply.

e. Print the screen. (See Independent Challenge 3, Step d for screen printing instructions.)

f. Restore the original date and time zone settings, then click OK.

g. Close the Control Panel window.

▶ Visual Workshop

Re-create the screen shown in Figure A-15, which shows the Windows desktop with the Recycle Bin and the Control Panel open. Print the screen. (See Independent Challenge 3, Step d for screen printing instructions.)

FIGURE A-15

Windows XP

Unit B

Working

with Windows Programs

Objectives

- ► Start a program
- ► Open and save a WordPad document
- ► Edit text in WordPad
- ► Format text in WordPad
- ► Create a graphic in Paint
- ► Copy data between programs
- ► Print a document
- ► Play a video or sound clip
- ► Create a movie

Now that you know how to work with common Windows graphical elements, you're ready to work with programs. A program is software you use to accomplish specific tasks, such as word processing and managing files on your computer. Windows comes with several **accessories**: built-in programs that, while not as feature-rich as many programs sold separately, are extremely useful for completing basic tasks. In this unit, you work with some of these accessories. John Casey owns Wired Coffee Company, a growing company that uses Windows XP. John needs to prepare a new coffee menu, so he plans to use two Windows accessories, WordPad and Paint, to create it. He also wants to use two other multimedia accessories, Windows Media Player and Windows Movie Maker, to play video and sound clips and work with a movie on his computer.

Starting a Program

A **Windows program** is software designed to run on computers using the Windows operating system. The most common way to start a Windows program is to use the Start menu, which provides easy access to programs installed on your computer. Clicking the Start button on the taskbar displays the Start menu, which lists common and recently used programs and the All Programs submenu, with additional programs on the left side. In this lesson, you will start a Windows accessory called **WordPad**, a word processing program that comes with Windows. As you look for WordPad on the Accessories submenu, you might notice an accessory called **Notepad**. The accessory names are similar, and both programs work with text. Notepad is a text-only editor, in which you can enter and edit text only with basic document formatting. WordPad is a word processing program, in which you can create and edit documents with complex formatting and graphics. With both programs, you can open only one document per open program window at a time. John wants to use WordPad to prepare the text of his new coffee menu, so he needs to start this program.

Steps

1. **Click the Start button on the taskbar**
   The Start menu opens.

QuickTip

If a single arrow appears at the top or bottom of the All Programs submenu, point to the arrow to scroll up or down the menu to view more elements.

2. **Point to All Programs on the Start menu**
   The All Programs submenu opens, listing the programs and submenus for programs installed on your computer. WordPad is in the submenu called Accessories.

3. **Point to Accessories on the All Programs submenu**
   The Accessories submenu opens, as shown in Figure B-1, containing several programs to help you complete common tasks. You want to start WordPad.

Trouble?

If the Toolbar, Format Bar, ruler, or status bar do not appear, click View on the menu bar, then click the element you want to view so that a checkmark appears.

4. **Click WordPad on the Accessories submenu**
   Your mouse pointer changes momentarily to ⬚, indicating that Windows is starting the WordPad program. The WordPad window then appears on your desktop, as shown in Figure B-2. The WordPad window includes two toolbars, called the Toolbar and Format Bar, as well as a ruler, a work area, and a status bar. A blinking line, known as the **insertion point**, appears in the work area of the WordPad window, indicating where new text will appear. The WordPad program button appears in the taskbar and is highlighted, indicating that WordPad is now open and running.

5. **Click the Maximize button in the WordPad window, if necessary**
   WordPad expands to fill the screen. In the next lesson you will open and save a document in WordPad.

Clues to Use

Creating documents in other languages

You can install multiple languages on your computer, such as Hebrew, Arabic, Japanese, French, Spanish, German, and many others. You can choose which language you want to use when you create a document, then Windows makes the characters for that language available. You can create documents in more than one language using WordPad or Notepad. To install additional languages, open the Control Panel in Classic View, double-click Regional and Language Options, click the Languages tab, click Details to open the Text Services and Input Languages dialog box, click Add to open the Add Input language dialog box, click the Input language list arrow, click the language you want to add, then click OK. Under Preferences, click Language Bar, click the check boxes to turn off advanced text services and turn on options to display the Language Bar on the desktop and language icons (the first two letters of the current input language, such as EN for English) in the notification area of the taskbar, then close the remaining dialog boxes. To compose a document that uses more than one language, click the language icon on the Language Bar or taskbar, click the language you want to use in the list that opens, then type your message. The language setting remains in place until you change it or shutdown your computer. Any recipient of multilanguage documents must also have the same languages installed on their computer to read and edit the documents.

FIGURE B-1: Starting WordPad using the Start menu

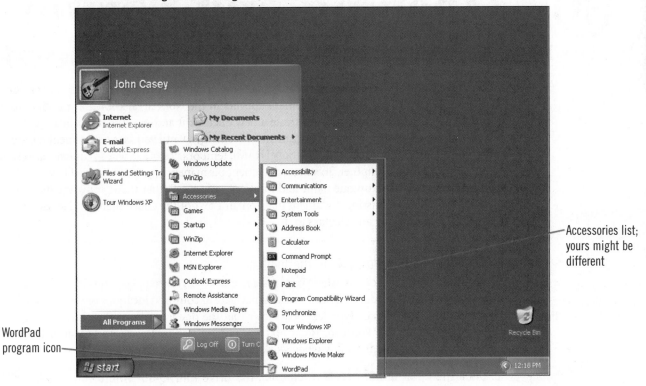

WordPad
program icon

Accessories list;
yours might be
different

FIGURE B-2: Windows desktop with the WordPad window open

Title bar with
document
name

Menu bar

Toolbar

Insertion
point

WordPad
program
button

Status bar

Format bar

Ruler

Work area

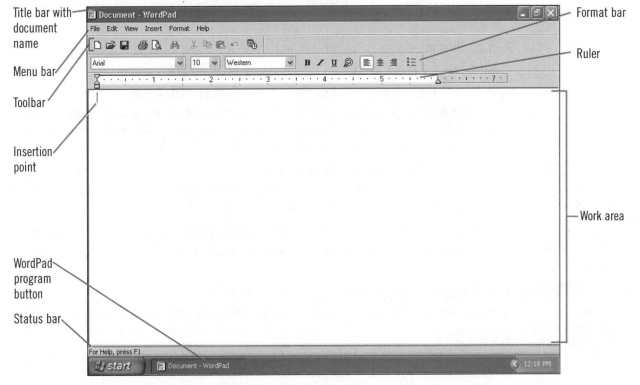

Opening and Saving a WordPad Document

A **document** is a file you create using a word processing program, such as a letter, memo, or resume. When you start WordPad, a blank document appears in the work area, known as the **document window**. You can enter information to create a new document and save the result in a file, or you can open an existing file and save the document with changes. Until you save a document it is stored in the computer's **Random Access Memory** (**RAM**), temporary storage whose contents are erased when you turn off the computer. To store a document permanently, you save it as a file, a collection of information that has a unique name and location. ▬▬▬ Rather than typing the menu from scratch, John opens an existing document that contains text of the coffee menu and saves it with a new name before making any changes to it.

Trouble?

In this book, files are displayed with file extensions. Your display may differ.

1. **Click the Open button 🗁 on the Toolbar**
   The Open dialog box opens, where you locate and choose a file to open. Icons in the **Places bar**, on the left side of the dialog box, are used to navigate to common locations or recently used files and folders. The Files of type text box shows that the document is of type Rich Text Format (.rtf), the default for WordPad. **Rich Text Format** is a standard text format that includes formatting and provides flexibility when working with other programs.

Trouble?

If you are not sure how to locate your Project Files, contact your instructor or technical support person.

2. **Click the Look in list arrow, then click the drive and folder where your Project Files are located**
   A list of files and folders appears in the file list, as shown in Figure B-3. The files shown are determined by the option chosen in the Files of type list. You can select a file from the file list or type the name of the file in the File name text box. When you type a name in the File name text box, **AutoComplete** suggests possible matches with previous filename entries. You can continue to type or click the File name list arrow, then click a matching filename from the list.

3. **If no filenames appear in the file list, click the Files of type list arrow, then click Rich Text Format (*.rtf)**

4. **In the file list, click Win B-1 to select the file, then click Open**
   The Win B-1 file opens a menu for the coffee company. To prevent accidental changes to the original, you save the document in another file with a new name. This makes a copy of it so that you can change the new document and leave the original file unaltered.

QuickTip

Windows saves all your documents in and opens them from the My Documents folder on your desktop unless you choose a different location.

5. **Click File on the menu bar, then click Save As**
   The Save As dialog box opens, as shown in Figure B-4, which you can use to save an existing document with a new name and in a different folder or drive.

6. **If necessary, select the filename Win B-1 by dragging the mouse pointer over it**
   You must select text before you can modify it. When you select text, any action you take affects it.

QuickTip

When a document is open, click the New button 🗋 on the Toolbar to create a blank new document.

7. **Type Coffee Menu to replace the selected text**
   When you start typing, the text you type replaces the selected text in the File name text box.

8. **Click Save**
   You saved the file with a new name in the same folder and drive as the Win B-1 file. The original file, called Win B-1, closes automatically, and the new filename, Coffee Menu, appears in the title bar of the WordPad window.

FIGURE B-3: **Open dialog box**

Places bar

AutoComplete suggests possible matches with previous filenames as you type

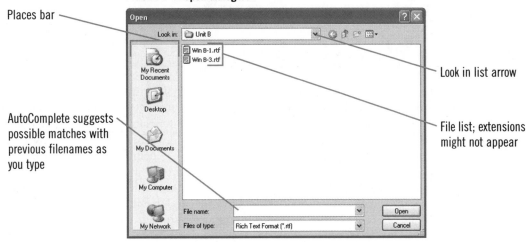

Look in list arrow

File list; extensions might not appear

FIGURE B-4: **Save As dialog box**

Save in list arrow

File name list arrow

File name text box

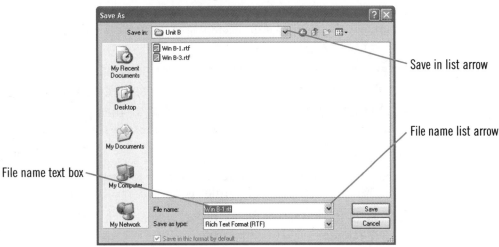

CLUES TO USE

File extensions

The program Windows uses to open a document depends on a three-letter extension to the document's filename, called a file extension. You might have never seen a document's file extension because your system might be set up to hide it. The file extension for simple text files is ".txt" (pronounced "dot t-x-t"), and many graphic files have the extension ".bmp". This means that the full name for a text file named Memo is Memo.txt. If you double-click a document whose filename ends with the three-letter extension ".txt," Windows automatically opens the document with Notepad, a text only editor. If you want to display or change file extension settings, click the Start button on the taskbar, click My Documents, click Tools on the menu bar, then click Folder Options. If you want to display file extensions in dialog boxes and windows, click the View tab in the Folder Options dialog box, then click the Hide extensions for known file types check box to deselect it in the Advanced settings list box. If you want to change the program Windows automatically starts with a given file extension, click the File Types tab in the Folder Options dialog box to see the list of the file extensions Windows recognizes and the programs associated with each of them, and make changes as appropriate.

Editing Text in WordPad

One of the advantages of using a word processing program is that you can **edit** a document, or change the contents without re-creating it. In the WordPad work area, the mouse pointer changes to the I-beam pointer, which you can use to reposition the insertion point (called **navigating**) and insert, delete, or select text. Table B-1 describes several methods for selecting text in a document. You can also move whole sections of a document from one place to another using the Cut and Paste commands or the drag-and-drop method. The **drag-and-drop** method allows you to simply drag text from one location to another, while the Cut and Paste commands require several steps. When selected text is cut from a document, Windows removes it from the document and places it on the **Clipboard**, a temporary storage place where it remains available to be pasted elsewhere. When you want to move a section of a document a short distance (within the same screen), the drag-and-drop method works best, while the Cut and Paste commands are better when dragging for a longer distance, or for text you want to insert in more than one location. John wants to add a greeting, modify the price of coffee, change the order of menu items so that they are alphabetical, and move text in the Coffee Menu document.

1. **Press [↓] three times**
   The insertion point appears at the beginning of the blank line just above the text "Specialty Coffee."

2. **Type Welcome to the taste tantalizing coffee selections offered to you by Wired Coffee Company. You will find a variety of specialty coffees, including Single Origin, Blends, Dark Roasts, and Decaffeinated., then press [Enter]**
   WordPad keeps the text on multiple lines together in the same paragraph, using **word wrap**. The text wraps to the edge of the window or to the right side of the ruler depending on your word wrap settings. When you press [Enter], you create a new paragraph. After inserting new text, you want to edit some existing text. To correct a mistake or to change text, you press [Backspace] to delete the character to the left of the insertion point until you delete the text, then retype the text.

3. **In the price of the Breakfast Blend (Decaf) coffee, click to the right of the last digit, press [Backspace] twice, then type 00**
   The number changes from "12.95" to "12.00." Now you want to rearrange the list so that the coffees are listed in alphabetical order. To do this, you first must select the text you want to move.

4. **Position the pointer in the margin to the left of the first character in the line "Espresso Dark Roast," the pointer changes to ⇗ shown in Figure B-5, then double-click**
   Double-clicking selects the entire paragraph, which in this case is only one line.

QuickTip

To view the Clipboard, click the Start button on the taskbar, point to All Programs, point to Accessories, point to System Tools, then click Clipboard Viewer.

5. **Click the Cut button ✂ on the Toolbar**
   The selected text is cut from the document and placed on the Clipboard.

6. **Click I to the left of the first character in the line that begins with Ethiopian Harrar, then click the Paste button 📋 on the Toolbar**
   The selection you paste is inserted at the location of the insertion point. The coffee list is now in alphabetical order.

7. **Double-click the word "gourmet" in the bottom paragraph to select it, then drag the selection to the left of the word "bean"**
   As you drag the pointer, the pointer changes from ⇖ to ⇖ and the insertion point moves, indicating where the selection is placed in the document.

8. **Click the Save button 💾 on the Toolbar**
   You saved the changes made to the Coffee Menu document.

FIGURE B-5: Editing a WordPad document

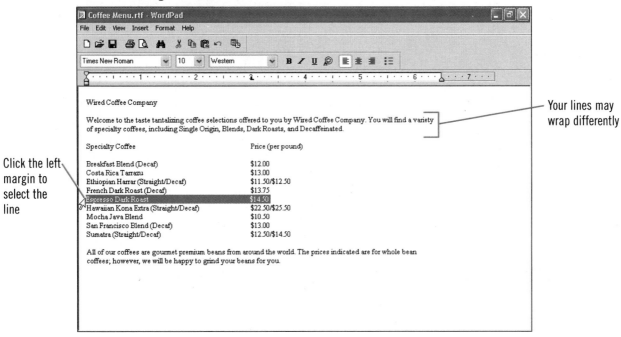

Your lines may wrap differently

Click the left margin to select the line

TABLE B-1: Methods for selecting text

to select	do this
A single word	Double-click the word
A single line	Click the left margin to the left of the first character in the line
A single paragraph	Triple-click a word within the paragraph or double-click the left margin to the left of the first character in the paragraph
Any part of a document	Drag the mouse to select the text you want to select
A large selection	Click at the beginning of the text you want to select, then press and hold [Shift] while you click at the end of the text you want to select
The entire document	Triple-click the left margin

CLUES TO USE

Setting paragraph tabs

Tabs set how text or numerical data aligns in relation to the edges of the document. A tab stop is a predefined stopping point along the document's typing line. Default tab stops are set every half-inch on the ruler, but you can set multiple tabs per paragraph at any location. Each paragraph in a document contains its own set of tab stops. The default tab stops do not appear on the ruler, but the manual tab stops **L** you set do appear. To display the tab stops for a paragraph on the ruler, click any word in the paragraph. To set a tab stop, click the ruler where you want to set it or use the Tabs command on the Format menu to open the Paragraph dialog box, from which you can set tabs. Once you place a tab stop, you can drag the tab stop to position it where you want. To delete a tab stop, drag it off the ruler. If you want to add or adjust tab stops in multiple paragraphs, simply select the paragraphs first.

Formatting Text in WordPad

You can change the **format**, or the appearance, of the text and graphics in a document so that the document is easier to read or more attractive. Formatting text is a quick and powerful way to add emphasis, such as bold, italics, underline, or color, to parts of a document. For special emphasis, you can combine formats, such as bold and italics. In addition, you can change the font style and size. A **font** is a set of characters with the same typeface or design, such as Arial or Times New Roman, that you can increase or decrease in size. Font size is measured in points; one **point** is 1/72 of an inch high. You can make almost all formatting changes in WordPad using the Format Bar, which appears below the Toolbar in the WordPad window. Table B-2 provides examples of each button on the Format Bar. You can determine the current formatting for text in a document by placing the insertion point anywhere in the text, then looking at the button settings on the Format Bar. John wants to make the Coffee Menu document more attractive and prominent by centering the title, bolding it, and increasing its size.

Steps

1. **Select the text Wired Coffee Company at the top of the document**

   Once you select the text you want to format, you can select formatting options on the Format Bar, such as the Center, Bold, or Italic buttons, to apply to the text.

2. **Click the Center button ≡ on the Format Bar**

   The title is now centered and the Center button is selected ("turned on"), while the Left Align button is deselected ("turned off"). Related buttons, such as Left Align, Center, and Right Align, on a toolbar act like options in a dialog box—only one button can be turned on and used at a time; click one to turn it on, and the other related ones turn off.

3. **Click the Bold button B on the Format Bar**

   The selected material appears in boldface. If you didn't like the way boldface looked, you would click the button again. Some buttons act as **toggle** switches—click once to turn the format feature on, click again to turn it off. The Bold, Italic, Underline, and Bullets buttons are examples of toggle buttons.

4. **Click the Italic button ╱ on the Format Bar**

   Bold and italics are both applied to the selected text. Italicizing does not provide the effect that you want, so you change it back to its previous look.

5. **Click the Undo button ↶ on the Toolbar**

   The **undo** command reverses the last change made, such as typing new text, deleting text, and formatting text. Undo cannot reverse all commands (such as scrolling or saving a document), but it is a quick way to reverse most editing and formatting changes.

6. **Click the Font list arrow [Times New Roman ▼] on the Format Bar, then click Arial**

   The font, or typeface, of the text changes to Arial.

7. **Click the Font Size list arrow [10 ▼] on the Format Bar, then click 14**

   The selected text changes in size to 14 point.

8. **Click the Color button 🖉 on the Format Bar, then click Blue**

   The selected text changes in color from Black to Blue.

9. **Click anywhere in the document to deselect the text, then click the Save button 🖫 on the Toolbar**

   Figure B-6 shows the changes made to the Coffee Menu document. Leave WordPad open for now, and continue to the next lesson.

FIGURE B-6: Formatted WordPad document

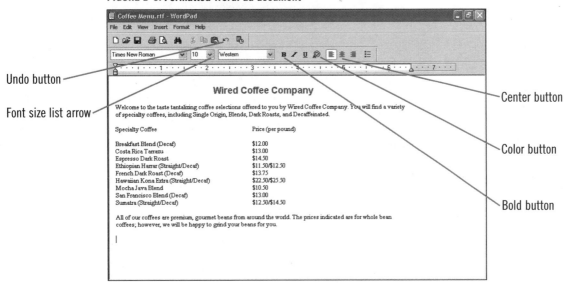

Undo button

Font size list arrow

Center button

Color button

Bold button

TABLE B-2: Format Bar buttons and list arrows

button or list arrow	name	function	example
Arial	**Font**	Select a font	Arial
10	**Font Size**	Select a font size	14 point
Western	**Font Script**	Select a language type	Western
B	**Bold**	Apply boldface style	**Bold**
I	**Italic**	Apply italic style	*Italic*
U	**Underline**	Apply underline style	Underline
	Color	Apply or change color	Color
	Align Left	Align paragraph to the left margin	Align left
	Center	Align paragraph to the center between left and right margin	Center
	Align Right	Align paragraph to the right margin	Align right
	Bullets	Create a bulleted list	• Bullet

CLUES TO USE

Setting paragraph indents

When you indent a paragraph, you move its edge in from the left or right margin. You can indent the entire left or right edge of a paragraph or just the first line. The markers on the ruler control the indentation of the current paragraph. The left side of the ruler has three markers. The top triangle, called the first-line indent marker ▽, controls where the first line of the paragraph begins. The bottom triangle, called the hanging indent marker △, controls where the remaining lines of the paragraph begin. The small square under the bottom triangle, called the left indent marker ☐, allows

you to move the first-line indent marker and the left indent marker simultaneously. When you move the left indent marker, the distance between the hanging indent and the first line indent remains the same. The triangle on the right side of the ruler, called the right indent marker △, controls where the right edge of the paragraph ends. You can also set paragraph indents using the Paragraph command on the Format menu, making your changes in the Paragraph dialog box, then clicking OK.

Creating a Graphic in Paint

Paint is a Windows accessory you can use to create and work with graphics or pictures. Paint is designed to create and edit bitmap (.bmp) files, but you can also open and save pictures created in or for other graphics programs and the Internet using several common file formats, such as .tiff, .gif, or .jpeg. A **bitmap** file is a map of a picture created from small dots or bits, black, white, or colored. You can find buttons, known as **tools**, for drawing and manipulating pictures in the Paint Toolbox, located along the left edge of the window, and described in Table B-3. Tools in the Toolbox act like options in a dialog box—only one tool can be turned on and used at a time. A tool remains turned on until another tool in the Toolbox is selected. In addition, you can use commands on the Image menu, such as rotate, stretch, and invert colors, to further modify pictures in Paint. You can open more than one Windows program at a time, called **multitasking**, so while WordPad is still running, you can open Paint and work on drawings and pictures. John has already created a logo for his coffee company. Now he wants to review the logo and revise it before using it in his promotional materials.

Steps

1. **Click the Start button on the taskbar, point to All Programs, point to Accessories, click Paint, then click the Maximize button in the Paint window, if necessary**
   The Paint window opens and is maximized in front of the WordPad window.

2. **Click File on the menu bar, click Open, click the Look in list arrow, then navigate to the drive and folder where your Project Files are located**
   A list of all the picture files in the selected folder appears.

QuickTip

Windows organizes all your picture files in and opens them from the My Pictures folder located, by default, in the My Documents folder to provide a consistent place to store all your pictures.

3. **In the file list, click Win B-2, then click Open**
   The file named Win B-2 opens in the Paint window, shown in Figure B-7. If you cannot see the logo on your screen, use the scroll buttons to adjust your view. You decide the logo could use some final modifications. Before you make any changes, you want to save this file with a more meaningful name so your changes don't affect the original file.

4. **Click File on the menu bar, click Save As, then save the file as Wired Coffee Logo to the drive and folder where your Project Files are located**
   As you type the new name of the file, Windows automatically determines the file type and changes the format in the Save as type list. In this case, the format changes to 256 Color Bitmap. You want to add a rounded border around the logo.

QuickTip

Press and hold [Shift] while you drag a drawing tool to create a proportional drawing, such as a square or circle.

5. **Click the Rounded Rectangle tool in the Toolbox, then click the third color from the left in the second row of the color box**
   The Rounded Rectangle tool is active, and color fill options appear below the Toolbox. The Foreground color (top color box) on the right side of the Paint Color box changes to red, while the Background color (bottom color box) remains white. The Foreground color is for lines, text, or brush strokes, while the Background color is for filling in a shape. You right-click a color in the Paint Color box to change the foreground color.

6. **Move the pointer into the Paint work area**
   When you move the mouse pointer into the work area, it changes to ┼, indicating that you are ready to draw a rounded rectangle.

Trouble?

If your rounded rectangle doesn't match Figure B-8, click the Eraser/Color tool in the Toolbox, drag to erase the rounded rectangle, then repeat Step 7.

7. **Beginning above and to the left of the logo, drag ┼ so that a rounded rectangle surrounds the image, then release the mouse button when the pointer is below and to the right of the image, as shown in Figure B-8**
   You like this new look. The logo is complete but you need to save it.

8. **Click File on the menu bar, then click Save**
   Now you can use the logo in your other documents.

FIGURE B-7: **Company logo in Paint**

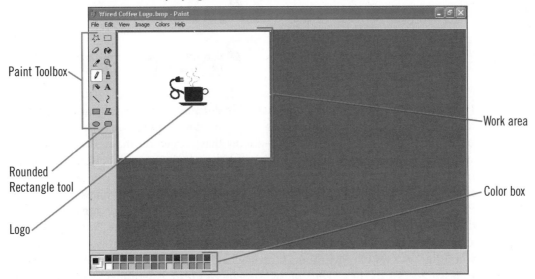

Paint Toolbox

Rounded
Rectangle tool

Logo

Work area

Color box

FIGURE B-8: **Company logo with rounded rectangle**

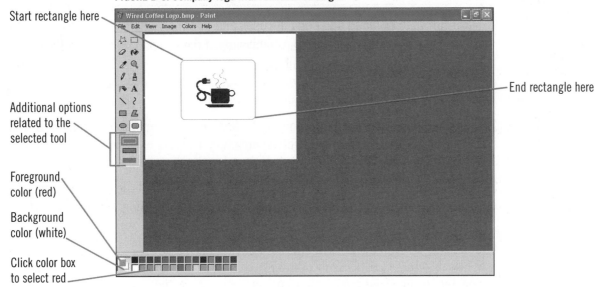

Start rectangle here

Additional options
related to the
selected tool

Foreground
color (red)

Background
color (white)

Click color box
to select red

End rectangle here

TABLE B-3: **Tools in the Paint Toolbox**

tool	used to	tool	used to
Free-Form Select	Select a free-form or irregular shape	Airbrush	Create dispersed lines and patterns
Select	Select a square or rectangular shape	Text	Enter text in drawings
Eraser/Color Eraser	Erase or color part of a drawing	Line	Draw a straight line
Fill With Color	Fill a closed shape with the current color or texture	Curve	Draw a free-form line
Pick Color	Pick up a color from the picture for drawing	Rectangle	Draw a rectangle or square shape
Magnifier	Magnify part of an image	Polygon	Draw a polygon or irregular shape from connected straight-line segments
Pencil	Draw a freehand line	Ellipse	Draw an oval or circle
Brush	Draw a brush stroke using a brush with the selected size and shape	Rounded Rectangle	Draw a rectangle or square with rounded corners

Windows XP

Copying Data Between Programs

One of the most useful features Windows offers is the ability to use data created in one file in another file, even if the two files were created in different Windows programs. To work with more than one program or file at a time, you simply need to open them on your desktop. A **program button** on the taskbar represents any window that is open on the desktop. When you want to switch from one open window to another, click the correct program button on the taskbar. If you **tile**, or arrange open windows on the desktop so that they are visible, you can switch among them simply by clicking in the window in which you want to work. Just as you worked with the Cut and Paste commands to rearrange text in WordPad, you can use the same commands to move and copy data between two different files. Table B-4 reviews the Cut, Copy, and Paste commands and their associated keyboard shortcuts. John wants to add the company logo, which he created with Paint, to the Coffee Menu document, which he created with WordPad. First he switches to Paint and copies the logo. Then he switches to WordPad, determines exactly where he wants to place the logo, and pastes the Paint logo into the WordPad document.

Steps

Trouble?

If your windows don't appear tiled, click the program button on the taskbar for each program, ensure that both windows are maximized, then repeat Step 1.

1. **Make sure both WordPad and Paint are open and that there are no other program windows open, place the mouse pointer on an empty area of the taskbar, right-click, then click Tile Windows Vertically on the shortcut menu**
   The windows (Paint and WordPad) are next to one another vertically, as shown in Figure B-9, so you can maneuver quickly between them while working.

2. **Click the Paint program button on the taskbar, or click anywhere in the Paint window**
   The Paint program becomes the **active program**. The title bar text changes from gray to white, and the Close button changes from purple to red.

3. **Click the Select button ⬚ in the Toolbox, then drag around the coffee logo to select it**
   Dragging with the Select tool selects an object in Paint for cutting, copying, or performing other modifications.

4. **Click Edit on the Paint menu bar, then click Copy**
   When an item is copied, a copy of it is placed in the Clipboard to be pasted in another location, but the item also remains in its original place in the file.

5. **Click the first line of the WordPad document**
   The WordPad program becomes active, and the insertion point is on the WordPad page, where you want the logo to appear. If you cannot see enough of the page, use the scroll buttons to adjust your view.

6. **Click the Paste button 📋 on the WordPad toolbar**
   The logo is pasted into the document, as shown in Figure B-9.

7. **Click the Maximize button in the WordPad window, click the Center button ☰ on the Format Bar, then click below the logo to deselect it**
   The logo is centered in the document.

8. **Click ⌶ at the bottom of the document, type your name, then click the Save button 💾 on the WordPad toolbar**
   The document is complete and ready for you to print.

9. **Click the Paint program button on the taskbar, then click the Close button in the Paint window**

FIGURE B-9: Logo copied from one program to another

Logo selected in Paint document

Resize handle

WordPad and Paint windows tiled vertically

Logo pasted in WordPad document

Program buttons for WordPad and Paint

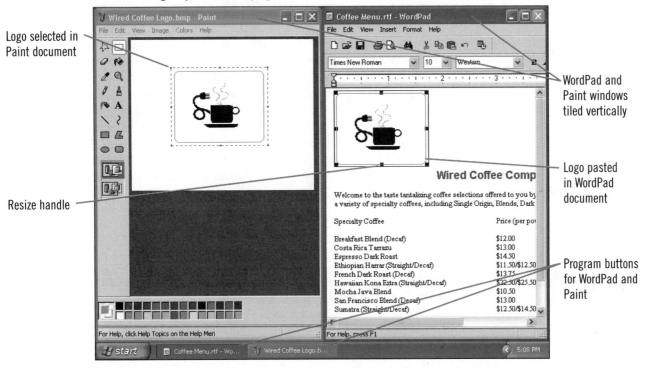

TABLE B-4: Overview of cutting, copying, and pasting

function	toolbar button	keyboard shortcut	drag-and-drop method
Cut: Removes selected information from a file and places it on the Clipboard	✂	[Ctrl][X]	Press and hold **[Shift]** as you drag selected text to move text without using the clipboard
Copy: Places a copy of selected information on the Clipboard, leaving the file intact	🗐	[Ctrl][C]	Press and hold **[Ctrl]** as you drag selected text to copy text without using the clipboard
Paste: Inserts whatever is currently on the Clipboard into another location (within the same file or in a different file)	📋	[Ctrl][V]	Release the left mouse button when you have moved text to the location you want

Switching between files

When you open many file and program windows, the taskbar groups related files together under one program button to reduce the clutter on the taskbar and save space. For example, if you have five windows open, and two of them are Paint files, the two Paint file buttons on the taskbar are grouped together into one button named *2 Paint*. When you click the *2 Paint* button on the taskbar, a menu appears listing the open Paint files, from which you can choose the file you want to view, as shown in Figure B-10. The taskbar only groups file buttons together if the taskbar is overcrowded with windows. If you have only two Paint windows opens, the Paint file buttons will not group together. To open more than one Paint window, you need to start two versions of the program using the Start menu.

FIGURE B-10: Program buttons grouped on taskbar

Windows XP

Printing a Document

Printing a document creates a **printout** or hard copy, a paper document that you can share with others or review as a work in progress. Most Windows programs have a print option that you access through the Print dialog box and a Print button on the Toolbar. Although your printing options vary from program to program, the process works similarly in all of them. It is a good idea to use the **Print Preview** feature to look at the layout and formatting of a document before you print it. You might catch a mistake, find that the document fits on more pages than you wanted, or notice formatting that you want to do differently. Making changes before you print saves paper. ✐ John decides to preview the coffee menu before printing the document. Satisfied with the result, John prints the Coffee Menu document.

1. In the WordPad window, click the **Print Preview button** 🔍 on the Toolbar
A reduced but proportionate image of the page appears in the Preview window, shown in Figure B-11.

QuickTip

To zoom out from the zoom in position, click the print preview area or click Zoom Out in Print Preview.

2. Move the pointer over the logo, the pointer changes to 🔍, then click the screen
The preview image of the page appears larger, and is easier to see. The space outside the dotted rectangle (not usable for text and graphics) is adjustable and determined by margin settings in the Page Setup dialog box. The **margin** is the space between the text and the edge of the document. The margin is too large, so you are not yet ready to print.

3. Click **Close** on the Print Preview toolbar
The Preview window closes, and you return to the Coffee Menu document.

4. Click **File** on the menu bar, then click **Page Setup**
The Page Setup dialog box opens. In this dialog box, you can change the margin setting to decrease or increase the area outside the dotted rectangle. You can control the length of a line by setting the left and right margins and the length of a page by setting the top and bottom margins. You can also change other printing options here, for example paper size, page orientation, and printer source, such as a paper bin or envelope feeder. Page orientation allows you to select **Portrait** (in which the page is taller than it is wide) or **Landscape** (in which the page is wider than it is tall).

5. In the Page Setup dialog box, select the number in the Left text box, type **1**, select the number in the Right text box, type **1**, then click **OK**
The document appears with new page margins. You should verify that you like the new margins before printing.

6. Click 🔍
The page margins are smaller.

7. Click **Print** on the Print Preview toolbar
The Print dialog box opens, as shown in Figure B-12, showing various options available for printing. Check to make sure the correct printer is specified. If you need to change printers, select a printer. When you are finished, accept all of the settings.

QuickTip

To print a document quickly, click the Print button 🖨 on the Toolbar. To open the Print dialog box from the WordPad window, click File on the menu bar, then click Print.

8. In the Print dialog box, click **Print**
The WordPad document prints. While a document prints, a printer icon 🖨 appears in the status area of the taskbar. You can point to the printer icon to get status information. To close a program and any of its currently open files, click Exit from the File menu or click the Close button in the upper-right corner of the program window.

9. Click the **Close button** in the WordPad window
If you made any changes to the open file and did not save them, you will be prompted to save your changes before the program closes.

FIGURE B-11: WordPad document in Print Preview

Click button to open Print dialog box

Click to magnify the view

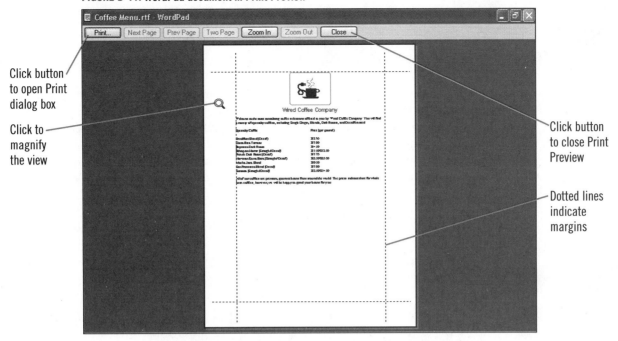

Click button to close Print Preview

Dotted lines indicate margins

FIGURE B-12: Print dialog box

Printer information

In a multiple page document, set which pages to print in the text box

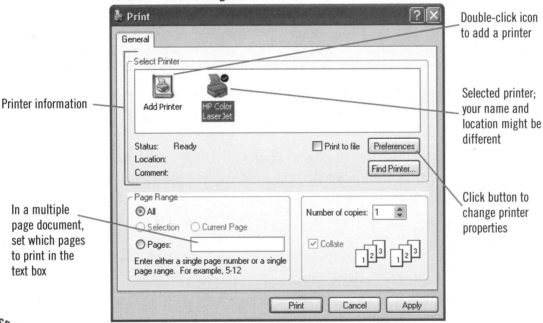

Double-click icon to add a printer

Selected printer; your name and location might be different

Click button to change printer properties

CLUES TO USE

Installing a printer

A new printer is one of the most common hardware devices that computer users install. Windows makes installing a printer quick and easy with the Add Printer Wizard. The Add Printer Wizard asks you a series of questions to help you set up either a local or network printer, install printer software, establish a connection, assign a name to the printer, and print a test page to make sure that the printer works properly. You can start the Add Printer Wizard from a Print dialog box in a program by double-clicking the Add Printer icon in the Select Printer box, or from the Control Panel by double-clicking the Printers and Faxes icon, then clicking Add a printer in the left pane under Printer Tasks. In the left pane of the Printers and Faxes window, you can also click Troubleshoot printing to help you fix a problem, or click Get help with printing to display printer information from the Help and Support Center or a Microsoft Product Support Services Web site.

Playing a Video or Sound Clip

Windows XP comes with a built-in accessory called **Windows Media Player**, which you can use to play video, sound, and mixed-media files. You can use it to play movies, music, sounds, and other multimedia files from your computer, a CD, a local network, or the Internet. The Windows Media Player delivers high-quality continuous video, live broadcasts, sound, and music playback, known as **streaming media**. You can also copy individual music tracks or entire CDs to your computer and create your own jukebox or playlist of media. With the Windows Media Player, you can modify the media, control the settings, and change the player's appearance, or **skin**. Windows XP comes with Windows Media Player version 8. To make sure you are using the most recent version of Windows Media Player, click Help on the Windows Media Player menu bar, then click Check for Player Upgrade or click Windows Update on the All Programs submenu on the Start menu. You must have an open connection to the Internet to perform this check. 🖎 John experiments using the Media Player to play a sample video and a sound.

Trouble?

If the Windows Media Player window doesn't match Figure B-13, press [Ctrl][1] to display the screen in full mode, press [Ctrl][M] to show the menu bar, then click the Show Taskbar button, if necessary.

1. Click the **Start button** on the taskbar, point to **All Programs**, point to **Accessories**, point to **Entertainment**, then click **Windows Media Player**
   The Windows Media Player opens in skin mode, in which the appearance varies, or full mode, which displays a Taskbar with tabs along the left side of the window and player controls that look and function similar to those on a CD player. The Windows Media Player opens to the Media Guide by default. If you are connected to the Internet, the WindowsMedia.com Web site appears, displaying current videos, music, and other entertainment. Otherwise, an information page appears.

2. Click **File** on the menu bar, click **Open**, click the **Look in list arrow**, then navigate to the drive and folder where your Project Files are located
   A list of all the media files in the selected folder appears in the Open dialog box.

3. Click **Coffee Cup**, then click **Open**
   The Coffee Cup video clip appears in the Now Playing tab and plays once, as shown in Figure B-13.

QuickTip

To play a music CD, insert the CD in the disc drive and wait for the Windows Media Player to start playing the CD. Double-click a track to play that track.

4. Click **File** on the menu bar, click **Open**, click the **Look in list arrow**, navigate to the drive and folder where your Project Files are located if necessary, click **AM Coffee**, then click **Open**
   The Coffee Cup video clip is closed and the AM Coffee sound clip appears in the Now Playing tab and plays once.

5. Click **Play** on the menu bar, then click **Repeat**
   You set the option to play the media clip continuously, or to **loop**.

6. Click the **Play button**
   When you play a sound in the Now Playing tab, a visual effect, known as a **visualization**, appears, displaying splashes of color and geometric shapes that change with the beat of the sound, as shown in Figure B-14.

QuickTip

To select a specific visualization, click the Select visualization or album art button 🔘, then click the visualization you want.

7. Click the **Previous Visualization button** 🔘 or the **Next Visualization button** 🔘 to change the visual effect as the sound plays, then click the **Stop button** after the audio repeats several times
   A new visual effect appears as the sound plays.

8. Click **Play** on the menu bar, click **Repeat** to turn off the option, then click the **Close button** in the Windows Media Player window

FIGURE B-13: Playing a video clip in Windows Media Player

Click button to show or hide menu bar

Full mode

Taskbar

Play button

Stop button

Playlist; your name might be different

Media clip name and length

Click button to show or hide Taskbar

FIGURE B-14: Playing an audio clip in Windows Media Player

Visualization

Visualization name; yours might be different

Media clip name and length

Volume slider

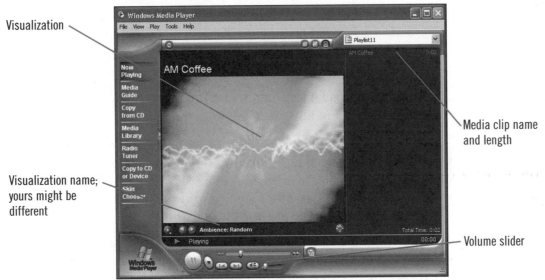

Playing media from the Internet

You can play media available on the Internet, such as videos, live broadcasts, and music tracks. You can stream the media directly from the Web site or by downloading the media file to your computer. When you stream the media, the video or music starts playing while the file is transmitted to you over the Internet. The streaming media is not stored on your computer. To stream media from the Internet, locate the Web site that contains the media you want to play using the Media Guide or Radio Tuner, click the link to the media, wait for Windows Media Player to start and the first data to be transmitted to a temporary memory storage area called the buffer, then listen to and watch the multimedia. When you download a media file, you wait for the entire file to be transferred to your computer. To download a file, use the Media Guide or a Web browser to locate the media you want to download from the Internet, click the download link to open the File Download dialog box, click the Save this file to disk option, click OK to open the Save As dialog box, specify the location in which you want to save the file, click Save, wait for the file download, then click Close.

Creating a Movie

Windows comes with a multimedia accessory called **Windows Movie Maker**, which allows you to create movies from a variety of sources. You can create a digital movie using a digital video camera or digital Web camera or use a video capture card or other device to convert images from an analog video camera, videotape, or TV. Clips are organized in a **collection** for use in movie projects. To create a movie, you assemble the clips from a collection in one of two views, storyboard or timeline, then rearrange and crop parts of the movie. Storyboard view shows the order of video clips, and timeline view shows the duration of clips. You can also add a fade-in or -out transition between clips, and add audio, music, or narration. When you finish your movie, Movie Maker can compress the file. ✐ John creates a movie from an existing collection.

Steps 1 2 3 4

1. Click the **Start button** on the taskbar, point to **All Programs**, point to **Accessories**, click **Windows Movie Maker**, then click **Exit**, if necessary, to close the tour
   The Movie Maker window opens.

2. Click **File** on the menu bar, click **Import** to open the Select the File to Import dialog box, click the **Look in list arrow**, navigate to the drive and folder where your Project Files are located, click **Coffee Cup**, then click **Open**
   Movie Maker creates a collection called Coffee Cup, which inludes the Coffee Cup video.

3. Click **File** on the menu bar, click **Import** to open the Select the File to Import dialog box, click the **Look in list arrow**, navigate to the drive and folder where your Project Files are located if necessary, click **AM Coffee**, then click **Open**
   The AM Coffee sound is added to the Coffee Cup collection, as shown in Figure B-15.

4. Drag the **Clip 1** video clip icon onto frame 1 of the storyboard
   When you drag the video clip onto the storyboard, an insertion point appears in frame 1.

5. Click the **Timeline button** 🎬 above the storyboard, then drag **AM Coffee** in the collection to the beginning of the audio track below the video clip
   When you drag the sound, an insertion point appears in the audio track to indicate where to place it. The sound appears at the beginning of the audio track with a blue border around it, indicating it is currently selected, as shown in Figure B-16.

6. Click **Play** on the menu bar, then click **Play Entire Storyboard/Timeline**
   As the movie plays, the movie time progresses, and a marker moves across the Seek Bar.

7. Click the **Save Project button** 💾 on the Toolbar to open the Save Project dialog box, click the **Look in list arrow**, navigate to the drive and folder where your Project Files are located, select the text in the File name text box, type **Coffee Meltdown**, then click **Save**
   The movie is saved in a form Movie Maker can recognize.

8. Click the **Save Movie button** 🎞 on the Toolbar to open the Save Movie dialog box, type **Coffee Meltdown** in the Title box, then type *Your Name* in the Author text box
   The Save Movie dialog box asks you to select playback quality settings and enter display information. The playback quality set affects the file size and the download time.

9. Click **OK**, click the **Save in list arrow** in the Save As dialog box, navigate to the drive and folder where your Project Files are located if necessary, click **Save**, click **Yes** to watch the movie, then close Windows Media Player and Windows Movie Maker
   The video is saved in the Windows Media Video Files (.wmv) format, and Windows Media Player plays the video.

QuickTip

To create a collection, select a folder in the Collections pane, click the New Collection button 📁, name the collection, then import existing media clips or click the Record button 📷 to create a video.

QuickTip

To adjust the length of a media clip, select the clip, then drag the End Trim handle ◢ in the Timeline. If a clip is not in the correct position, drag it in the Timeline to reposition it or click it and press [Delete].

QuickTip

To play an individual media clip, select the clip in the Timeline or Storyboard, then click the Play button ▶ on the playback controls.

Trouble?

If a warning box appears asking to backup the collection, click No.

FIGURE B-15: Adding a video to a movie in Windows Movie Maker

Video clip icon

Audio clip icon

Coffee Cup collection

Contents of the Coffee Cup collection

Preview of selected media clip

Timeline button

Storyboard

Frame 1

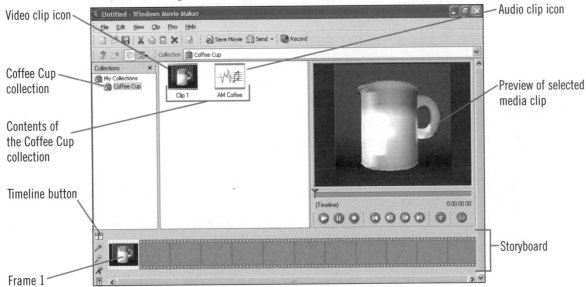

FIGURE B-16: Adding a sound to a movie in Windows Movie Maker

Save Project button

Save Movie button

Seek Bar

Media clip duration; drag End Trim handle to adjust length

Playback controls for selected media clip

Storyboard button

Video track in timeline

Audio track in timeline; selected media clip

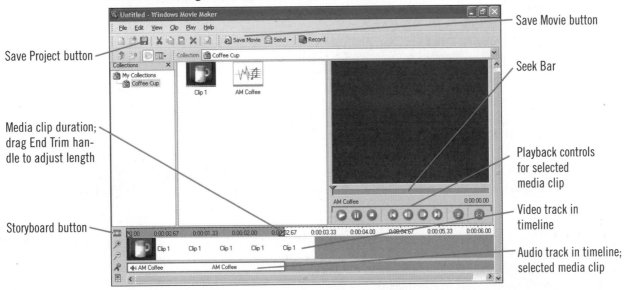

CLUES TO USE

Using copyrighted materials

When creating movies, documents, or other work on your computer where you are compiling elements from different sources, you have to consider whose property you are using. Videos, images, text, and sounds that you have created on your computer or with a digital camera, film camera, or sound recorder are your property to use as you want. However, media from other sources, including magazines, books, and the Internet are the intellectual property of others and may be copyrighted and have limitations placed on their use. Permission for you to use the material may be granted by the copyright holder. Sometimes permission is received just by asking, and other times you may be required to pay a fee. It is your legal and ethical responsibility to use only images that belong to you or that you have permission to use. Once you receive permission, you can use a scanner to transfer images to your computer or download videos, images, and sounds from the Internet.

Practice

▶ Concepts Review

Label each of the elements of the screen shown in Figure B-17.

FIGURE B-17

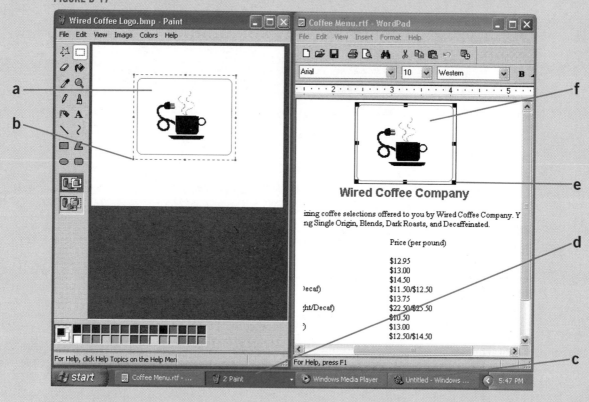

1. Which element points to a selected logo in Paint?
2. Which element points to the selected logo in WordPad?
3. Which element points to the original logo?
4. Which element points to the copied logo?
5. Which element points to a grouped program button?
6. Which element points to a nongrouped program button?

Match each term with the statement that describes its function.

7. **Accessories**
8. **Filename**
9. **Select**
10. **Cut**
11. **Copy**

a. Removes selected text or an image from its current location
b. Copies selected text or an image from its current location
c. A set of characters you assign to a collection of information
d. A collection of programs that come built-in with Windows and enable you to perform certain tasks
e. What you must first do to existing text before you can format, move, or copy it

Select the best answers from the following lists of choices.

12. **What program command makes a copy of a file?**
    a. Copy
    b. Duplicate
    c. Save As
    d. Save

13. **When WordPad automatically moves words to the next line, it is called:**
    a. Margin.
    b. Word wrap.
    c. Tab.
    d. Format insert.

14. **Which of the following is not a way to select text?**
    a. Drag over the text
    b. Click the left margin in a line of text
    c. Click File on the menu bar, then click Select
    d. Double-click a word

15. **What is the name of the Windows location that stores cut or copied information?**
    a. Start menu
    b. Hard drive
    c. Paint
    d. Clipboard

16. **Which of the following controls the size of the empty border around a document?**
    a. Paper Size
    b. Paper Source
    c. Orientation
    d. Margins

▶ Skills Review

1. **Open and save a WordPad document.**
   a. Start WordPad.
   b. Open the WordPad file named **Win B-3** from the drive and folder where your Project Files are located.
   c. Save the file as **Choose Coffee** to the drive and folder where your Project Files are located.

2. **Edit text in a WordPad document.**
   a. Change the spelling of the word "neuances" to "nuances" in the last paragraph.
   b. Insert a space between the characters "r" and "a" in the word "ora" in the last line of the first paragraph.
   c. Delete the word "heavy" in the last line of the first paragraph, then replace it with "medium."
   d. Move the first paragraph and its title to one line below the second paragraph and title.

3. **Format text in WordPad.**
   a. Select all the text in the file named **Choose Coffee**.
   b. Change the text font to Garamond (or another available font), then change its size to 12 point.
   c. Center the text "Wired Coffee," then change it to 16 point boldface.
   d. Underline the text "How to Choose a Coffee" and "How to Taste the Difference," and change both to 14 point font size and blue color.
   e. Click anywhere in the WordPad window outside of the selected text, then save the document.

4. **Use Paint.**
   a. Start Paint, then open the file **Win B-2** from the drive and folder where your Project Files are located.
   b. Save this file as **Wired Coffee Logo 2** to the drive and folder where your Project Files are located.
   c. Draw a green circle around the logo.
   d. Use the Undo command or Eraser/Color tool as necessary if the circle doesn't fit around the logo.
   e. Save the file.

5. Copy data between programs.

a. Tile the WordPad and Paint windows vertically. (*Hint:* Maximize both windows first.)

b. Select the logo in the Paint window, then copy it to the Clipboard.

c. In WordPad, place the insertion point at the beginning of the document, then maximize WordPad.

d. Paste the logo in the blank line, then center it.

e. Save the Choose Coffee file. Close the Wired Coffee Logo 2 file, then close Paint.

6. Print a document.

a. Add your name to the bottom of the document, then print the Choose Coffee file.

b. Close all open documents, then close WordPad.

7. Play a video clip or sound.

a. Start Windows Media Player.

b. Open the Better Coffee sound from the drive and folder where your Project Files are located.

c. Play the sound, change the visualization, then close Windows Media Player.

8. Create a movie.

a. Start Windows Movie Maker.

b. Import the Coffee Cup video and the Better Coffee sound from the drive and folder where your Project Files are located.

c. Drag the video clip to frame 1, then drag the sound clip to the audio track.

d. Drag another copy of the video clip after the first one, drag the End Trim handle to reduce the size of the video clip to end with the audio track, then play the movie.

e. Save the project as **Coffee Time**, give the movie file the same name, save it with medium quality, then close Windows Movie Maker.

► Independent Challenge 1

You own an international bookstore, and you need to create a bestsellers list of international books that you can give to customers. Use WordPad to create a new document that lists the top 10 bestselling international books in your stock. In the document include the name of your bookstore and its street address, city, state, zip code, and phone number, and for each book, the author's name (last name first), title, and publication date. You will make up this information.

a. Start WordPad. Enter the heading (the name of the bookstore, address, city, state, zip code, and phone number), pressing [Enter] after the name, address, and zip code.

b. Center the heading information and add color to the heading text.

c. Enter the title **Bestsellers List**, center it, then change the font size to 18 point.

d. Enter the information for at least 10 books, using [Tab] to create columns for the author's name, the title, and the publication date. Be sure that the columns line up with one another.

e. Italicize the title of each book, then format the last and first names of each author with boldface.

f. Add your name to the bottom of the document.

g. Save the list as **Bestsellers List** to the drive and folder where your Project Files are located.

h. Print the document, then close WordPad.

▶ Independent Challenge 2

Your parents are celebrating their twenty-fifth wedding anniversary. Using WordPad, you want to create an invitation to a party for them. Using Paint, you then want to paste a map of the party location onto the invitation.

a. Start WordPad, then type the information for the invitation, which includes the invitation title, your parents' names; date, time, and location of the party; directions; your name and phone number; and the date to respond by.

b. Change the title text to 18 point, boldface, center align, then add color.

c. Change the rest of the text to 14 point Times New Roman.

d. Save the WordPad document as **Invitation** to the drive and folder where your Project Files are located.

e. Start Paint, then open the file **Invitation Map** from the drive and folder where your Project Files are located.

f. Copy the map to the Clipboard.

g. Place the insertion point above the instructions in the invitation, then paste the map into the WordPad document.

h. Add your name to the bottom of the document.

i. Save the document, preview the document, make any necessary changes, then print the document.

j. Close WordPad and Paint.

▶ Independent Challenge 3

As vice president of Things-That-Fly, a kite and juggling store, you need to design a new type of logo, consisting of three simple circles, each colored differently. You use Paint to design the logo, then you paste the logo into a WordPad document.

a. Start Paint, then create a small circle, using the [Shift] key and the Ellipse tool.

b. Select the circle using the Select tool, then copy the circle.

c. Paste the circle from the Clipboard in the Paint window, then use the mouse to drag the second circle below and a bit to the right of the first.

d. Paste the circle again, then use the mouse to drag the third circle below and a bit to the left of the first.

e. For each circle, use the Fill With Color tool in the Toolbox, select the color in the Color box you want the circle to be, then click inside the circle you want to fill with that color.

f. Using the Select tool, select the completed logo, then copy it.

g. Save the Paint file as **Stationery Logo** to the drive and folder where your Project Files are located.

h. Open WordPad, place the insertion point on the first line, then center it.

i. Paste the logo in the document, deselect the logo, press [Enter] twice, then type **Things-That-Fly**.

j. Change the text to 18 point boldface, then add several colors that coordinate with the logo.

k. Add your name to the bottom of the document.

l. Save the WordPad document as **Stationery** to the drive and folder where your Project Files are located.

m. Preview the document, make any changes, print the document, then close WordPad and Paint.

▶ Independent Challenge 4

As creative director at Digital Arts, a music company, you need to find sample sounds for a demo CD. You use Windows Media Player to open sound files located on your computer or the Internet (if available) and play them. You also use the Media Library in Windows Media Player to keep track of the sounds you like best.

a. Open Windows Media Player.

b. Open all the sound files in the Media folder (in the Windows folder) on your computer, or play sounds on the Internet using the Media Guide. (*Hint:* You can use the Search Computer For Media command on the Tools menu to help you find the sounds.)

c. Play each sound file. Close the Windows Media Player.

▶ Visual Workshop

Re-create the screen shown in Figure B-18, which displays the Windows desktop with more than one program window open. You can use the file **Win B-2** for the coffee cup logo (Save it as **A Cup of Coffee** to the drive and folder where your Project Files are located) and the file **Wired Coffee Logo**. Create a new WordPad document, save it as **Good Time Coffee Club** to the drive and folder where your Project Files are located, and enter the text shown in the figure. Print the screen. (Press [Print Screen] to make a copy of the screen, open Paint, click Edit on the menu bar, click Paste to paste the screen into Paint, then click Yes to paste the large image, if necessary. Click the Text button on the Toolbox, click an empty space in the Paint work area, then type your name. Click File on the menu bar, click Page Setup, change 100% normal size to 50% in the scaling area, then click OK. Click File on the menu bar, click Print, then click Print.)

FIGURE B-18

Managing
Files and Folders

Objectives

- ► **Understand file management**
- ► **Open and view My Computer**
- ► **View files and folders**
- ► **View the Folders list**
- ► **Create and rename files and folders**
- ► **Search for files and folders**
- ► **Copy and move files and folders**
- ► **Delete and restore files and folders**
- ► **Create a shortcut to a file or folder**

File management is organizing and keeping track of files and folders. A **folder** is a container for storing programs and files, similar to a folder in a file cabinet. Windows XP provides you with two file management programs: **My Computer** and **Windows Explorer**. My Computer and Windows Explorer allow you to work with more than one computer, folder, or file at once by using a split window with two **panes**, or frames, to accommodate comparison of information from two different locations. Windows Explorer displays the split window by default, while in My Computer, you need to click a button to display the split window.

In this unit, John Casey, the owner of Wired Coffee Company, reviews the files on his computer and learns about how to keep them organized and also to prepare for the upcoming Wired Coffee Spring Catalog. John keeps the Project Files for this unit on a floppy disk, but yours might be in a different location; if you are not sure how to locate your Project Files, contact your instructor or technical support person.

Understanding File Management

Managing files and folders enables you to quickly locate any file that you created and need to use again. Working with poorly managed files is like looking for a needle in a haystack—it is frustrating and time-consuming to search through several irrelevant, misnamed, and out-of-date files to find the one you want. Windows allows you to organize folders and files in a file hierarchy, imitating the way you store paper documents in real folders. Just as a filing cabinet contains several folders, each containing a set of related documents and several dividers grouping related folders together, a **file hierarchy** allows you to place files in folders, then place folders in other folders, so that your files are neat and organized. Figure C-1 shows the Wired Coffee folder hierarchy, with the files and folders that John uses in his business. At the top of the hierarchy is the name of the folder, Wired Coffee. This folder contains several files and folders, and each folder contains related files and folders.

As you examine the figure, note that file management can help you to do the following:

▶ **Organize files and folders in a file hierarchy so that information is easy to locate and use**
John stores all of his correspondence files in a folder called Letters. Within that folder are two more folders. One named Business Letters holds all business correspondence. The other, Personal Letters, holds all of John's personal correspondence.

▶ **Save files in a folder with an appropriate name for easy identification**
John has a folder named Sales in which he stores all information about sales for the current year. He also places files related to accounting information in this folder.

▶ **Create a new folder so you can reorganize information**
Now that John does more advertising for Wired Coffee Company, he wants to create a new folder to store files related to these marketing efforts.

▶ **Delete files and folders that you no longer need**
John deletes files when he's sure he will not use them again, to free disk space and keep his disk organized and uncluttered.

▶ **Find a file when you cannot remember where you stored it**
John knows he created a letter to a supplier earlier this week, but now that he is ready to revise the letter, he cannot find it. Using the Search command, he can find that letter quickly and revise it in no time.

▶ **Create shortcuts to files and folders**
John created a file within a folder, within another folder to keep it organized with other related files. When he wants to access the file, he has to open several folders, which can take several steps. To save him time in accessing the files, folders, and programs he uses most frequently, John can create shortcuts, or links, in any location, such as the desktop or Start menu, to gain instant access to them. All John needs to do is double-click the shortcut icon to open the file or a program, or view the contents of a folder.

FIGURE C-1: How John uses Windows to organize his files

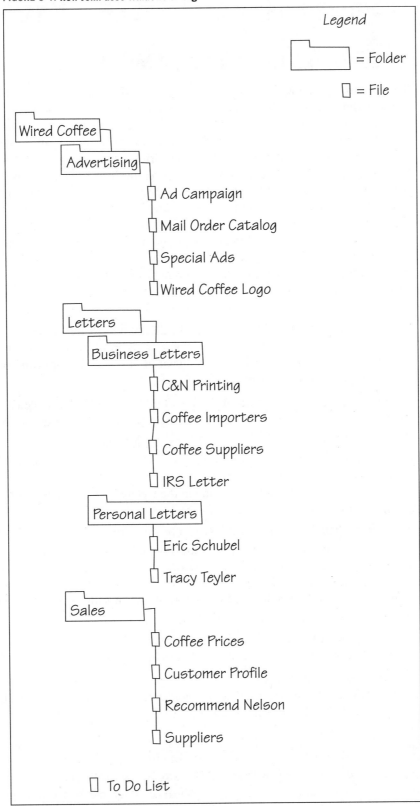

Legend

= Folder

= File

Wired Coffee

Advertising

Ad Campaign

Mail Order Catalog

Special Ads

Wired Coffee Logo

Letters

Business Letters

C&N Printing

Coffee Importers

Coffee Suppliers

IRS Letter

Personal Letters

Eric Schubel

Tracy Teyler

Sales

Coffee Prices

Customer Profile

Recommend Nelson

Suppliers

To Do List

Opening and Viewing My Computer

The keys to organizing files and folders effectively within a hierarchy are to store related items together and to name folders informatively. Proper hierarchy and relevant names allow you to get a good idea of what's on your system just by looking at the higher levels of your file hierarchy; you don't have to examine every individual file or memorize a coding system. Drives and folders are represented by icons. Table C-1 lists the typical drives on a computer and how you use them. Each drive is assigned a drive letter, denoted with parenthesis and a colon, such as Local Disk (C:), to help make it easier to identify. Typically, the floppy is drive A, the hard (also known as local) disk is drive C, and the CD is drive D. If your computer includes additional drives, they are assigned letters by your computer in alphabetical order. Like most other windows, the My Computer window contains a toolbar, a status bar (which might not be activated) providing information about the contents of the window, a menu bar, and a list of contents. ✎ The file hierarchy on John's disk contains several folders and files organized by topic. He will use My Computer to review this organization and see if it needs changes.

1. **Click the Start button on the taskbar, then click My Computer**
   The My Computer window opens, displaying the contents of your computer, including all disk drives and common folders, as shown in Figure C-2. Since computers differ, your My Computer window probably looks different.

2. **Click the Maximize button in the My Computer window, if necessary**
   Now you can see the entire toolbar and the contents of the window as you work.

3. **Click the drive where your Project Files are located**
   The left pane in the Details section displays details about the selected drive and other related management tasks. In this example, details about the 3½ Floppy (A:) disk drive appear. If you select a hard disk drive, the left pane in the Details section displays additional information, including free space and total disk size.

4. **Double-click the drive and folder where your Project Files are located**
   You can see the folders contained on the disk drive. When you open a disk drive or folder, the Address bar changes to indicate the new location. In this example, the Address bar changed from My Computer to disk drive A (A:\), and the title bar for the My Computer window changed to 3½ Floppy (A:). To see what the folders stored on the disk drive contain, you need to open them.

5. **Double-click the Wired Coffee folder**
   You can see the files and folders that the Wired Coffee folder contains. Different types of icons represent files created using different applications. You want to see what files the Sales folder contains.

6. **Double-click the Sales folder**
   You can now see the files that the Sales folder contains. You created these files using WordPad and saved them in the Sales folder.

Opening a document with a different program

Most documents on your desktop are associated with a specific program. For example, if you double-click a document whose filename ends with the three-letter extension ".txt," Windows XP automatically opens the document with Notepad, a text only editor. There are situations, though, when you need to open a document with a program other than the one Windows chooses, or when you want to choose a different default program.

For example, you might want to open a text document in WordPad rather than Notepad so that you can add formatting and graphics. To do this, right-click the document icon you want to open, point to Open With, then click the application you want to use to open the document, or click Choose Program to access more program options. Once you open a text file using WordPad, this option is automatically added to the Open With menu.

FIGURE C-2: My Computer window

Standard Buttons toolbar

Left pane; common tasks related to drives and folders

Floppy disk drive

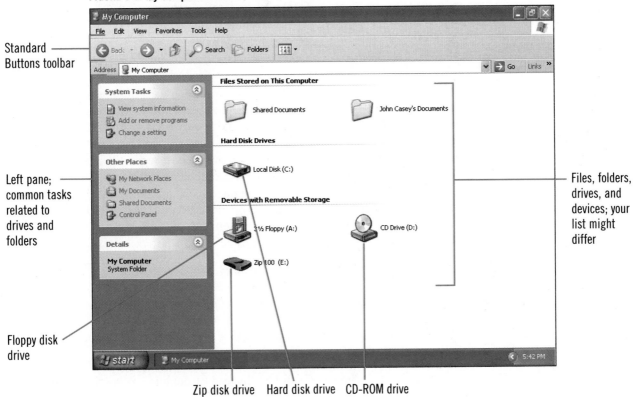

Zip disk drive   Hard disk drive   CD-ROM drive

Files, folders, drives, and devices; your list might differ

TABLE C-1: Typical disk drives on a computer

icon	type	description
	Local	A hard magnetic disk on which you can store large amounts of data. The disk is faster to access than a floppy disk and typically not removable from the computer
	Floppy	A soft magnetic removable disk that comes in two sizes: 5 ¼-inch (the common size for computers through the early 1990s), which stores up to 1.2 MB (megabytes) of data, and 3 ½-inch, which stores up to 1.44 MB of data. Floppy disks are slower to access than a hard disk, but are portable and much less expensive
	Zip	A soft magnetic removable disk on which you can store 100 MB to 500 MB of computer data. Zip drives are not standard on all computers
	Compact Disc-Read-Only Memory (CD-ROM)	An optical disk on which you can stamp, or burn, up to 1 GB (typical size is 650 MB) of data in only one session. The disc cannot be erased or burned again with additional new data
	Compact Disc-Recordable (CD-R)	A type of CD-ROM on which you can burn up to 1 GB of data in multiple sessions. The disc can be burned again with additional new data, but cannot be erased
	Compact Disc-Rewritable (CD-RW)	A type of CD-ROM on which you can read, write, and erase data, just like a floppy or hard disk
	Digital Video Disc (DVD)	A type of CD-ROM that holds a minimum of 4.7 GB, enough for a full-length movie

Viewing Files and Folders

Once you have opened more than one folder, buttons on the Standard Buttons toolbar help you move quickly between folders in My Computer. When you open a folder, Windows XP keeps track of where you have been. To go back or forward to a folder you already visited, click the Back or Forward button. To go to a folder you visited two or more locations ago, click the Back or Forward list arrow to display a menu of places you visited. To move up one step in the hierarchy, you can click the Up button. When you view a folder in the My Computer window, you can use the Views button on the Standard Buttons toolbar to change the way you view file and folder icons. Table C-2 lists the Standard Buttons toolbar buttons. ✍ John moves between folders and changes the way he views folders and files, depending upon the information he needs.

Steps 1 2 3 4

Trouble?

If Microsoft Word or another word processing program is installed on your computer, your document icons may be different.

1. **Click the Up button 🗁 on the Standard Buttons toolbar**
   The Wired Coffee folder and its contents appear in the Wired Coffee window, as shown in Figure C-3. Each time you click the Up button, you move up one step in the folder hierarchy. In this example, the descending hierarchy is 3 ½ Floppy (A:) to Wired Coffee folder to Sales folder. You moved up one step from the Sales folder to the Wired Coffee folder.

2. **Click 🗁 again**
   You should now see the Wired Coffee folder. Instead of double-clicking the Wired Coffee folder icon again to reopen the folder, you can click the Back button on the Standard Buttons toolbar to go back to the previous folder you visited, which, in this case, is Wired Coffee.

QuickTip

You can also press [Backspace] to go back to a previous folder you visited.

3. **Click the Back button ⬅ Back ▾ on the Standard Buttons toolbar**
   The Wired Coffee folder and its contents appear in the My Computer window. You want to open other folders.

4. **Double-click the Advertising folder**
   The Advertising window appears, displaying its contents. You want to go back to the Sales folder. You can click the Back list arrow to display a menu, then select the Sales folder.

5. **Click the Back list arrow ⬅ Back ▾ on the toolbar**
   The Back list arrow, shown in Figure C-4, displays the folders you visited recently. You can click the Forward button on the Standard Buttons toolbar to return to the folder that you visited recently, in this case, the Wired Coffee folder.

6. **Click Sales, then click the Forward button ➡ ▾ on the Standard Buttons toolbar**
   The Wired Coffee window appears, displaying the contents of the folder. You want to switch the view to Details view.

QuickTip

To display additional file and folder information, click View on the menu bar, click Choose Details, select the items you want to add, then click OK in the Choose Details dialog box.

7. **Click the Views button ▦▾ on the Standard Buttons toolbar, then click Details**
   The display changes to Details view, which shows the name, size of the object, type of file, and date on which each folder or file was last modified, as shown in Figure C-5.

8. **Click ▦▾, then click Tiles**
   The display changes to Tiles view, which displays summary information (file name, file type, and size) next to each icon. Instead of using the toolbar for navigating between folders and drives, you can use the **Address bar**, which makes it easy to open items on the desktop and the drives and in the folders and system folders on your computer.

9. **Click the Address list arrow on the Address bar, then click My Computer**
   The My Computer window appears, displaying drives and common folders.

FIGURE C-3: Viewing files and folders in Tiles view

Back button—

Up button—

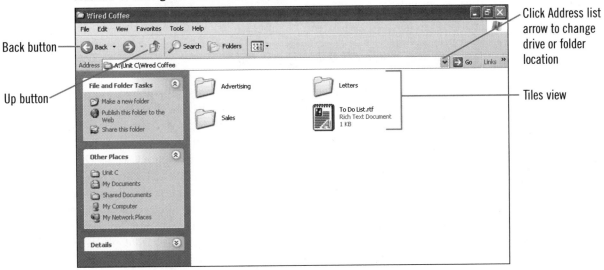

Click Address list
arrow to change
drive or folder
location

Tiles view

FIGURE C-4: Moving between folders

Back list arrow—

FIGURE C-5: Viewing files and folders in Details view

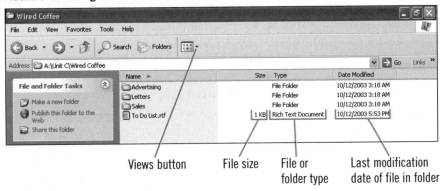

Views button   File size   File or   Last modification
folder type   date of file in folder

TABLE C-2: My Computer toolbar buttons

button	name	function
Back ▾	**Back**	Moves to the previous location you visited
⊙ ▾	**Forward**	Moves forward to the previous location you visited
⬆	**Up**	Moves up one level in the file hierarchy
🔍	**Search**	Lets you search for folders or files
📁	**Folders**	Displays a list of folders on your computer
▦ ▾	**Views**	Displays the contents of My Computer using different views

Windows XP

Viewing the Folders List

Windows XP offers another useful feature for managing files and folders, called the **Folders list** (also known as the **Folders Explorer bar**), which displays the file hierarchy of the drives and folders on your computer. At the top of the file hierarchy is the desktop, followed by My Documents, My Computer, My Network Places, then other drives and their folders. The Folders Explorer bar splits the window into two panes, or frames, as shown in Figure C-6, which allows you to view information from two different locations. The left pane of the Folders Explorer bar displays all drives and folders on the computer, and the right pane displays the contents of the selected drive or folder. This arrangement enables you to view the file hierarchy of your computer and the contents of a folder simultaneously. Using the Expand indicator ⊞ and Collapse indicator ⊟ to the left of an icon in the Folders Explorer bar allows you to display different levels of the drives and folders on your computer without opening and displaying the contents of each folder. With its split window, the Folders Explorer bar makes it easy to copy, move, delete, and rename files and folders. You can move back and forth to the last drive or folder you opened using the Back and Forward buttons on the Standard Buttons toolbar just as you did in the My Computer window. If you are working in My Computer, you can click the Folders button on the Standard Buttons toolbar to display the Folders Explorer bar. Windows Explorer displays the Folders Explorer bar in a split window by default. ✐ John wants to open the Letters folder without opening and displaying the contents of each folder in the file hierarchy.

QuickTip

To open Windows Explorer, click the Start button, point to All Programs, point to Accessories, then click Windows Explorer.

1. Click the **Folders button** 🗀 on the Standard Buttons toolbar
   The Folders Explorer bar opens, displaying the contents of your computer's hard drive. Note that the contents of your Folders Explorer bar will vary, depending on the programs and files installed on your computer and on where Windows is installed on your hard disk or network.

2. Click the **Expand indicator** ⊞ next to the drive icon where your Project Files are located in the Folders Explorer bar
   The drive where your Project Files are located expands the folder structure for the drive under the icon in the Folders Explorer bar, as shown in Figure C-6. ⊞ changes to the Collapse indicator ⊟, indicating all the folders on the drive or folder are displayed. Because you did not click the floppy drive icon, the right pane displays My Computer as it did before. You decide to display the folders on the floppy disk drive.

QuickTip

When neither ⊞ nor ⊟ appears next to an icon, the item has no folders in it. However, it might contain files, whose names you can display in the right pane by clicking the icon.

3. Click the drive icon where your Project Files are located in the Folders Explorer bar
   When you click a drive or folder in the Folders Explorer bar, the contents of that drive or folder appear in the right pane. In this case, the 3½ Floppy (A:) opens.

4. Click ⊞ next to the folder where your Project Files are located in the Folders Explorer bar, then click ⊞ next to the Wired Coffee folder in the Folders Explorer bar
   The folders in the Wired Coffee folder expand and appear in the Folders Explorer bar. Because you did not click the Wired Coffee folder icon, the right pane still displays the contents of the 3½ Floppy (A:). You can open a folder or a document in the right pane of the window.

QuickTip

To change the size of the left and right panes, place the mouse pointer on the vertical bar separating the two window panes, the pointer changes to ↔, then drag to change the size of the panes.

5. Click the **Letters folder** in the Folders Explorer bar
   The right pane shows the contents of the Letters folder and the Folders Explorer bar shows the folders in the expanded Letters folder. When you double-click a drive or folder in the right pane, the right pane of the window shows the contents of that item. When you double-click a document, the program associated with the document starts and opens the document.

6. Double-click the **Business Letters folder** in the right pane
   The Business Letters folder opens, as shown in Figure C-7. The right pane shows the contents of the Business Letters folder.

FIGURE C-6: **Folders on the 3½ floppy disk drive**

Address bar

Folders Explorer bar

Project Disk folders; yours may differ

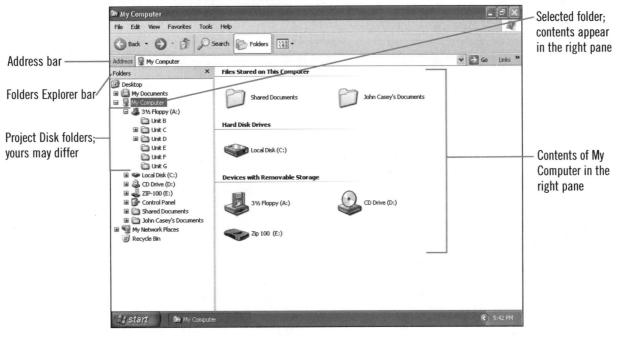

Selected folder; contents appear in the right pane

Contents of My Computer in the right pane

FIGURE C-7: **Business Letters folder**

Open folder icon indicates the folder is open and its contents appear in the right pane

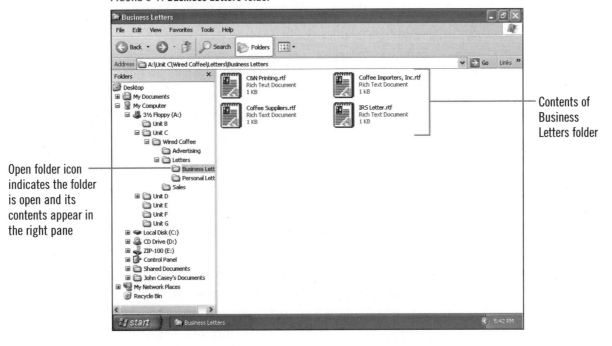

Contents of Business Letters folder

Viewing files using the History list

Windows keeps a list of your most recently used files, folders, and network computers in the History folder. Instead of navigating through a long list of folders to open a recently used file, you can use the History Explorer bar to find it quickly. To display the History Explorer bar on the left side of the screen, click View on the menu bar, point to Explorer bar, then click History. You can view the History Explorer bar in several ways: by date, by site, by most visited, and by order visited today. In the History Explorer bar, click the Views button, then click the view you want. To open a file, double-click the file name in the History Explorer bar. When you double-click a file, the program associated with the file starts and opens the file.

Creating and Renaming Files and Folders

Creating a new folder can help you organize and keep track of files and other folders. In order to create a folder, you select the location where you want the new folder, then create the folder, then lastly, name the folder. You should name each folder meaningfully, so that just by reading the folder's name you know its contents. After you name a folder or file, you can rename it at any time. You can change the way individual files and folders are sorted by using other Arrange Icons options on the View menu, as described in Table C-2. ✐ John wants to create a set of new folders to hold the files for the Wired Coffee Spring Catalog. Then, he renames a file.

1. **Click the Wired Coffee folder in the Folders Explorer bar**
   Next, you will create a new folder in the Wired Coffee folder.

2. **Click File on the menu bar, point to New, then click Folder**
   A new folder, temporarily named New Folder, appears highlighted with a rectangle around the title in the right pane of Windows Explorer, as shown in Figure C-8. To enter a new folder name, you simply type the new name. You name the new folder Spring Catalog.

Trouble?

If nothing happens when you type the name, click the folder, click the name "New Folder" so that a rectangle surrounds it and the insertion point is inside, then repeat Step 3.

3. **Type Spring Catalog, then press [Enter]**
   The Spring Catalog folder appears in both panes. When you create a new folder, the icon for the new folder is placed at the end of the list of files and folders. You can rearrange, or sort, the icons in the folder to make them easier to find.

4. **Click View on the menu bar, point to Arrange Icons by, then click Name to select it if necessary**
   The folder and file icons in the Wired Coffee folder are sorted by name in alphabetical order (folders first, then files) and automatically aligned with the other icons. You want to create folders within the Spring Catalog folder.

5. **In the right pane, double-click the Spring Catalog folder**
   Nothing appears in the right pane because the folder is empty; no new files or folders have been created or moved here.

6. **Right-click anywhere in the right pane, point to New on the shortcut menu, click Folder, type Catalog Pages as the new folder name, then press [Enter]**
   The folder is now named Catalog Pages. Notice that the Expand indicator ⊞ appears next to the Spring Catalog folder in the left pane, indicating that this folder contains other folders or files.

7. **Click the Back button ⬅ Back ▾ on the Standard Buttons toolbar**
   The Wired Coffee folder is displayed. Now you will rename a file.

QuickTip

To quickly change a file or folder name, select the icon, click the name, then type a new name.

8. **Right-click the To Do List file in the right pane, then click Rename on the shortcut menu, as shown in Figure C-9**
   The file appears highlighted, in the right pane. When the text is highlighted, you can click in the title to place the insertion point and make changes to part of the filename.

Trouble?

If a warning box appears, click No, then retype the file name, typing ".rtf" at the end of the filename.

9. **Type Important, then press [Enter]**
   The file is renamed Important. You can use the same procedure to rename a folder.

FIGURE C-8: Creating a new folder

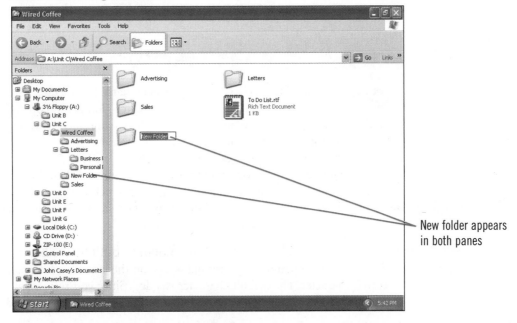

New folder appears in both panes

FIGURE C-9: Renaming a file using the right-click method

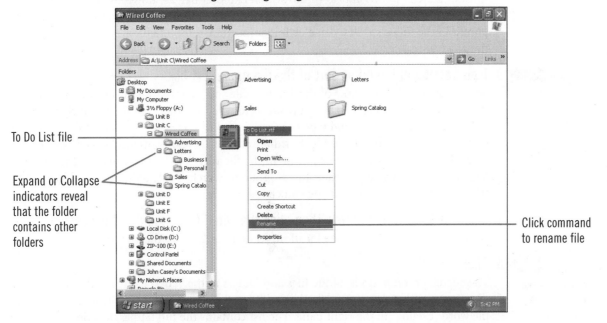

To Do List file

Expand or Collapse indicators reveal that the folder contains other folders

Click command to rename file

TABLE C-2: Options for arranging files and folders

option	arranges files and folders
Name	Alphabetically
Size	By size, with the largest folder or file listed first
Type	By type, such as all documents created using the WordPad program
Modified	Chronologically by their last modification date, with the latest modification date listed last
Show in Groups	In letter groups by alphabetical order
Auto Arrange	Automatically in orderly rows and columns
Align to Grid	Automatically in rows and columns by invisible grid points

Searching for Files and Folders

Sometimes remembering precisely where you stored a file is difficult. Windows provides a Search Companion to help you find files or folders. The Search Companion opens in the Search Explorer bar and gives you the option to find files or folders by name, location, size, type, and the creation or last modification date. You can also narrow your search by selecting categories, listed in the Search Companion. The Search Companion is also accessible from the Start menu to help you locate files and folders when you are not using My Computer or Windows Explorer. John wants to find a file he created several months ago with a preliminary outline for the Spring Catalog. He cannot remember the exact title of the file or where he stored it, so he needs to do a search.

1. Click the Search button 🔍 on the Standard Buttons toolbar

The Search Companion Explorer bar opens on the left side of the screen with an animated search character. The default character is a dog. Since you remember part of the name, but not the location, of the file you need, you will use the All files and folders option.

QuickTip

To turn off the animated search character, click Change preferences in the Search Explorer bar, then click Without an animated screen character.

2. In the Search Companion Explorer bar, click All files and folders

A list of search options appear in the Search Explorer bar, as shown in Figure C-10. You can enter search information to find folders and files by all or part of the file name, a word or phrase in the file, a specific drive or folder location, a modified date, a size range, or additional advanced criteria.

QuickTip

Use the * (asterisk) wild-card symbol in a filename when you're unsure of the entire name. For example, type "S*rs" to find all files beginning with "S" and ending with "rs," such as Stars and Sports cars.

3. Type catalog in the All or part of the file name text box

You can supply the full name of the folder or file you want to find or only the part you know for sure. If, for example, you were unsure as to whether you saved the file as Spring Catalog or Catalog Outline, you could type Catalog, since you're sure of that part of the name. If you didn't know the name of the file, but did know some text contained in the file, you could enter the text in the A word or phrase in the file text box. Before you start the search, you need to indicate where you want the program to search. By default, the search will occur in the currently open folder, but you can choose any location.

4. Click the Look in list arrow, then click the Wired Coffee folder if necessary

Now that you have defined the location, you are ready to do the search.

5. Click Search

The Search program finds all the files and folders in the Wired Coffee folder, switches from the current folder view to Details view, and lists those files and folders whose names contain the word "catalog" in the right pane. The list contains the full names, locations, sizes, types, and the creation or last modification dates of the folders or files.

QuickTip

To cancel a search, click the Close button in the Search Companion Explorer bar.

6. Position the pointer between the In Folder column indicator button and the Size column indicator button, the pointer changes to ↔, then drag to the right to display the location of the file if necessary, as shown in Figure C-11.

At this point, you can either double-click the file to start the associated program and open the file, or you can note the file's location and close the Search Explorer bar. You decide to note the file's location and return to viewing folders.

7. In the Search Companion Explorer bar, click Yes, finished searching to complete the search and close the Search Companion Explorer bar

8. Click the Folders button 📂 on the Standard Buttons toolbar to open the Folders Explorer bar

FIGURE C-10: Search Explorer bar with All files and folders option

Click button to
begin the search
process

Enter name or
partial name of
the file you are
looking for here

Enter text
contained in
the file here

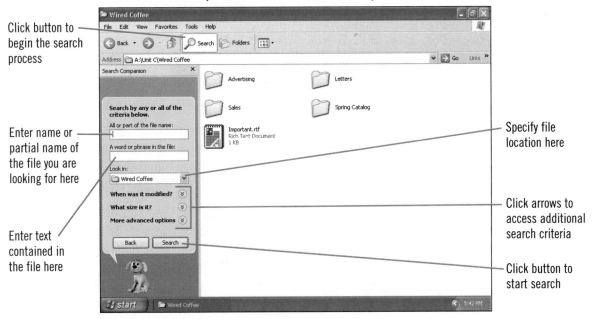

Specify file
location here

Click arrows to
access additional
search criteria

Click button to
start search

FIGURE C-11: Results of search for "catalog"

Drag to resize
column size

Additional
search options
with the results

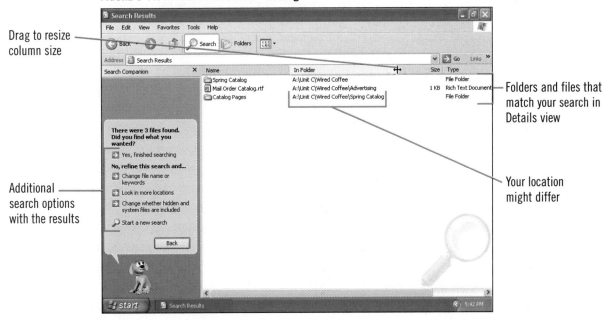

Folders and files that
match your search in
Details view

Your location
might differ

Performing an advanced search

You can also perform an advanced search that uses criteria beyond just the name or partial name of the file. If you do not know what the name or content of the file is, but can recall the type of file (such as a WordPad document), click All Files and Folders, click More Advanced Options, then select a file type using the Type of file list arrow and other location specific or case sensitive options. When you click Search, Windows searches for and displays all the files for the type you specify. In some cases, this can take a long time, although probably less time than re-creating the missing files would take.

Windows XP

Copying and Moving Files and Folders

Sometimes you will need to move a file from one folder to another, or copy a file from one folder to another, leaving it in the first location and placing a copy of it in the second. You can move or copy a file or folder using a variety of methods. If the file or folder and the location where you want to move it are visible in a window or on the desktop, you can simply drag the item from one location to the other. Moving a file or folder on the same disk relocates it; whereas dragging it from one disk to another copies it so that it appears in both locations. To make sure that you move or copy an item properly, right-click the file or folder, drag the item to the destination location, then choose the appropriate command from the shortcut menu. When the destination folder or drive is not visible, you can use the Cut, Copy, and Paste commands on the Edit menu or the buttons on the Standard Buttons toolbar. John plans to use and revise the text from the Mail Order Catalog file, currently located in the Advertising folder, which is in the Spring Catalog folder. The Mail Order Catalog file is no longer needed in the Advertising folder, so John moves it from the Advertising folder to the Catalog Pages folder to keep related files together. He also wants to make a copy of the Wired Coffee Logo file and place it in the Spring Catalog folder.

QuickTip

To select files or folders that are not consecutive, press and hold [Ctrl], then click each item in the right pane.

1. **Click the Expand indicator ⊞ next to the Spring Catalog folder in the Folders Explorer bar**
   The Spring Catalog folder expands, displaying the folder it contains. The right pane shows the results of the search. When moving or copying files or folders, make sure the files or folders you want to move or copy appear in the right pane. To move the Mail Order Catalog file, you drag it from the right pane to the Catalog Pages folder in the Folders Explorer bar.

Trouble?

If the search results are not available, click the Advertising folder in the Folders Explorer bar.

2. **Drag the Mail Order Catalog file in the right pane from the list of search results across the vertical line separating the two panes to the Catalog Pages folder as shown in Figure C-12, then release the mouse button**
   Once you release the mouse button, the Mail Order Catalog file is relocated to the Catalog Pages folder. If you decide that you don't want the file moved, you could move it back easily using the Undo command on the Edit menu. Now you copy the Wired Coffee Logo file in the Advertising folder to the Spring Catalog folder.

3. **Click the Advertising folder in the Folders Explorer bar**
   Notice that the Mail Order Catalog file is no longer stored in the Advertising folder.

4. **Point to the Wired Coffee Logo file, press and hold the right mouse button, drag the file across the vertical line separating the two panes to the Spring Catalog folder, then release the mouse button**
   As shown in Figure C-13, a shortcut menu appears, offering a choice of options. Another way to copy or move the file to a new location is by right-clicking a file in the right pane, then clicking the appropriate option on the shortcut menu.

QuickTip

To copy a file quickly from one folder to another on the same disk, select the file, press and hold [Ctrl], then drag the file to the folder.

5. **Click Copy Here on the shortcut menu**
   The original Wired Coffee Logo file remains in the Advertising folder, and a copy of the file is in the Spring Catalog folder.

6. **Click the Spring Catalog folder in the Folders Explorer bar**
   A copy of the Wired Coffee Logo file appears in the Advertising folder.

7. **Click the Catalog Pages folder in the Folders Explorer bar**
   The folder opens and the Mail Order Catalog file appears in the right pane.

8. **Click the Advertising folder in the Folders Explorer bar, then click the Folders button ▣ on the Standard Buttons toolbar to close the Folders Explorer bar**

FIGURE C-12: **Moving a file from one folder to another**

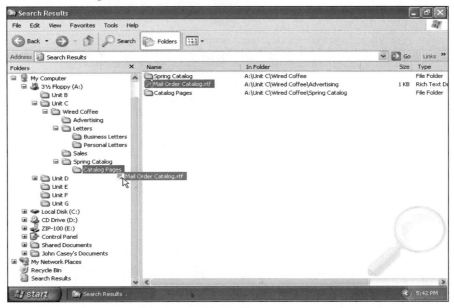

FIGURE C-13: **Copying a file from one location to another**

Copied file will appear here

Click command to move the file

Click command to copy the file

Sending files and folders

When you right-click most objects on the desktop or in My Computer or Windows Explorer, the Send To command, located on the shortcut menu, lets you send, or move, a file or folder to a new location on your computer. For example, you can send a file or folder to a floppy disk to make a quick backup copy of the file or folder, to a mail recipient as an electronic message, or to the desktop to create a shortcut. You can also use the Send To command to move a file or folder from one folder to another. To send a file or folder, right-click the file or folder you want to send, point to Send To on the shortcut menu, then click the destination you want.

Deleting and Restoring Files and Folders

When you organize the contents of a folder, disk, or the desktop, you might find files and folders that you no longer need. You can **delete** these items, or remove them from the disk. If you delete a file or folder from the desktop or from the hard disk, it goes into the Recycle Bin. The **Recycle Bin**, located on your desktop, is a temporary storage area for deleted files. The Recycle Bin stores all the items you delete from your hard disk, so that if you accidentally delete an item, you can remove it from the Recycle Bin to restore it. If the deletion is a recent operation, you can also use the Undo command on the Edit menu to restore a deleted file or folder. Be aware that if you delete a file from your floppy disk, it is permanently deleted, not stored in the Recycle Bin. Table C-3 summarizes deleting and restoring options. ► John is not sure how the Recycle Bin works, so he deletes a file, then restores it to find out.

Steps

1. **Click the Restore Down button** in the Advertising window, then resize and move the window so that you can see the Recycle Bin icon on the desktop
   Because you cannot restore files deleted from a floppy disk, you start by moving a file from the drive where your Project Files are located to the desktop.

2. Point to the **Ad Campaign file** in the right pane, press and hold the **right mouse button**, drag it to the desktop, then click **Move Here** on the shortcut menu
   You moved the Ad Campaign file to the desktop, as shown in Figure C-14.

Trouble?

If a message box appears, click Yes to confirm the deletion.

3. Drag the **Ad Campaign file** from the desktop to the Recycle Bin
   The Recycle Bin icon should now look like it contains paper 🗑.

4. Double-click the **Recycle Bin icon** on the desktop
   The Recycle Bin window opens, containing the Ad Campaign file and any other deleted files. Like most other windows, the Recycle Bin window has a menu bar, a toolbar, and a status bar. Your deleted files remain in the Recycle Bin until you empty it, permanently removing the contents of the Recycle Bin from your hard disk. Because you still need this file, you decide to restore it.

QuickTip

To empty the Recycle Bin, click Empty the Recycle Bin in the left pane under Recycle Bin Tasks, or right-click the Recycle Bin icon on the desktop, then click Empty Recycle Bin.

5. Select the **Ad Campaign file** in the Recycle Bin window, as shown in Figure C-15, then click **Restore this item** in the left pane under Recycle Bin Tasks
   You restored the file back to its previous location on the desktop. It is intact and identical to the form it was in before you deleted it.

6. Click the **Close button** in the Recycle Bin window
   The Recycle Bin window closes, and the desktop appears with the Ad Campaign file and the Advertising window open.

7. In the Advertising window, click **Edit** on the menu bar, then click **Undo Move**
   The Ad Campaign file is moved back to the Advertising folder and no longer appears on the desktop.

FIGURE C-14: Selecting a file to drag to the Recycle Bin

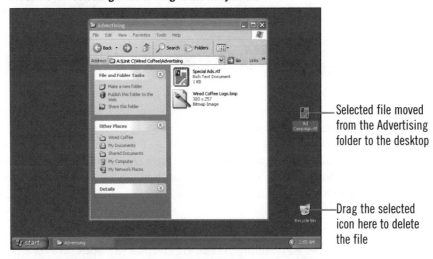

— Selected file moved from the Advertising folder to the desktop

— Drag the selected icon here to delete the file

FIGURE C-15: Deleted file from the Advertising folder in the Recycle Bin

Click link to empty the Recycle Bin and permanently delete the file

Click link to restore the selected file

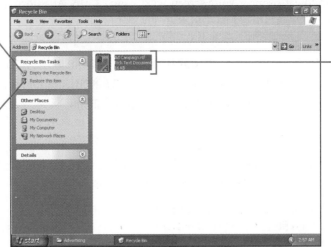

— Contents of the Recycle Bin; yours might differ

TABLE C-3: Deleting and restoring files

ways to delete a file or folder	ways to restore a file or folder from the Recycle Bin
Select the file or folder, click File on the menu bar, then click Delete	Select the file or folder, click File on the menu bar, then click Restore
Select the file or folder, then press [Delete]	Click Edit on the menu bar, then click Undo
Right-click the file or folder, then click Delete	Right-click the file or folder, then click Restore
Drag the file or folder to the Recycle Bin	Drag the file or folder from the Recycle Bin to any location

CLUES TO USE

Recycle Bin properties

You can adjust several Recycle Bin settings by using the Properties option on the Recycle Bin shortcut menu. For example, if you do not want to place files in the Recycle Bin when you delete them, but, rather, want to delete them immediately, right-click the Recycle Bin, click Properties, then click the Do not move files to the Recycle Bin check box to select it.

Also, if you find that the Recycle Bin is full and cannot accept any more files, you can increase the amount of disk space allotted to the Recycle Bin by moving the Maximum size of Recycle Bin slider to the right. The percentage shown represents how much space the contents of the Recycle Bin takes on the drive.

Windows XP

Creating a Shortcut to a File or Folder

It could take you a while to access a file or folder buried several levels down in a file hierarchy. You can create shortcuts to the items you use frequently. A **shortcut** is a link that you can place in any location to gain instant access to a particular file, folder, or program on your hard disk or on a network just by double-clicking. The actual file, folder, or program remains stored in its original location, and you place an icon representing the shortcut in a convenient location, such as a folder or the desktop. John is always updating a file that lists special ads. Rather than having to take steps to start WordPad and then open the file, he places a shortcut to this file on the desktop.

Steps

1. **In the Advertising folder, right-click the Special Ads file, then click Create Shortcut**
   An icon with a small arrow for a shortcut to the Special Ads now appears in the Advertising window. Compare your screen with Figure C-16. All shortcuts are named the same as the files to which they link, but with the words "Shortcut to" in front of the original name. You want to place the shortcut on the desktop for easy file access.

2. **Position ⌖ over the Shortcut to Special Ads file in the Advertising folder, press and hold the right mouse button, drag it from the Advertising folder to an empty area of the desktop, then click Move Here on the shortcut menu**
   The shortcut appears on the desktop, as shown in Figure C-17. You can place a shortcut anywhere on the desktop. You should test the shortcut.

Trouble?

Depending on your file association settings, another word processing program might open instead of WordPad.

3. **Double-click the Shortcut to Special Ads icon on the desktop**
   The Special Ads document opens in WordPad.

4. **Click the Close button in the WordPad window**
   The logo file and the WordPad program close. The Special Ads shortcut remains on the desktop until you delete it, so you can use it again and again.

5. **Right-click the Shortcut to Special Ads icon**
   A shortcut menu opens that offers several file management commands. The commands on your shortcut menu might differ, depending on the item you right-click, or the Windows features installed on your computer.

6. **Click Delete on the shortcut menu, then click Yes to confirm the deletion to the Recycle Bin**
   You delete the shortcut from the desktop and place it in the Recycle Bin, where it remains until you empty the Recycle Bin or restore the shortcut. When you delete a shortcut, you remove only the shortcut. The original file remains intact in its original location.

7. **Click the Close button in the Advertising window**

FIGURE C-16: **Creating a shortcut**

Original file ——

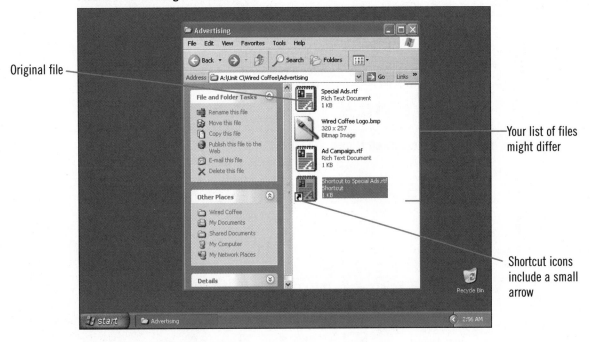

——— Your list of files
might differ

——— Shortcut icons
include a small
arrow

FIGURE C-17: **Shortcut moved to a new location**

Relocated shortcut
on the desktop ——

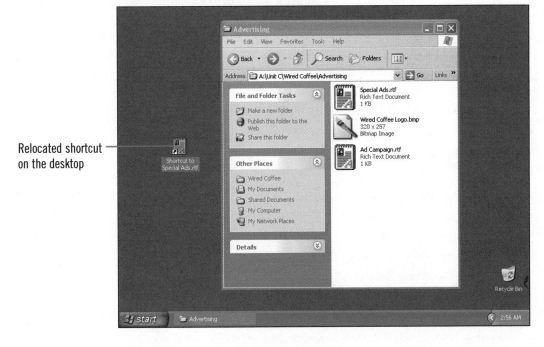

Placing shortcuts on the Start menu and the taskbar

You can place shortcuts to frequently-used files, folders, and programs on the Start menu or on a toolbar on the taskbar. To do this, simply drag the shortcut file, folder, or program to the Start button, wait until the Start menu opens, drag to the All Programs submenu, wait until the submenu opens, then drag the shortcut to the appropriate place on the menu. You can also drag a shortcut to a toolbar on the taskbar using the same method. When you release the mouse, the item appears on the menu or toolbar.

Practice

► Concepts Review

Label each of the elements of the screen shown in Figure C-18.

FIGURE C-18

1. Which element do you click to display folder contents in the right pane?
2. Which element is ready to be deleted or restored?
3. Which element do you click to expand a folder?
4. Which element holds items to be deleted or restored?
5. Which element do you click to collapse a folder?
6. Which element is copied?
7. Which element is a shortcut?

Match each term with the statement that describes its function.

8. **My Computer**   a. A display of drives and folders on the computer
9. **Folders list**   b. A file and folder management tool
10. **File**   c. A storage container for deleted files
11. **Recycle Bin**   d. A storage container for files and folders
12. **Folder**   e. A collection of information that has a unique name

Select the best answer from the following list of choices.

13. My Computer is used to:
    a. Delete files.   **c.** Manage files and folders.
    b. Add folders.   **d.** All of the above.

14. Which of the following is NOT a valid search criterion for a file using the Search program?
    a. Date modified   **c.** Name
    b. Date opened   **d.** Location

15. Which of the following is a method for copying a file or folder:
    a. Press [Ctrl], then drag the folder or file.   **c.** Double-click the folder or file.
    b. Drag the folder or file on the same disk drive.   **d.** Left-click the folder or file, then click Copy.

16. Which of the following locations is NOT a valid place from which to delete a file and send it to the Recycle Bin?
    a. Floppy disk   **c.** Hard drive
    b. My Documents folder   **d.** My Computer

17. What graphical element appears on a shortcut icon?
    a. pencil   **c.** pointer
    b. chain link   **d.** arrow

▶ Skills Review

1. Open and view My Computer.
    a. Insert your disk where your Project Files are located in the appropriate disk drive if necessary.
    b. Open and maximize My Computer.
    c. Navigate to the Wired Coffee folder on the drive and folder where your Project Files are located.
    d. Double-click the Letters folder, then double-click the Personal Letters folder.

2. View folders and files.
    a. Click the Views list arrow, then click List. Click the Up button on the Standard Buttons toolbar twice.
    b. Click the Back button on the Standard Buttons toolbar, then open the Business Letters folder.
    c. Click the Back list arrow on the Standard Buttons toolbar, then click Personal Letters.
    d. Click the Forward button on the Standard Buttons toolbar.
    e. Click View on the menu bar, then click Details. Click View on the menu bar, then click Tiles.

3. View the Folders list.
    a. Click the Folders button on the Standard Buttons toolbar.
    b. Click the Expand indicator next to the drive icon where your Project Files are located in the Folders Explorer bar.
    c. Click the drive icon where your Project Files are located in the Folders Explorer bar.
    d. Click the Expand indicator next to the drive and folder icons where your Project Files are located in the Folders Explorer bar, then click the Wired Coffee folder in the Folders Explorer bar.
    e. Double-click the Sales folder in the right pane to open it.

4. Create and rename files and folders.
    a. In the Sales folder, right-click a blank area of the window, point to New, then click Folder.
    b. Name the folder **Sales & Marketing**, then press [Enter].
    c. Rename the Sales & Marketing folder to **Marketing**, then press [Enter]. Arrange the icons by name.

5. Search for files and folders.
   a. Open the Search Companion Explorer bar, then click All file and folders in Search Companion Explorer bar.
   b. Search in the Wired Coffee folder for files that are named or contain the word "customer" as part of the filename.
   c. Close the Search Companion Explorer bar.

6. Copy and move files and folders.
   a. Click the Customer Profile file to select it in the right pane. Click Edit on the menu bar, then click Copy.
   b. Open the Folders Explorer bar. Click the Sales folder in the Folders Explorer bar (expand folders if necessary).
   c. Click Edit on the menu bar, then click Paste.
   d. Move the copy of the Customer Profile file into the Marketing folder.
   e. Move the Marketing folder into the Wired Coffee folder.

7. Delete and restore files and folders.
   a. Open the Wired Coffee folder, click the Restore Down button, then resize to display part of the desktop.
   b. Right-click the Marketing folder, drag it to the desktop, then click Move Here on the shortcut menu.
   c. Drag the Marketing folder from the desktop to the Recycle Bin, then click Yes to confirm the deletion, if necessary.
   d. Double-click the Recycle Bin. Right-click a blank area of the taskbar, then click Tile Windows Vertically.
   e. Click File on the Recycle Bin menu bar, click Empty Recycle Bin, then click Yes.
   f. Drag the Marketing folder back to the Wired Coffee folder to restore it, then click the Recycle Bin Close button.

8. Create a shortcut to a file or folder.
   a. Open the Marketing folder.
   b. Create a shortcut to the Customer Profile file, then move the shortcut to the desktop.
   c. Rename the shortcut "Customer Profile," then delete the shortcut on the desktop.

▶ Independent Challenge 1

As a human resources manager at World Wide Books, you need to organize the folders and files on the company's computer for new employees at store locations around the world. Your job is to create and organize company files and folders.

   a. Open My Computer and create a new folder named **World Wide Books** on the drive and in the folder where your Project Files are located, within which the rest of the organization of files and folders for this independent challenge will appear.
   b. Create a file using WordPad listing at least six international store locations. Save it as **New Store Locations**.
   c. Create a file using WordPad listing employee names. Save it as **Employee App**.
   d. In the World Wide Books folder, create folders named **Store Locations** and **Employees**.
   e. In the Employees folder, create four new folders named with employee names.
   f. Copy the Employee App file into each of the employee folders, then rename each file using the employees' names.
   g. In the folder named Store Locations, create a new folder named **New Stores**.
   h. Move the New Store Locations file to the New Stores folder.
   i. Using paper and pencil, draw the file hierarchy of the World Wide Books folder, then Close My Computer.

▶ Independent Challenge 2

You are vice president of a carton manufacturing company, Apex Cartons, and you need to organize your Windows files and folders. In addition to folders for typical business related functions, such as correspondence, contracts, inventory, and payroll, you have folders related to company functions, such as manufacturing and material suppliers.

a. Open My Computer and create a new folder named **Apex Cartons** in the drive and in the folder where your Project Files are located, within which the rest of the organization of files and folders for this independent challenge will appear.

b. Create folders named **Manufacturing, Material Suppliers, East Coast** and **West Coast.**

c. Move the East Coast and West Coast folders into the Material Suppliers folder.

d. Create a blank file using WordPad, then save it as **Suppliers Bid** in the Manufacturing folder.

e. Move the Suppliers Bid file into the Material Suppliers folder.

f. Copy the Suppliers Bid file into the Manufacturing folder and rename the copied file **Manufacturing Bids.**

g. Using paper and pencil, draw the file hierarchy of your Apex Cartons folder, then close My Computer.

▶ Independent Challenge 3

You start a mail-order PC business called MO PC, and you use Windows to organize your business files.

a. Open My Computer and create a new folder named **MO PC** on the drive and in the folder where your Project Files are located, within which the files and folders for this independent challenge will appear.

b. Create folders named **Advertising** and **Customers.**

c. Use WordPad to create a letter welcoming new customers. Save it as **Customer Letter** in the Customers folder.

d. Use WordPad to create a list of five tasks to do. Save it as **Business Plan** in the MO PC folder.

e. Use Paint to create a simple logo, then save it as **MO Logo** in the MO PC folder.

f. Move the MO Logo file into the Advertising folder.

g. Create a shortcut to the MO Logo file, then move it into the MO PC folder.

h. Delete the Business Plan file, then restore it.

i. Using paper and pencil, draw the file hierarchy of your MO PC folder, then close My Computer.

 Independent Challenge 4

You are a new administrative assistant at Sunrise Bakeries, which recently opened. Your job is to help the owners organize their recipes into different categories and help keep files and folder organized in the future.

a. Open My Computer and create a new folder named **Sunrise Bakeries** on the drive and in the folder where your Project Files are located, within which the files and folders for this independent challenge will appear.

b. Create three files using WordPad and save them as **French Bread, Torte,** and **7-Layer Chocolate** in the Sunrise Bakeries folder on the drive and in the folder where your Project Files are located.

c. In the Sunrise Bakeries folder, create a folder named **Desserts.**

d. Create folders named **Flourless Cakes** and **Flour Cakes** and move them into the Desserts folder.

e. In the Sunrise Bakeries folder, create a folder named **Breads.**

f. Move the Torte file into the Flourless Cakes folder and move 7-Layer Chocolate into the Flour Cakes folder.

g. Move the French Bread file into the Breads folder.

h. Copy the French Bread file into the Breads folder and rename it **Sweet Bread.**

i. Move the Sweet Bread file to your desktop, then drag the file to the Recycle Bin.

j. Double-click to open the Recycle Bin, then restore the Sweet Bread file to the Breads folder.

k. Create a shortcut to the Torte file in the Flourless Cakes folder, then move it into the Sunrise Bakeries folder.

l. Using paper and pencil, draw the file hierarchy of your Sunrise Bakeries folder, then close My Computer.

► Visual Workshop

Re-create the screen shown in Figure C-19, which displays the Search Results window with files from the drive and folder where your Project Files are located. Print the screen. (Press [Print Screen] to make a copy of the screen, open Paint, click Edit on the menu bar, click Paste to paste the screen into Paint, then click Yes to paste the large image if necessary. Click the Text button on the Toolbox, click a blank area in the Paint work area, then type your name. Click File on the Menu bar, click Page Setup, change 100% normal size to 50% in the scaling area, then click OK. Click File on the menu bar, click Print, then click Print.)

FIGURE C-19

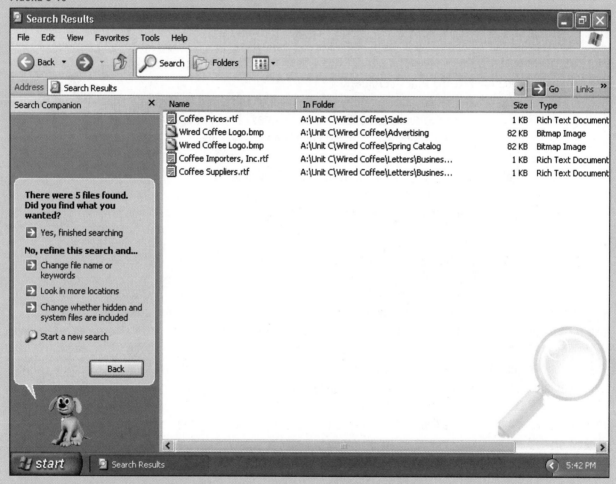

Unit
D

Customizing
File and Folder Management

Objectives

- ► **Add a folder to the Favorites list**
- ► **Change folder options**
- ► **Change file details to list**
- ► **Change file and folder list views**
- ► **Display disk and folder information**
- ► **Compress files and folders**
- ► **Use personal folders**
- ► **Customize a personal folder**
- ► **Manage files and folders on a CD**

As you work with files and folders, you'll discover that navigating through a long list of folders can be time consuming. To be more efficient, you can customize the way you work with files and folders to save you time and effort and to suit your personal needs and preferences. In this unit you'll learn how to create links to access files and folders quickly, change folder view options to display the file and folder information you need, store a file in a custom personal folder to quickly view its contents, display disk and folder size information, compress files and folders to save disk space, and use a compact disc to backup and store files for later use in case of problems. ✐ John Casey, the owner of Wired Coffee Company, customizes some file management tasks to suit his personal needs.

Windows XP

Adding a Folder to the Favorites List

Rather than navigating through a long list of folders to get to the location you want to display, you can use a Favorites list to locate and organize folders. When you view a folder in My Computer or Windows Explorer that you want to display at a later time, you can add the folder to your Favorites list. Once you add the folder to the Favorites list, you can return to the folder in My Computer or Windows Explorer by opening your Favorites list and selecting the link to the folder you want. In addition to adding folders to the Favorites list, you can also add locations on the Internet. If your list of favorites grows long, you can delete favorites you don't use anymore or move favorites into folders. ➤ John wants to add the Wired Coffee folder to his Favorites list.

1. **Click the Start button on the taskbar, then click My Computer**
   The My Computer window opens, displaying the contents of your computer, including all disk drives and common folders.

2. **Double-click the drive and folder where your Project Files are located, then double-click the Wired Coffee folder**
   The Wired Coffee window appears, displaying the contents of the Wired Coffee folder.

3. **Click Favorites on the menu bar, then click Add to Favorites**
   The Add Favorite dialog box opens, as shown in Figure D-1.

QuickTip

To specify the location of a favorite on the Favorites list, click Create in in the Add Favorite dialog box, then select a location.

4. **Click to the right of the text to place the insertion point in the Name text box, press [Spacebar], type Company, then click OK**
   You named the favorite "Wired Coffee Company," and added the folder to your Favorites list.

5. **In the left pane under Other Places, click My Computer**
   The My Computer window appears, displaying the contents of your computer.

QuickTip

To display the Favorites list in the Explorer bar, click View on the menu bar, point to Explorer bar, then click Favorites. To close it, click the Close button in the Explorer bar.

6. **Click Favorites on the menu bar, then click Wired Coffee Company**
   The Wired Coffee window appears, displaying the contents of the Wired Coffee folder. To keep the Favorites list organized, you can delete, rename, or move the favorites.

7. **Click Favorites on the menu bar, then click Organize Favorites**
   The Organize Favorites dialog box opens, as shown in Figure D-2.

8. **Click Wired Coffee Company in the Favorites list, click Delete, then click Yes to confirm the deletion to the Recycle Bin**
   The favorite is deleted from the Favorites list and sent to the Recycle Bin.

9. **Click Close**
   The Organize Favorites dialog box closes, and the Wired Coffee window remains open.

FIGURE D-1: **Add Favorite dialog box**

Name text box

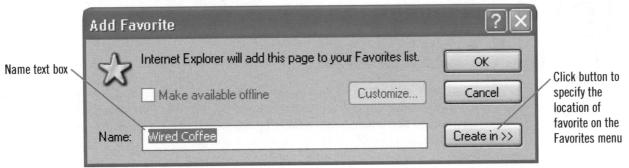

Click button to specify the location of favorite on the Favorites menu

FIGURE D-2: **Organize Favorites dialog box**

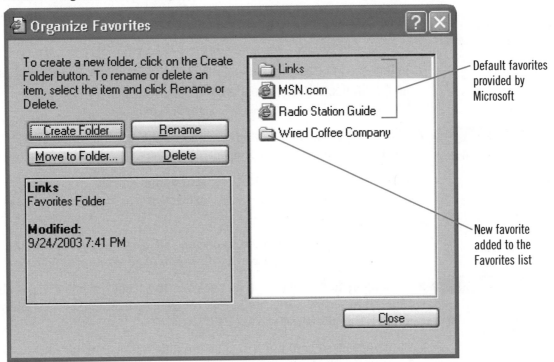

Default favorites provided by Microsoft

New favorite added to the Favorites list

CLUES TO USE

Organizing favorites in folders

If your list of favorites grows long, you can move favorites into folders. To move your favorites, click Favorites on the menu bar, click Organize Favorites, select one or more files or folders from the Favorites list, click Move to Folder to open the Browse for Folder dialog box, select a folder, then click OK. If you want to add a new folder to your Favorites list,

click Create Folder, type the new folder name, then press [Enter]. If you prefer to use another name for a favorite, you can select the favorite you want to rename, click the Rename button, type the new name, then press [Enter]. When you finish making changes, click Close in the Organize Favorites dialog box.

Changing Folder Options

When you work with files and folders, Windows displays folder contents in a standard way, known as the default. The default folder view settings are: Tiles view displays files and folders as icons; common task links appear in the left pane; folders open in the same window; and items open when you double-click them, for example. Depending on previous installation or users, your folder view settings might differ. Instead of changing the folder view to your preferred view—Thumbnails, Icons, List, or Details—each time you open a folder, you can change the view permanently to the one you prefer. To change the default view for all the folders or the current folder on your computer, use the View tab in the Folder Options dialog box to apply new folder settings. In addition to the defaults, you can change options such as folder settings to show or hide file extensions for known file types, show or hide hidden files and folders, show the Control Panel in My Computer, and show pop-up descriptions of folders and desktop items. If you don't like the options you set in the Folder Options dialog box, you can restore the dialog box settings to Windows default settings. John wants to experiment with customizing the folder settings to suit his needs.

Steps

1. In the Wired Coffee folder, double-click the **Sales folder**, click the **Views button** ▦ ▾ on the Standard Buttons toolbar, then click **Details**

The files and folders in the Sales folder appear in Details view.

QuickTip
If you don't like the options you set in the Folder Options dialog box, you can restore the dialog box settings to Windows default settings by clicking Restore Defaults.

2. Click **Tools** on the menu bar, then click **Folder Options**

The Folder Options dialog box opens, displaying the General tab, as shown in Figure D-3.

3. Click the **Use Windows classic folders option button**

This option hides the left pane in the folder view that shows common tasks in folders.

4. Click the **View tab**

The View tab appears, as shown in Figure D-4, displaying folder options relating to the way files and folders appear in My Computer and Windows Explorer.

QuickTip
To restore all folders to original Windows settings, click Reset All Folders.

5. Click **Apply to All Folders**, then click **Yes** to accept the folder views change

This feature sets all the folders on your computer to match the current folder's view settings, which is currently Details view.

6. In the Advanced settings box, click the **Hide extensions for known file types check box** to select it if necessary

This option hides the three letter file extension, such as .rtf.

7. In the Advanced settings box, scroll down the list, then click the **Show Control Panel in My Computer check box** to select it

This option shows a Control Panel icon when you open the My Computer window.

8. Click **OK**

The Sales window appears without the left pane of common tasks and file extensions at the end of filenames, as shown in Figure D-5.

QuickTip
To display the Control Panel in My Computer, double-click the Control Panel icon.

9. Click the **Back list arrow** ◀ Back ▾ on the Standard Buttons toolbar, click **My Computer** to display the Control Panel icon in My Computer, click the **Forward list arrow** ▶ ▾ on the Standard Buttons toolbar, then click **Wired Coffee**

The Wired Coffee window appears, displaying the contents of the folder in Details view. Based on the new folder option settings, all folders appear in Details view.

FIGURE D-3: Folder Options dialog box with the General tab

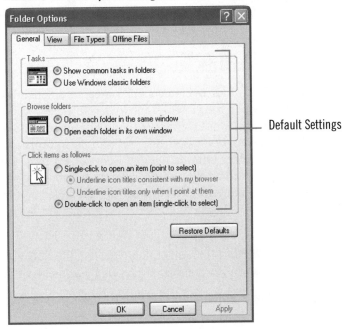

Default Settings

FIGURE D-4: Folder Options dialog box with the View tab

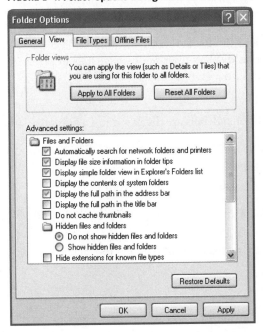

FIGURE D-5: Sales folder with new folder options

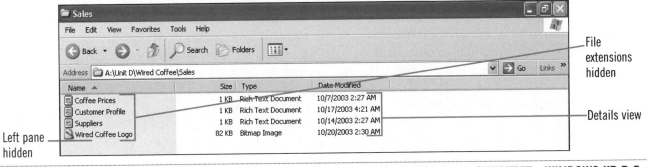

File extensions hidden

Details view

Left pane hidden

Changing File Details to List

You can display files and folders in a variety of different ways, depending on what you want to see and do. When you view files and folders in Details view, a default list of file and folder information appears, which consists of Name, Size, Type, and Date Modified. If the default list of file and folder details doesn't provide you with the information you need, you can add and remove the file and folder information you want to and from the Details view. You use the Choose Details command or right-click a column indicator button to make changes to the details list. John wants to add the owner of a file and image size of picture files to the details list in Details view.

1. **In the Wired Coffee folder, double-click the Sales folder**
   The Sales window appears, displaying the contents of the folder in Details view.

QuickTip
When you set the default view to Details view, the items you add or remove from the Choose Details dialog box are not included in Details view.

2. **Click View on the menu bar, then click Choose Details**
   The Choose Details dialog box opens, as shown in Figure D-6. The selected check boxes indicate the current columns shown in Details view.

3. **In the Details box, click the Owner check box to select it**
   This options displays the owner (the person who can make changes) of files. Yours will be different.

4. **In the Details box, scroll down, then click the Dimensions check box to select it**
   This option displays the size of image files in pixels. A pixel, short for picture element, is a single point in a graphic image.

5. **Click OK**
   The additional details are displayed in Details view, as shown in Figure D-7.

6. **Right-click any column indicator button, then click Owner on the shortcut menu to deselect it**
   The Owner column is removed from Details view.

7. **Right-click any column indicator button, then click Date Created on the shortcut menu to select it**
   The Date Created column is added to Details view, as shown in Figure D-8.

Moving columns in Details view

When you display files and folders in Details view, you can change the order of the column details to make it easier to locate the information you need to find. You can change the order of columns by using the Choose Details dialog box or the mouse pointer. The easiest way to move a column detail a short distance on the screen is to drag the column indicator button between the two columns where you want to place the column. As you drag the column indicator button, a blue bar appears, indicating where the column will be placed. If you need to move a column several columns across the screen, the best way to move it is to use the Choose Details dialog box. Click View on the menu bar, click Choose Details to open the Choose Details dialog box, click the column detail you want to move, then click Move Up or Move Down. When you're done, click OK to close the Choose Details dialog box.

FIGURE D-6: **Choose Details dialog box**

Current column details in order of appearance

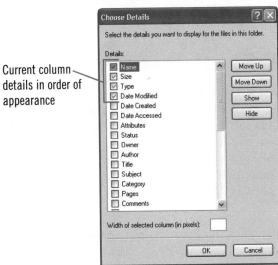

FIGURE D-7: **Columns added in Details view**

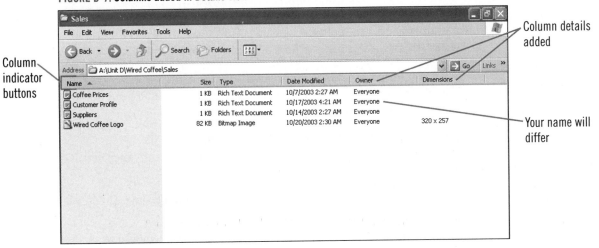

Column indicator buttons

Column details added

Your name will differ

FIGURE D-8: **Columns modified in Details view**

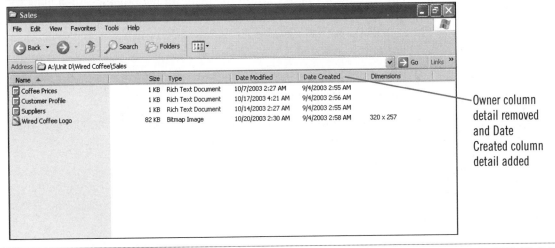

Owner column detail removed and Date Created column detail added

Windows XP

Changing File and Folder List Views

Once you choose the details that you want to list in Details view, you can change the order in which the file and folder information is displayed in the columns. If you need to change the way Windows sorts your files and folders, you can use the column indicator buttons in the right pane of Details view. Clicking one of the column indicator buttons, such as Name, Size, Type, or Date Modified in Details view, sorts the files and folders by the type of information listed in the column. ✎ John wants to find the date he wrote a letter to the coffee suppliers, so he decides to sort the files in the Business Letters folder by date.

QuickTip

If ellipses appear at the end of file information in a column, additional information is hidden. To show the information, drag the edge of the column indicator button to resize the column.

1. In the Sales folder, click the **Date Modified column indicator button**

The files and folders are now sorted by their last modification date, as shown in Figure D-9. The gray up arrow in the column indicator button indicates that the list is sorted from earliest (at the top) to latest (at the bottom), and the gray column background indicates that the column is selected. When you point to a column indicator button, a bold orange line appears under the column title.

2. Click the **Date Modified column indicator button**

The gray arrow changes from up to down, indicating that the list is sorted from latest (at the top) to earliest (at the bottom), as shown in Figure D-10. Each of the column indicator buttons works as a toggle; clicking once sorts the file in one order, and clicking again reverses the order.

QuickTip

Instead of using the column indicator buttons, you can also click View on the menu bar, point to Arrange Icons by, then click a details category to sort by.

3. Click the **Name column indicator button**

The files and folders are now sorted alphabetically by name from top to bottom. You want to restore folder settings.

4. Click **View** on the menu bar, then click **Choose Details**

The Choose Details dialog box opens, displaying the currently used details checked at the top of the list.

5. In the Details box, click the **Date Created check box** to deselect it, click the **Dimensions check box** to deselect it, then click **OK**

The Date Created and Dimensions Column details are removed from Details view.

6. Click **Tools** on the menu bar, then click **Folder Options**

The folder Options dialog box opens, displaying the file hierarchy.

7. Click **Restore Defaults**, click the **View tab**, click **Restore Defaults**, click **Reset All Folders**, click **Yes** to confirm the reset all folder views, then click **OK**

The folder options are restored to the Windows default settings. Although Tiles view is the default, the current view doesn't automatically switch back to it when you restore the settings unless you close and re-open the folder.

8. Click the **Views button** 🏐 ▾ on the Standard Buttons toolbar, then click **Tiles**

The folder view changes to Tiles, as shown in Figure D-11.

9. Click the **Back button** ⬅ Back on the Standard Buttons toolbar

The Wired Coffee window appears in Tiles view.

FIGURE D-9: Sorting files and folders by date modified (earliest to latest)

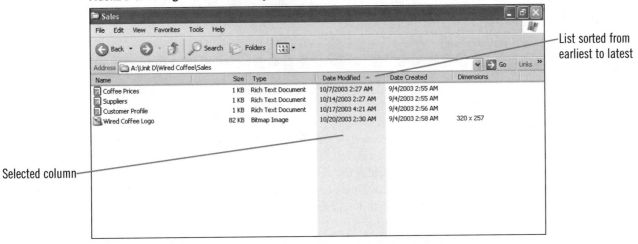

List sorted from
earliest to latest

Selected column

FIGURE D-10: Sorting files and folders by date modified (latest to earliest)

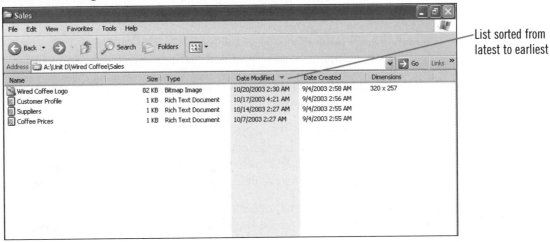

List sorted from
latest to earliest

FIGURE D-11: Restoring folder options

Left pane of
common tasks

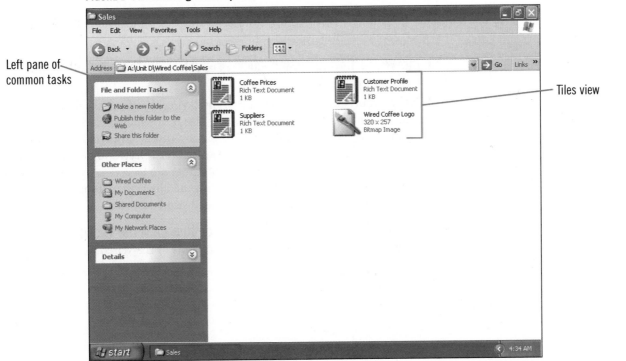

Tiles view

Displaying Disk and Folder Information

As you work with files, folders, and programs, it's important to know the size of the disk and how much space remains available. A disk can store only a limited amount of data. Hard disks can store large amounts of data, up to 10 gigabytes of data, while floppy disks are limited to 1.4 megabytes of data. A disk that can store 1.44 megabytes of data, for example, is capable of storing approximately 1.4 million characters, or about 3,000 pages of information. You can use the Properties command on a disk to display the disk size, used and free space, and change a **disk label**, which is a name you can assign to a hard or floppy disk. When you label a hard disk, the label appears in the My Computer and Windows Explorer windows. Besides checking hard disk drive or floppy disk information, you can also use the Properties command on a folder to find out the size of its contents. This can be helpful when you want to copy or move a folder to a removable disk or CD. John wants to find out how much space is available on his floppy disk and the size of a folder's contents.

Steps

1. **In the left pane under Other Places, click My Computer**
   The My Computer window opens, displaying the disk drives available on your computer.

2. **Right-click the icon for the drive where your Project Files are located**
   In this example, the drive is the 3½" disk.

3. **Click Properties on the shortcut menu, then click the General tab if necessary**
   The 3½ Floppy (A:) Properties dialog box opens, displaying the General tab, as shown in Figure D-12. There is a pie chart showing the amount of space being used relative to the amount available for the disk. In this example, 872 kilobytes are used and 551 kilobytes are free.

   Trouble?

   If you are working in a lab and your Project Files are located on a hard or network disk, skip Step 4.

4. **Click in the text box if necessary, then type ProjectDisk**
   A disk label cannot contain any spaces, but can be up to 11 characters long.

5. **Click OK**
   The Properties dialog box closes.

6. **Double-click the icon for the drive and folder where your Project Files are located**
   The Wired Coffee folder is displayed.

7. **Right-click the Wired Coffee folder, click Properties on the shortcut menu, then click the General tab if necessary**
   The Wired Coffee Properties dialog box opens, displaying the General tab, as shown in Figure D-13. The Properties dialog box displays the size of the folder (Size) and the actual amount of disk space used by the selected folder (Size on disk). The actual amount of disk space used is either the cluster size or compressed size of the selected folder. A **cluster** is a group of sectors on a disk. A **sector** is the smallest unit that can be accessed on a disk. A sector on a disk cannot always be filled, so the amount is generally higher. If the file or folder is compressed, the Size on disk amount is the compressed size.

8. **Click OK to close the Properties dialog box, then double-click the Wired Coffee folder**
   The Wired Coffee window appears, displaying the contents of the Wired Coffee folder.

FIGURE D-12: **General tab in the 3½ Floppy (A:) Properties dialog box**

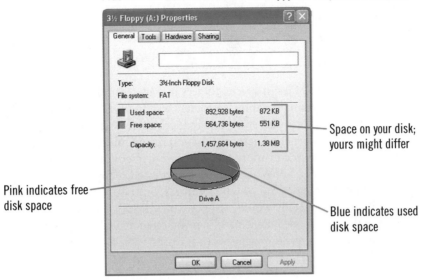

Pink indicates free
disk space

Space on your disk;
yours might differ

Blue indicates used
disk space

FIGURE D-13: **General tab in the Wired Coffee Properties dialog box**

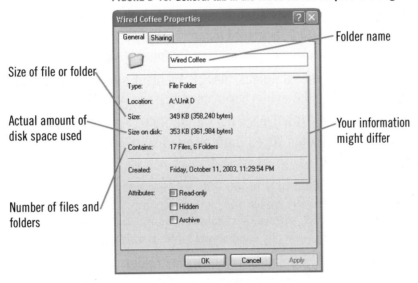

Size of file or folder

Actual amount of
disk space used

Number of files and
folders

Folder name

Your information
might differ

Understanding file sizes

When you create a file, it takes up space on a disk. Files with text are smaller than files with graphics. The size of a file is measured in bytes. A byte is a unit of storage capable of holding a single character or pixel. It's the base measurement for all other incremental units, which are kilobyte, megabyte, and gigabyte. A kilobyte (KB) is 1,024 bytes of information while a megabyte (MB) is 1,048,576 bytes, which is equal to 1,024 kilobytes. A gigabyte (GB) is equal to 1,024 megabytes.

Compressing Files and Folders

You can **compress** files in special folders that use compressing software to decrease the size of the files they contain. Compressed folders are useful for reducing the file size of one or more large files, which frees disk space and reduces the time it takes to transfer files to another computer over the Internet or network. A compressed folder is denoted by a zippered folder icon. You can compress one or more files in a compressed folder by simply dragging them onto the compressed folder icon. When a file is compressed, a copy is used in the compression, and the original remains intact. You can uncompress, or **extract**, a file from the compressed folder and open it as you normally would, or open a file directly from the compressed folder by double-clicking the compressed file icon. When you open a file directly, Windows extracts the file when it opens and compresses it again when it closes. ✎ John wants to compress Wired Coffee graphics in a folder.

Steps

🛑 *If you have a compression program, such as WinZip, installed, you need to uninstall it to perform these steps. See your instructor or technical support person.*

1. In the Wired Coffee folder, double-click the **Graphics folder**, click the **Views button** ▦ ▾ on the Standard Buttons toolbar, then click **Details**
The Graphics window appears, displaying the contents of the folder in Details view.

2. Right-click an empty area of the window, point to **New** on the shortcut menu, then click **Compressed (zipped) Folder**
A new folder, temporarily named New Compressed (zipped) Folder, appears in the right pane.

3. Type **Compressed Graphics**, then click a blank area of the window to deselect the folder
The Compressed Graphics folder appears, as shown in Figure D-14.

> **Trouble?**
> If a warning dialog box appears, click No to change the name. The filename needs a file extension (.zip). You need to type ".zip" at the end of the folder name.

4. Press and hold [Ctrl], click the **Coffee Roast Logo** file, click the **Wired Coffee Color Logo** file, click the **Wired Coffee Logo** file, then release [Ctrl]
The three graphic files are selected.

> **QuickTip**
> To compress a folder and its contents, right-click the folder, point to Send To, then click Compressed (zipped) Folder.

5. Drag the selected files to the **Compressed Graphics folder**
The selected files are copied and compressed into the Compressed Graphics folder. The Size column in Details view shows that the uncompressed graphic files combined are approximately 183 KB, while the compressed folder is only 5 KB.

6. Double-click the **Compressed Graphics folder**
The Compressed Graphics folder appears, as shown in Figure D-15.

7. In the left pane under Folder Tasks, click **Extract all files** to start the Extraction Wizard, then click **Next** to continue
The second Extraction Wizard dialog box appears, as shown in Figure D-16.

> **QuickTip**
> To extract individual files, click the file, click Move this file in the left pane, select a folder location in the Move Items dialog box, then click Move.

8. In the text box with the directory, select the word **Compressed**, type **Extracted**, click **Next** to extract the files, click the **Show extracted files check box** to deselect it if necessary, then click **Finish**
The three files are extracted into a folder called Extracted Graphics.

9. Click the **Up button** 🗁 on the Standard Buttons toolbar, press and hold [Ctrl], click the **Extracted Graphics** folder, click the **Compressed Graphics** folder, press [Delete], click **Yes** to confirm the deletion, then click the Graphics window **Close button**
The graphics are deleted from the Graphics folder, and the Graphics window closes.

FIGURE D-14: **Creating a compressed folder**

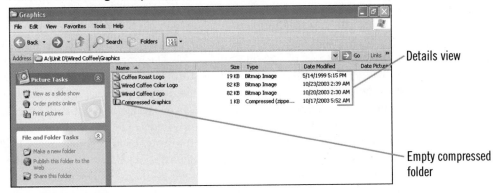

Details view

Empty compressed
folder

FIGURE D-15: **Contents of the compressed folder**

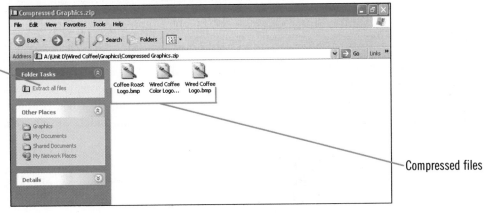

Click link to extract
all files

Compressed files

FIGURE D-16: **Extraction Wizard dialog box**

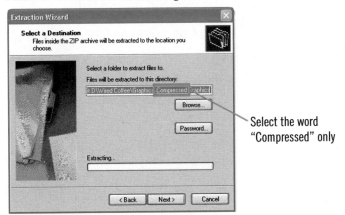

Select the word
"Compressed" only

CLUES TO USE

Compressing existing files and folders on an NTFS drive

If your hard disk is formatted as NTFS, you need to use a different method to compress existing files and folders. NTFS is an advanced file system that provides additional performance, security, and reliability over the standard file system FAT (File Allocation Table) or FAT32. To display the file system, select your hard disk icon in My Computer in the left pane under Details. To compress an existing file or folder on an NTFS drive, right-click the file or folder you want to compress, click Properties, click Advanced on the General tab, click the Compress contents to save disk space check box to select it, then click OK twice. In the Confirm Attribute Changes dialog box, select the option you want, then click OK.

Using Personal Folders

Windows makes it easy to manage the personal and business files and folders you work with everyday with a set of **personal folders**. My Documents is a personal folder, which contains additional personal folders, such as My Pictures, My Music, and My Videos. Depending on previous installation, devices installed, or other users, your personal folders might differ. The contents of your personal folders are private, unless you decide to share the contents with others who use your computer. Windows creates personal folders for everyone on your computer to make sure the contents of personal folders remain private. Each personal folder is identified by the user's name. For example, if John Casey and an associate Shawn Brooks use the same computer, there are two sets of personal folders, one named John Casey's Documents and another named Shawn Brooks' Documents. When John logs on to the computer, his personal folders appear as My Documents and Shawn's appear as Shawn Brooks' Documents, but John cannot access them. John wants to open his personal folders and find out more about their functionality.

1. Click the **Start button** on the taskbar, then click **My Documents**

   The My Documents window opens, as shown in Figure D-17.

QuickTip
To open the My Pictures folder from the Start Menu, click the Start button, then click My Pictures.

2. Double-click the **My Pictures folder**

   The My Pictures window opens, displaying the contents of the folder as thumbnails. A **thumbnail** is a miniature image of the contents of a file; thumbnails are often used to quickly browse through multiple images. If the folder doesn't contain images, Windows inserts icons instead of thumbnails.

3. Double-click the **Sample Pictures folder**

   The Sample Pictures window opens, displaying the contents of the picture folder as a filmstrip, as shown in Figure D-18. Filmstrip is a special view, located on the Views button or View menu, available only for folders with many pictures.

QuickTip
To rotate pictures in Filmstrip view, click the Rotate Clockwise button or the Rotate Counterclockwise button.

4. Click the **Next Image (Right Arrow) button** until the last image in the Sample Pictures folder appears in the filmstrip

5. Click the **Back button** Back on the Standard Buttons toolbar twice to display the My Documents folder

6. Double-click the **My Videos folder**

   The My Videos folder opens, displaying the contents of the folder as thumbnails. For videos, the first frame appears in the thumbnail.

7. In the left pane under Video tasks, click **Play all**

   Windows Media Player opens and plays the sample Windows Movie Maker video.

8. When the video is finished, click the in Windows Media Player **Close button**

   Windows Media Player closes.

9. Click the **Back button** Back on the Standard Buttons toolbar to display the My Documents folder, then click a blank area to deselect the folder

FIGURE D-17: **My Documents folder**

General file and folder task links

Personal folders; yours might differ

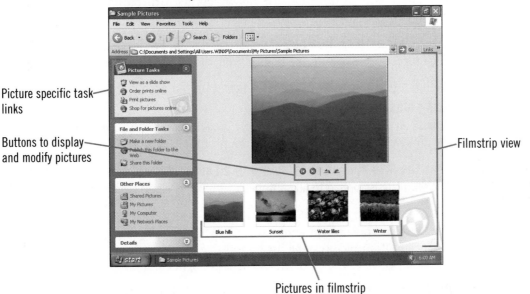

FIGURE D-18: **Sample Pictures folder**

Picture specific task links

Buttons to display and modify pictures

Filmstrip view

Pictures in filmstrip

Using the Shared Documents folder

Shared folders are related to your personal folders on a shared computer. They provide a place for you to make files, pictures, and music available to everyone who uses your computer. Your personal folders: My Documents, My Pictures, My Music, and My Videos each have a shared counterpart: Shared Documents, Shared Pictures, etc., in which you can copy files and folders to share with others. To share files and folders on your computer, click the Start button on the taskbar, click My Documents, click the file or folder you want to share, then drag the file or folder to Shared Documents in the left pane under Other Places. To share pictures and music on your computer, open My Documents, double-click the My Pictures or My Music folder, click the file or folder you want to share, click Move this file or Move this folder to open the Move Items dialog box, click the Shared Documents folder, click Shared Pictures or Shared Music, then click Move.

Customizing a Personal Folder

In the My Documents folder you can create your own folders and customize view options based on the contents. In the left pane of the My Pictures, My Music, and My Videos folders, Windows provides links to file management activities specifically related to the contents of the folder and other places on your computer, such as Print pictures in the My Pictures folder, or Play all in the My Music or My Video folders. When you create a new folder, you can customize it for pictures, music, and videos by applying a folder template, which is a collection of folder task links and viewing options. When you apply a template to a folder, you apply specific features to the folder, such as specialized task links and viewing options for working with pictures, music, and videos. John wants to customize a folder for pictures in the My Documents folder.

Trouble?

If a folder is selected, this will not be an option. Click a blank area of the window to deselect the folder, then try again.

QuickTip

To choose the picture that displays on a folder icon in Thumbnails view, click Choose Picture in the Customize tab of the Properties dialog box, navigate to the picture, then double-click it.

1. In the My Documents folder, click **Make a new folder** in the left pane under File and Folder tasks, type **Wired Coffee Pictures**, then press **[Enter]**
   The new folder appears.

2. Double-click the **Wired Coffee Pictures folder**
   The empty Wired Coffee Pictures folder appears. General links for file and folder tasks appear in the left pane.

3. Right-click a blank area of the folder, then click **Customize This Folder**
   The Properties dialog box opens, displaying the Customize tab, as shown in Figure D-19.

4. Click the **Use this folder type as a template list arrow**, then click **Pictures (best for many files)**
   When you choose a template, you apply specific features to your folder, such as specialized task links and viewing options for working with pictures, music, and videos.

5. Click the **Also apply this template to all subfolders check box** to select it
   The template is applied to all subfolders within the Wired Coffee Pictures folder.

6. Click **OK**
   The left pane contains common tasks related specifically to pictures, such as Order prints online and Print pictures; the list of available picture tasks changes based on the current selection. See Table D-1 for a list and description of common picture tasks.

7. Click the **Back button** ◁ Back to display the My Documents folder

8. Click the **Wired Coffee Pictures folder** to select it if necessary, click **Delete this folder** in the left pane under File and Folder Tasks, then click **Yes** to confirm the deletion to the Recycle Bin
   The Wired Coffee Pictures folder is deleted and sent to the Recycle Bin.

9. Click the **Close button** in the My Documents window
   The My Documents window closes.

FIGURE D-19: **Properties dialog box with Customize tab**

Folder template

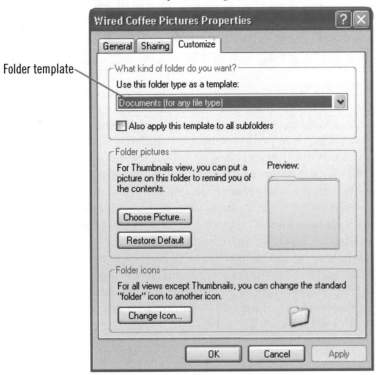

TABLE D-1: **Picture tasks in the My Pictures folder**

picture task	description
View as a slide show	Displays a full screen version of each picture in the folder for five seconds; click buttons on the Slide Show toolbar to start, pause, and stop the show
Order prints online	Opens the Online Print Ordering Wizard, which helps you order prints of your digital photographs over the Internet
Print this picture or Print the selected pictures	Opens the Photo Printing Wizard, which helps you format and print photographs from a digital camera or scanner
Set as desktop background	Sets the selected picture as the desktop background
Show for pictures online	Opens the Windows XP Pictures Online Web site in your Web browser, where you can find and download pictures over the Internet

Managing Files and Folders on a CD

A **compact disc**, or CD, is a small circular disc that is used to store large amounts of information. The low cost and convenient size of CDs and the popularity of CD recording hardware make using CDs an effective approach to some file management tasks. For example, CDs are an effective way to backup information or transfer large amounts of information to another computer without a network. You can copy, or **write**, files and folders to either a **compact disc-recordable (CD-R)** or a **compact disc rewritable (CD-RW)**. With CD-Rs, you can write files and folders only once, read them many times, but can't erase them. With CD-RWs, you can read, write, and erase files and folders many times, just like a floppy or hard disk. To create a CD, you must have a CD recorder (also known as a writer or burner) and blank CDs. Do not copy more files and folders to the CD than it will hold; anything beyond the limit will not be copied to the CD. Standard CDs hold up to 700 megabytes (MB). High-capacity CDs hold up to 850 MB. When you write to, or **burn**, a CD, Windows needs disk space on your hard disk to store temporary files that are created during the process, so make sure you have 700 MB of free hard disk space when using a standard CD and 1 gigabyte (GB) for a high-capacity CD. John wants to copy the Wired Coffee folder to a CD-RW.

Steps

🛑 *If you don't have a CD-RW drive, read the steps but do not perform any actions.*

1. Insert a blank CD-RW into the CD recorder, click the **Start button** on the taskbar, then click **My Computer**
My Computer opens, displaying the drives, including a CD recording drive.

2. Double-click the drive and folder where your Project Files are located, then click the **Wired Coffee folder** to select it

3. In the left pane under File and Folder Tasks, click **Copy this folder**
The Copy Items dialog box opens.

4. In the Folder list, scroll down, click the **CD recording drive**, then click **Copy**
The Wired Coffee folder is copied to the CD recording drive.

5. In the left pane under Other Places, click **My Computer**, then double-click the **CD recording drive**
Windows displays a temporary area where files are held before they are copied to the CD, as shown in Figure D-20. Verify that the files and folders that you intend to copy to the CD appear under Files Ready to be Written to the CD

6. In the left pane under CD Writing Tasks, click **Write these files to CD**
The CD Writing Wizard dialog box appears, as shown in Figure D-21.

7. In the CD name text box with the selected text, type **Wired Coffee**, then click the **Next button** to continue
A progress meter appears while the wizard writes the data files to the CD. Then, when finished, the final CD Writing Wizard dialog box appears.

8. Click **Finish**
The CD recording drive opens, displaying the contents of the drive.

9. Click the **Close button** in the CD recording drive window

FIGURE D-20: **Files ready to be copied to a CD**

Click link to start writing to the CD

Folder ready to be written to the CD

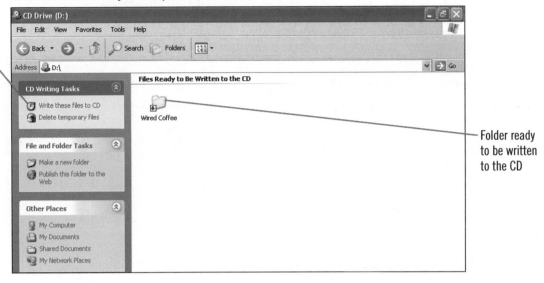

FIGURE D-21: **CD Writing Wizard dialog box**

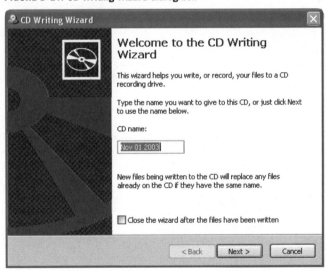

CLUES TO USE

Creating music CDs

With Windows Media Player, you can create your own CDs from music tracks you have stored in Media Library. To create a music CD, you must have a CD recorder and blank CDs (either CD-Rs or CD-RWs). If you use a CD-R to make a one time recording, make sure that the music fits on the CD and that you copy all the music at the same time. A standard CD (700 MB) holds 76 minutes of music, while a high-capacity CD holds 80 minutes. You can copy Windows Media (.wma), mp3, and wav files from the Media Library to a CD. To burn a music CD, insert a blank CD-R or CD-RW in the CD recording drive, start Windows Media Player, add music you want on CD to the Media Library, click Copy to CD or Device on the Taskbar, select the playlist or category of music tracks you want to copy from Media Library, click the recordable CD drive in the Music on Device pane, then click Copy Music. While the burning takes place, do not try to perform any other action on your computer, especially those that access the hard drive, such as opening or saving a file, as that could stop the recording.

Practice

► Concepts Review

Label each element of the screen shown in Figure D-22.

FIGURE D-22

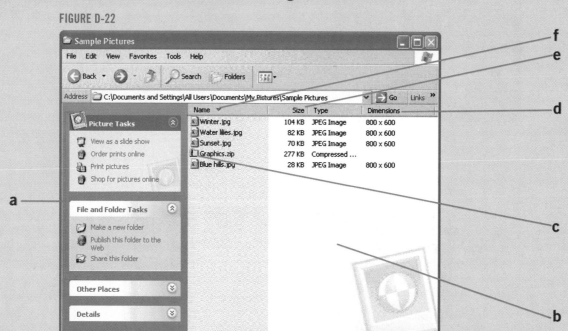

1. Which element points to the sorted column?
2. Which element sorts files and folders by image size?
3. Which element sorts files and folders by file size?
4. Which element contains links?
5. Which element contains personal files and folders?
6. Which element contains compressed files?

Match each term with the statement that describes its function.

7. Favorite
8. Byte
9. Personal folder
10. Compressed folder
11. Extract

a. A place to store files
b. A way to revisit a folder
c. A place to decrease file sizes
d. A term for uncompressing files
e. A unit of storage

Select the best answers from the following lists of choices.

12. Which of the following is NOT a default folder view setting?
    a. Icons view
    b. Show common tasks in folders
    c. Open each folder in the same window
    d. Double-click to open an item

13. **Which of the following folder sizes is the largest?**
    a. 1 megabyte
    b. 2000 kilobytes
    c. 1 gigabyte
    d. 1,248,896 bytes

14. **A cluster is a group of:**
    a. Sectors.
    b. Files.
    c. Folders.
    d. Bytes.

15. **Extract is another name for:**
    a. Uncompress.
    b. Expand.
    c. Compress.
    d. Zipped.

16. **Which of the following can read, write, and erase files and folders?**
    a. CD-ROM
    b. CD-R
    c. CD-RW
    d. DVD

▶ Skills Review

1. **Add a folder to the Favorites list.**
    a. Open My Computer.
    b. Navigate to the drive and folder where your Project Files are located, then open the Wired Coffee folder.
    c. Create a favorite to the Letters folder named **Wired Coffee Letters**, then click the Back button on the toolbar.
    d. Navigate to the Wired Coffee Letters favorite, then delete the Wired Coffee Letters favorite.

2. **Change Folder Options.**
    a. Change the view to Details. Change the folder option to use Windows classic folders.
    b. Change the folder option to display the full path in the title bar, then apply the folder options to all folders.
    c. Display the Wired Coffee folder to verify the new folder options.

3. **Change file details to list.**
    a. Open the Graphics folder in Details view. Add Dimensions and Date Accessed to Details view.
    b. Remove Date Accessed from Details view, then add Date Created to Details view.

4. **Change file and folder list views.**
    a. In the Graphics folder, sort by smallest to largest, then by date created earliest to latest, then by name in alphabetical order.
    b. Remove Date Created and Dimensions from Details view.
    c. Restore all folder option defaults and reset all folders, change to Tiles view, then display the Wired Coffee folder.

5. **Examine disk and folder capacity.**
    a. Go to My Computer, then display disk size information for the drive where your Project Files are located.
    b. On paper, write the disk capacity, how much is in use, and how much is available for further use.
    c. Display the Wired Coffee folder, then display folder size information for the Advertising and Letters folders.
    d. On paper, write down the actual size of the folder.
    e. Create a file using WordPad listing the information gathered in Steps b and c. Save it as **Disk Info** in the folder where your Project Files are located, then click the Close button in the WordPad window.

6. **Compress files and folders.**
    a. Create a compressed folder named **Compressed Logos**. Drag the Graphics folder to the Compressed Logos folder.
    b. Open the Compressed Logos folder, then open the Graphics folder inside.
    c. Extract the Coffee Roast Logo file to the Wired Coffee folder.
    d. In the Wired Coffee folder, delete the Compressed Logos folder and the Coffee Roast Logo file.
    e. Close the Wired Coffee window.

7. Use personal folders.

a. Open My Documents, then open the My Pictures folder and the Sample Pictures folder.

b. View all the graphics in the folder, then display My Documents, then open the My Music folder.

c. Play all the music in the folder, then close Windows Media Player. Display My Documents, then deselect all the folders.

8. Customize a personal folder.

a. In My Documents, create a folder named **Wired Coffee Music**, then open it.

b. Customize the folder with a music folder template.

c. Verify that the common task links changed to Music tasks.

d. Display My Documents. Delete the Wired Coffee Music folder, then close My Documents.

9. Manage files and folders on a CD.

a. Insert a CD-RW into the CD recorder. Copy the Advertising and Letters folders to the CD-RW.

b. Write the file to the CD-RW. Verify that the folders appear on the CD-RW, then close My Computer.

▶ Independent Challenge 1

You own a sewing machine repair business, and you want to use Windows to organize your documents.

a. Create a WordPad file named **Wilson Letter** thanking Mr. Wilson for his business. Save this file and the other files you create to the drive and folder where your Project Files are located.

b. Create another WordPad file named **Suppliers**. List the following suppliers in the file:

Apex Sewing Machine Parts	Jones Sewing Repair
PO Box 3645	18th and 3rd Avenues
Tempe, AZ 12345	Brooklyn, NY 09091

c. Create a third WordPad file named **Bills**. List the following information in the file:

Apex	16453	$34.56
Jones	47354	$88.45
Ott	44412	$98.56

d. Open My Computer, navigate to the drive and folder where your Project Files are located, then create a folder named **Sewing Works**.

e. In the Sewing Works folder, create three new folders: **Letters**, **Contacts**, and **Accounts**.

f. Expand the Sewing Works folder in the Folders Explorer Bar.

g. Move the file named Wilson Letter to the Letters folder, the file named Suppliers to the Contacts folder, and the file named Bills to the Accounts folder, then add a favorites link to the Letters folder.

h. Press [Print Screen], open Paint, click Edit on the menu bar, click Paste to paste the screen into Paint, then click Yes to paste the large image if necessary. Click the Text button on the Toolbox, click a blank area in the Paint work area, then type your name. Click File on the menu bar, click Page Setup, change 100 % normal size to 50% in the Scaling area, then click OK. Click File on the menu bar, click Print, then click Print.

i. Remove the favorites link to the Letters folder.

j. Close My Computer.

▶ Independent Challenge 2

As manager of the summer program at a day camp, you need to keep your files and folders organized.

a. Open My Computer, navigate to the drive and folder where your Project Files are located, then create three folders named **Day Camp**, **Campers**, and **Activities**.

b. Create a WordPad file named **Camper Data**. Save this and other files to the drive and folder where your Project Files are located. Create information on five campers, including names, ages, bunks, and sports.

c. Move the file named Camper Data into the folder named Campers.

d. Create a WordPad file named **Activities Overview**. Add information on five activities, including the activity names, equipment the children need to supply, number of children, and the activity leaders.

e. Move the file named Activities Overview into the folder named Activities.

f. Move the Activities folder and the Campers folder into the Day Camp folder.

g. Apply to all folders: Details view, Windows classic folders, and show extensions for known file types.

h. Open the Campers folder, then copy the Camper Data file to the Activities folder.

i. Open the Activities folder, then print the screen. (See Independent Challenge 1, Step h.)

j. Restore folder options to default settings, then close My Computer.

▶ Independent Challenge 3

The summer fine arts program you manage has different categories of participation for young adults, including two- and four-week programs. To keep track of who participates in each program, you must organize two lists into folders.

a. Open My Computer, navigate to the drive and folder where your Project Files are located, then create a folder named **Summer Program**.

b. In the Summer Program folder, create a folder named **Fine Arts**.

c. In the Fine Arts folder, create two other folders named **2 Weeks** and **4 Weeks**.

d. Create a WordPad file named **2 Weeks Art** on the drive and in the folder where your Project Files are located. Include the following information:

Leni Welitoff	2 weeks	painting
Tom Stacey	2 weeks	ceramics and jewelry

e. Create a WordPad file named **4 Weeks Art** on the drive and in the folder where your Project Files are located. Include the following information:

Kim Dayton	4 weeks	painting and landscape design
Sara Jackson	4 weeks	set construction

f. Move the files you created into their respective folders: 2 Weeks and 4 Weeks.

g. Change folder options to Details view, open each folder in its own window, and do not display the full path in the address bar. Apply to all folders.

h. Open the 4 Weeks folder in the Fine Arts folder, then print the screen (see Independent Challenge 1, Step h.)

i. Restore the folder setting defaults and reset the folders to Tiles view, then close My Computer.

▶ Independent Challenge 4

As head of the graphics department in a small design firm, one of your jobs is to organize the clip-art images used by the company. The two categories in which you want to place images are Lines and Shapes. You can place clip-art images in more than one category as well.

a. In the drive and folder where your Project Files are located, create three different small Paint images and save them using the names: **Ellipses**, **Lines**, and **Curves**.

b. Open My Computer, navigate to the drive and folder where your Project Files are located, then create two folders named **Lines** and **Shapes**.

c. Move the Curves and Lines files into the Lines folder, then move the Ellipses file into the Shapes folder.

d. Copy the Curves file into the Shapes folder, then rename the Ellipses file **Ovals**.

e. Create a compressed folder named **Clip Art**.

f. Place the Lines and Shapes folders in the compressed Clip Art folder.

g. Print the screen (see Independent Challenge 1, Step h), then close My Computer.

► Visual Workshop

Re-create the screen shown in Figure D-23, which displays the desktop and a compressed folder with pictures from the Sample Pictures folder on the hard disk. Print the screen. (See Independent Challenge 1, Step h for screen printing instructions.)

FIGURE D-23

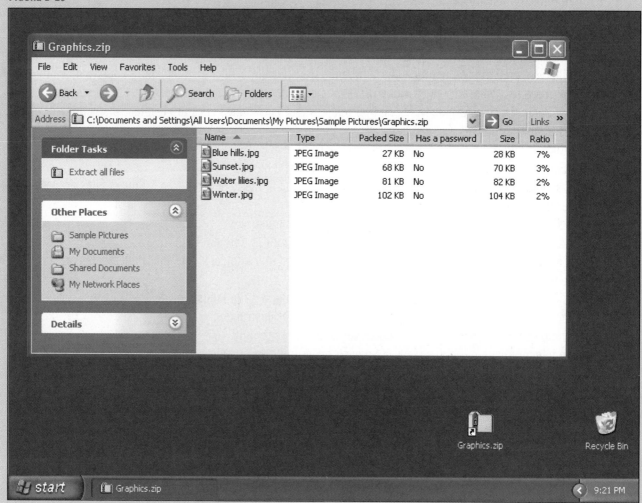

Customizing

Windows Using the Control Panel

Objectives

- ► **Change the desktop background**
- ► **Customize the desktop**
- ► **Change the desktop appearance**
- ► **Change desktop screen settings**
- ► **Set the date and time**
- ► **Work with fonts**
- ► **Add a scheduled task**
- ► **Customize the taskbar**
- ► **Customize the Start menu**

(STOP) *If you are concerned about changing the aspects of Windows XP and do not wish to customize, simply read through this unit without completing the steps, or click the Cancel button in any dialog box where you could make a change and don't click the Apply button when instructed.*

In this unit you'll learn how to customize Windows XP to suit your personal needs and preferences. You can adjust most Windows features through the Control Panel, a central location for changing Windows settings. The **Control Panel** contains several icons, each of which opens a dialog box or window for changing the **properties**, or characteristics, of a specific element of your computer, such as the desktop, the taskbar, or the Start menu. Each icon represents an aspect of Windows that you can change to fit your own working habits and personal needs. For example, you can use the Display icon to change the background picture or color of the desktop, or the Taskbar and Start Menu icon to customize the taskbar and Start menu. John Casey needs to change some of the settings on his computer to make his computing environment more attractive and efficient.

Changing the Desktop Background

The desktop **background**, or wallpaper, is a picture that serves as your desktop's backdrop, the basic surface on which icons and windows appear. You can select a background picture and change how it looks using the Desktop tab in the Display Properties dialog box. Once you select a background picture, you can display it on the screen three different ways: **Tile** displays the picture consecutively across the screen; **Center** displays the picture in the center of the screen; and **Stretch** enlarges the picture and displays it in the center of the screen. Instead of selecting a background picture, which can sometimes make icons on the desktop difficult to see, you can also change the background to a color. ✎ John wants to choose a background for his desktop.

Steps

1. **Click the Start button on the taskbar, click Control Panel, then click Switch to Classic View in the left pane under Control Panel if necessary**
   The Control Panel opens, as shown in Figure E-1. Each icon represents an aspect of Windows that you can change to fit your own working habits and personal needs.

2. **Click the Restore Down button in the Control Panel window if necessary, then resize the Control Panel window so you can see desktop changes**

QuickTip

To open the Display Properties dialog box from the desktop, right-click an empty area on the desktop, then click Properties.

3. **Double-click the Display icon 🖳 in the Control Panel, then click the Desktop tab**
   The Display Properties dialog box opens, displaying the Desktop tab, as shown in Figure E-2.

4. **Scroll through the Background list, then click Coffee Bean, or make another selection if this one is not available**
   The preview window shows how the background will look on your screen. The Coffee Bean picture is a small picture, so you decide to tile it across the desktop.

5. **Click the Position list arrow, then click Tile, if necessary**
   The background picture appears tiled in the preview window.

6. **Click Apply**
   The background picture appears tiled on the desktop. When you click the Apply button, Windows performs the changes you've made and keeps the dialog box open so that you can select additional options.

7. **In the Background list, click (None)**
   The current color in the Color list appears in the preview window.

8. **Click the Color list arrow, click a color in the list, then click Apply**
   The color in the Color list appears in the preview window and on the desktop.

9. **Select your original background picture or color to restore the desktop, then click Apply**
   The Display Properties dialog box remains open.

FIGURE E-1: Control Panel window

Depending on your
computer, your
icons might differ

FIGURE E-2: Display Properties dialog box with Desktop tab

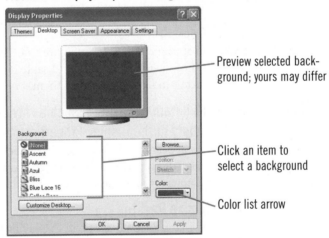

Preview selected back-
ground; yours may differ

Click an item to
select a background

Color list arrow

Setting a picture as the desktop background

Instead of using one of the pictures in the Background list on the Desktop tab in the Display Properties dialog box, you can select a picture on your hard disk or from a Web page as the desktop background. To set a picture as the background, right-click the picture you want to use in My Computer or Windows Explorer, then click Set as Desktop Background, or right-click the picture you want to use on a Web page in your Web browser, then click Set as Background. Acceptable formats for background files are Bitmap (the format of a Paint file), JPEG (the format of an Internet graphic file), or HTM (the format of a Web page). You can use Paint or any graphics program to create new background designs or change existing ones. After you set a picture as the desktop background, the picture is added to the Background list on the Desktop tab in the Display Properties dialog box. When you use a picture from a Web page, it is saved in the Background list as Internet Explorer Background. Each new picture from a Web page you set as a background replaces the previous one. To access the files in the Background list, open the Windows folder, then the Web folder, then the Wallpaper folder, from which you can remove, rename, or modify them.

Customizing the Desktop

Because more and more people are using the Internet, Windows allows you to view Web content on your desktop as you would in a **Web browser**, such as **Internet Explorer**, a program specifically designed to view Web content on the Internet. **Web items** are elements you can place on the desktop to access or display information from the Internet. For example, you can add a Web item to display stock prices or weather information continuously. When you place Web items on the desktop, they are active, which means the Web content is automatically updated as the content changes, while you're connected to the Internet. Using the Display Properties dialog box, you can customize the desktop to display the Web items you want to use. In addition, you can also customize the desktop to show or hide the icons My Documents, My Computer, My Network Places, or Internet Explorer. ⬛ John wants to learn how to customize the desktop.

QuickTip

To select your own picture as a background, click Browse, navigate to the drive and folder where your picture is located, select it, then click Open.

1. **On the Desktop tab of the Display Properties dialog box, click Customize Desktop**
   The Desktop Items dialog box opens, displaying the General tab, as shown in Figure E-3. The General tab provides options to display and clean up desktop icons.

2. **Click the My Documents check box to select it, then click the My Computer check box to select it if necessary**
   The My Documents and My Computer icons are set to display on the desktop.

3. **Click the Web tab**
   The Web tab appears, as shown in Figure E-4. The Web tab provides a list of Web items and previews of those items. To enable or disable items on the desktop, you must click the Web item check boxes to select or deselect them.

QuickTip

To add a new desktop item, click New, enter the Web address in the Location text box, then click OK, or click Visit Gallery to access and display Microsoft's Desktop Gallery on the Internet, select the item which you want to add, then click Add to Active Desktop.

4. **Click any Web item check box (such as My Current Home Page) to select it, click OK, then click Apply in the Display Properties dialog box**
   The Web item appears on the desktop. Some Web items require a connection to the Internet. If you don't currently have an Internet connection, you can still add a Web item to your desktop, and an error message will appear in the Web content window.

5. **Click Customize Desktop**
   The Desktop Items dialog box opens, displaying the General tab.

6. **Click the My Documents check box to deselect it, then click the My Computer check box to deselect it if necessary to restore the desktop settings**

7. **Click the Web tab, click the same Web item check box you checked before to deselect it, then click OK**
   You remove the Web item from the desktop.

8. **Click Apply**
   The Display Properties dialog box remains open, and the desktop appears as before.

FIGURE E-3: **Desktop Items dialog box with General tab**

Click check boxes to show or hide desktop icons →

Click button to clean up desktop icons

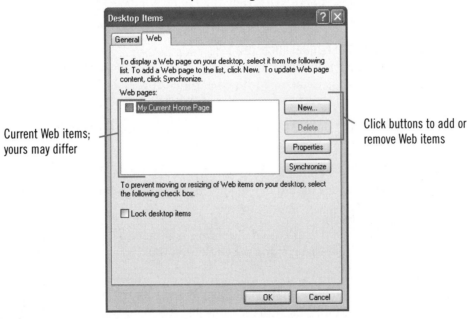

FIGURE E-4: **Desktop Items dialog box with Web tab**

Current Web items; yours may differ

Click buttons to add or remove Web items

Cleaning up the desktop

If your desktop gets cluttered with shortcut icons, you can use the Desktop Cleanup Wizard to move shortcuts that you don't use anymore into a folder. The wizard automatically runs every 60 days, or you can start it at any time. To start the wizard, double-click the Display icon 🖥 in the Control Panel in Classic View, click the Desktop tab, click Customize Desktop, then click Clean Desktop Now. Or, right-click an empty area of the desktop, point to Arrange Icons By, then click Run Desktop Cleanup Wizard. In the Desktop Cleanup Wizard dialog box, click Next, click the check boxes for the shortcuts you want to remove in the list to select them, click Next, then click Finish. Windows moves the selected shortcuts into the Unused Desktop Shortcuts folder on the desktop. If you don't want the wizard to run automatically every 60 days, click the Run Desktop Cleanup Wizard every 60 days check box to deselect it in the Desktop Items dialog box.

Windows XP

Changing the Desktop Appearance

You can change the entire appearance of the desktop by using desktop themes. A desktop **theme** changes the desktop background, screen saver, mouse pointers, sounds, icons, and fonts based on a set theme, such as baseball, science, sports, travel, or underwater. You can use one of the predefined desktop themes or create your own. If a theme isn't exactly what you want, you can change the appearance of colors, fonts, and sizes used for major window elements such as title bars, icons, menus, borders, and the desktop itself. You can change each item individually, or use a **scheme**, which is a predefined combination of settings that assures visual coordination of all items. Windows includes many predefined schemes, or you can create your own. When you create a custom scheme or modify an existing scheme, you save your changes with a unique name. ✐ Ray Adams, a visually impaired employee of Wired Coffee, needs the Windows classic display that he is more comfortable using and a display configuration with window elements larger than standard size. John decides to create a theme for Ray, who can switch to the theme whenever he uses the computer.

1. Click the **Themes tab** in the Display Properties dialog box
   The Themes tab, shown in Figure E-5, allows you to change the appearance of several desktop elements at once.

2. Click the **Theme list arrow**, then click **Windows Classic**
   The Sample box changes to Windows Classic settings.

3. Click the **Appearance tab**
   The Appearance tab, shown in Figure E-6, allows you to change the appearance of individual desktop elements, such as the menu bar, message box, and selected text, or to select one of several predefined schemes that Windows provides, then modify it as necessary.

4. Click the **Color scheme list arrow**, then click **Windows Classic**
   The color scheme changes to Windows Classic.

5. Click the **Font size list arrow**, then click **Large**
   The font size for text in windows increases in size to make it easier to read.

6. Click **Apply**
   The desktop changes, and the dialog box remains open. Use the Apply button when you want to test your changes, and the OK button when you want to keep your changes and close the dialog box.

7. Click the **Themes tab**, click **Save As**, type **Ray** in the File name text box, then click **Save**
   You save the theme with the name Ray. Now, anytime Ray wants to use the computer, he can easily set up the computer for his needs by clicking the Theme list arrow, then selecting Ray.

8. Click **Delete** to remove the selected theme

9. Click the **Appearance tab**, click the **Windows and buttons list arrow**, click **Windows XP style**, then click **Apply**
   The desktop, windows, and buttons are restored to the Windows XP style and the Display Properties dialog box remains open.

FIGURE E-5: Display Properties dialog box with Themes tab

Theme list arrow

Preview of selected theme; yours may differ

Click button to save a custom designed theme

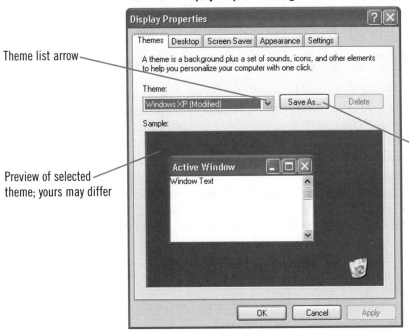

FIGURE E-6: Display Properties dialog box with Appearance tab

Preview of selected scheme

Windows, buttons, and desktop color schemes

Click list arrow to change the title bar font size

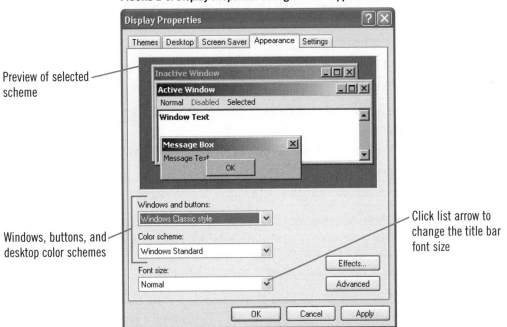

Adding sound effects

Besides customizing the desktop appearance of Windows XP, you can also add sound effects to common Windows commands and functions, such as starting and exiting Windows, printing complete, opening and closing folders, or emptying the Recycle Bin. To add sound effects, double-click the Sounds and Audio Devices icon 🔊 in the Control Panel in Classic View, then click the Sounds tab. In the Program events list,

click the event to which you want to apply a sound, such as Start Windows. Click the Sounds list arrow, then click the sound you want to link to the event. To hear the sound, click the Play sound button to the right of the Sounds list arrow. To save your settings into a sound scheme, click Save As, type a name, then click OK. When you're done, click OK to apply the sound effect changes to Windows.

Changing Desktop Screen Settings

If you find yourself frequently scrolling within windows as you work or squinting to read small text, you might want to change the size of the desktop on your monitor. A monitor displays pictures by dividing the display screen into thousands or millions of dots, or pixels, arranged in rows and columns. The pixels are so close together that they appear connected. The **screen resolution** refers to the number of pixels on the entire screen, which determines the amount of information your monitor displays. A low screen resolution setting, such as 640 by 480 pixels (width by height), displays less information on the screen, but the items on the screen appear relatively large, while a high setting, such as 1024 by 768 pixels, displays more information on the screen, but the items on the screen appear smaller. You can also change the color quality. The higher the color quality, the more colors can be displayed, which requires greater system memory. The most common color quality settings are: 16-bit, which displays 768 colors, and 24-bit and 32-bit, both of which display 16.7 million colors. If you frequently leave your computer idle, with no movement on your screen for a long time, you should select a **screen saver**, a continually moving display, to protect your monitor from **burn-in**, which occurs when the same display remains on the screen for extended periods of time and becomes part of the screen. John wants to change the size of the desktop and set a screen saver to start when his computer remains idle for more than five minutes.

1. **Click the Settings tab in the Display Properties dialog box**
   The Settings tab, shown in Figure E-7, allows you to change the appearance of several desktop elements at once.

2. **Drag the Screen resolution slider to a different setting**
   The new desktop size appears under the slider and in the preview window.

3. **Click Apply, then click Yes in the Monitor Settings dialog box to confirm the change if necessary**
   The desktop screen size changes based on your screen resolution setting.

4. **Click the Screen Saver tab**
   The Screen Saver tab, shown in Figure E-8, allows you to select a screen saver.

> **QuickTip**
>
> When (None) is the selected screen saver, no matter how long your computer remains idle, no screen saver appears.

5. **Click the Screen saver list arrow, then click Marquee**
   The Marquee screen saver appears in the preview window. To assign a password to your screen saver, click the On resume, password protect check box or the On resume, display Welcome check box to select it, then click Apply.

6. **Click Settings to open the Marquee Setup dialog box, type Wired Coffee Company in the Text text box if necessary, drag the Speed scroll box to the left (slowest speed), then click OK**
   The options for the Marquee screen saver are set. Not all screen savers have settings.

> **QuickTip**
>
> To create your own screen saver slide show, click My Pictures Slideshow from the Screen saver list arrow, then click Settings to add pictures from your hard disk.

7. **In the Wait box, click the up arrow or down arrow until it reads 5**
   Your computer will wait five minutes, during which it detects no mouse or keyboard activity, to begin the screen saver.

8. **Click Preview, move the mouse or press any key to stop the preview, then click Apply**
   When you preview the screen saver, the entire desktop displays the screen saver pattern.

9. **Restore the screen saver to Windows XP, and the screen resolution on the Settings tab to its original settings, then click OK**
   The Display Properties dialog box closes, and the screen saver and resolution settings are restored.

FIGURE E-7: Display Properties dialog box with Settings tab

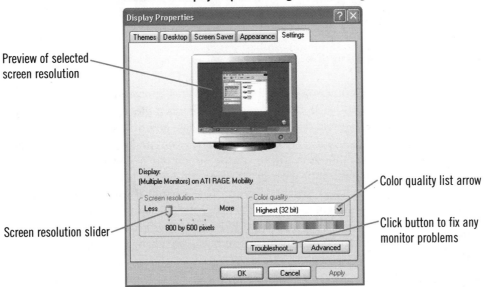

Preview of selected screen resolution

Screen resolution slider

Color quality list arrow

Click button to fix any monitor problems

FIGURE E-8: Display Properties dialog box with Screen Saver tab

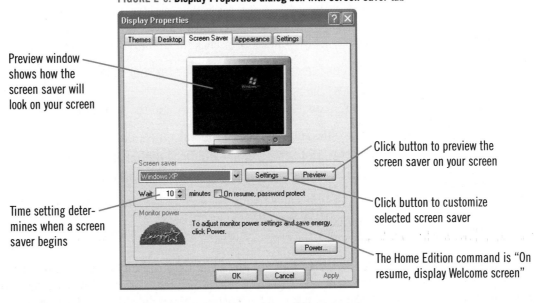

Preview window shows how the screen saver will look on your screen

Time setting determines when a screen saver begins

Click button to preview the screen saver on your screen

Click button to customize selected screen saver

The Home Edition command is "On resume, display Welcome screen"

Using more than one monitor

You can increase the size of your workspace on the desktop and your productivity by adding another monitor to your computer. For example, you can work on a document in WordPad on one monitor and search for Web content in your Web browser on the other monitor. One monitor is the primary monitor, which displays the dialog boxes that appear when you start your computer and most programs, and the other monitor is the secondary monitor, which displays windows, icons, and programs you drag to it from the primary monitor. Before you can use more than one monitor, you need to install another display adapter, a hardware device that allows a computer to communicate with its monitor, on your computer

that supports multiple monitors. After you install the display adapter according to the manufacturer's instructions and restart the computer, Windows detects the new device and installs the related software. In the Control Panel, double-click the Display icon 🖳 in Classic View, click the Settings tab, click the monitor icon that represents the secondary monitor that you want to use, click the Extend my Windows desktop onto this monitor check box to select it, then click Apply to activate the secondary monitor. To arrange multiple monitors, click the monitor icons and drag them in the preview window to the positions you want. You can set different screen resolutions and color settings for each monitor.

Windows XP

Setting the Date and Time

The date and time you set in the Control Panel appear in the lower-right corner of the taskbar. Programs use the date and time to establish when files and folders are created and modified. To change the date and time, you modify the date and time settings on the Date & Time tab in the Date and Time Properties dialog box. When you modify the time, it is important to also verify or update the time zone setting on the Time Zone tab, which is used to accurately display creation and modification dates in a different time zone. In addition to changing the date and time, you can also change their appearance. This is handy if you work on documents from a different country or region of the world. To change the date and time display, you modify the date or settings on the Date/Time tab in the Regional Settings Properties dialog box. John is working on an international document and wants to change his date and time settings.

QuickTip

To open the Date and Time Properties dialog box quickly, double-click the time in the notification area on the taskbar.

1. Double-click the Date and Time icon 🕒 in the Control Panel

The Date and Time Properties dialog box opens, displaying the Date & Time tab, as shown in Figure E-9. To change the date, you choose the month and year you want in the Date section, then click the day you want in the calendar. To change the time, you choose the time increment (hours, minutes, or seconds) you want to modify in the text box in the Time section, then type a new number or click the up or down arrow to select the new time.

2. Double-click the current minute in the text box in the Time section, click the up arrow three times, then click Apply

The new time appears in the running clock in the notification area.

QuickTip

If you have a connection to the Internet, you can click Update Now on the Internet Time tab to update the time on your computer with an accurate time on the Internet.

3. Click the Time Zone tab, click the list arrow, click (GMT) Greenwich Mean Time : Dublin, Edinburgh, Lisbon, London, then click Apply

The adjusted time appears in the running clock in the notification area.

4. Restore the time zone on the Time Zone tab and the time on the Date & Time tab to their original settings, then click OK

The Date and Time Properties dialog box closes.

QuickTip

To change regional format by language and country, click the Standards and formats list arrow, then click a language.

5. Double-click the Regional and Language Options icon 🌐 in the Control Panel

The Regional and Language Options dialog box opens, displaying the Regional Options tab, which shows sample number, currency, time, short date, and long date of the current format settings, as shown in Figure E-10.

6. Click Customize

The Customize Regional Options dialog box opens, displaying tabs that allow you to change the format and symbols used for numbers, currency, time, and date in your files and programs.

7. Click the Date tab

The Date tab appears, as shown in Figure E-11.

8. Click the Short date format list arrow, click dd-MMM-yy, then click OK

The short date format is changed and appears as 07-Sep-03, for example, in the Short date text box on the Regional Options tab.

9. Click Cancel

The Regional and Language Options dialog box closes and the short date format is restored to its original setting.

FIGURE E-9: **Date and Time Properties dialog box with Date & Time tab**

Month list arrow

Click arrows to change year

Click day to change date

Select time item, then click arrows to change time

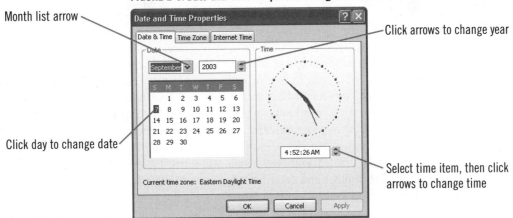

FIGURE E-10: **Regional and Language Options dialog box**

Standards and formats list arrow

Click button to change standards and formats

Current formatting samples

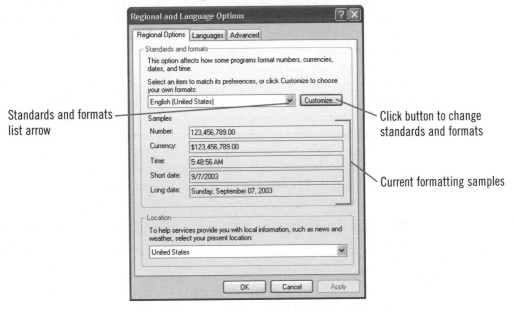

FIGURE E-11: **Customize Regional Options dialog box with Date tab**

Short date sample of current format

Short date format list arrow

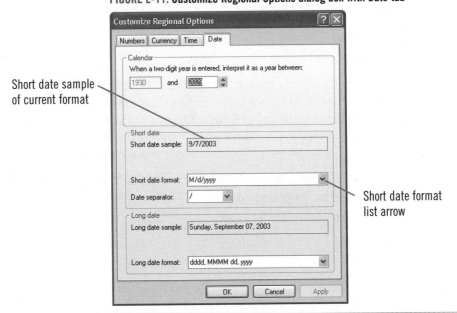

Working with Fonts

Everything you type appears in a **font**, or typeface, a particular design set of letters, numbers, and other characters. The height of characters in a font is measured in points, each point being approximately 1/72 inch, while the width is measured by **pitch**, which refers to how many characters can fit in an inch. You might have heard common font names, such as Times New Roman, Arial, Courier, or Symbol. Windows comes with a variety of fonts for displaying text and printing documents created with programs that are part of Windows, such as WordPad and Paint. Using the Fonts window, you can view these fonts, compare them to each other, see a sample of how a font appears when printed, and even install new fonts. Table E-1 lists the various font-related options on the Fonts toolbar and describes what they do. ✎ John wants to examine different fonts to prepare for a flyer he wants to create.

Steps 1 2 3 4

1. **Double-click the Fonts icon 🗁 in the Control Panel, then click the Maximize button in the Fonts window if necessary**
   The Fonts window opens. The window lists the fonts available on your system and indicates whether each is a TrueType, OpenType, or screen font. **TrueType** and **OpenType** fonts are outline (sometimes called vector or scalable) fonts based on a mathematical equation that creates resizable, or scalable, letters with smooth curves and sharp corners. OpenType is a newer technology and an extension of TrueType, but provides features such as multiplatform support and support for international characters. A **screen font** consists of **bitmapped characters**, which are small dots organized to form a letter. TrueType and OpenType fonts are designed for quality screen display and desktop printer output at any size, while screen fonts are designed for quality screen display and desktop printer output at only the font sizes installed on the computer. Besides the scalability, the main advantage of outline fonts over screen fonts is that they look better, the higher the resolution. Despite the advantages of outline fonts, small outline fonts do not look very good on low-resolution devices, such as display monitors.

2. **Click View on the menu bar, then click Hide Variations (Bold, Italic, etc.)**
   The main font styles appear in the Font window, as shown in Figure E-12.

3. **Double-click the Arial font icon**
   The window displays information about this font and shows samples of it in different sizes, as shown in Figure E-13.

4. **Click Print in the Arial (OpenType) window, then click Print in the Print dialog box**
   A copy of the font information prints.

5. **Click Done**
   The Arial (OpenType) window closes.

6. **Click the Similarity button 🆎 on the Fonts toolbar**
   The Similarity tool helps you find fonts similar to the selected font. All the fonts are listed by how similar they are to Arial, the font listed in the List fonts by similarity to box. You can choose a different font to check which fonts are similar to it by clicking the List fonts by similarity to list arrow, then selecting the font you want to check.

7. **Click the Large Icons button 🖿 on the Fonts toolbar, then click the Back button ◁ Back on the Fonts toolbar**
   You return to the Control Panel.

FIGURE E-12: **Fonts window**

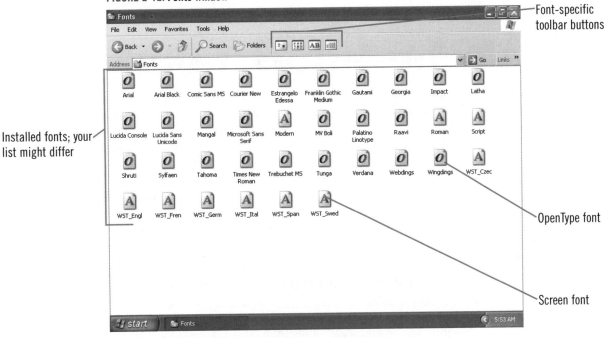

Font-specific toolbar buttons

Installed fonts; your list might differ

OpenType font

Screen font

FIGURE E-13: **Selected font and how it appears in different sizes**

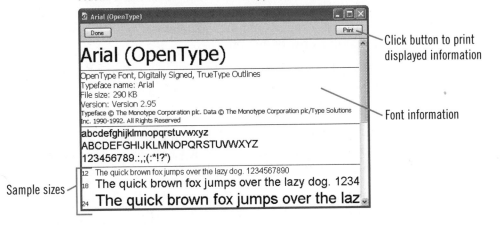

Click button to print displayed information

Font information

Sample sizes

TABLE E-1: **Font-related buttons on the toolbar**

button	description
	Lists fonts by large icon
	Lists fonts alphabetically
AB	Lists fonts by similarity to the selected font
	Lists details of fonts, including filename, font name, size, and date last modified

CLUES TO USE

Installing a font

Although many fonts come with Windows, you can purchase additional fonts and install them easily. To install a new font, click Install New Font on the File menu in the Fonts window, in the Add Fonts dialog box indicate the location of the font you want to install (on the hard drive, a network, or a floppy disk drive), then click OK. This installs the new font so that it's available in the Fonts window of the Control Panel and with all your Windows programs.

Windows XP

Adding a Scheduled Task

Task Scheduler is a tool that enables you to schedule tasks such as Disk Cleanup, a program that removes unnecessary files, to run regularly, at a time convenient for you. Task Scheduler starts each time you start Windows. When Task Scheduler is running on your computer, its icon appears next to the clock on the taskbar. You can double-click the Task Scheduler icon 🔘 on the taskbar in the notification area to open Task Scheduler. With Task Scheduler, you can schedule a task to run daily, weekly, monthly, or at certain times (such as when the computer starts or idles), change the schedule for or turn off an existing task, or customize how a task runs at its scheduled time. Before you schedule a task, be sure that the system date and time on your computer are accurate, as Task Scheduler relies on this information to run. ✐ John schedules a task to scan his hard disk for corrupted files.

Steps

1. **Double-click the Scheduled Tasks icon** 📂 **in the Control Panel**
   The Scheduled Tasks window opens, as shown in Figure E-14.

2. **Double-click the Add Scheduled Task icon** 🔲, **then click Next in the Scheduled Task Wizard dialog box**
   The Scheduled Task Wizard displays a list of programs you can schedule to run. If the program or document you want to use is not in the list, click Browse to locate the program on your disk drive or network.

3. **In the list of programs, click Disk Cleanup, then click Next**
   The next Scheduled Task Wizard dialog box opens, as shown in Figure E-15, asking you to name and select when you want the task to start.

4. **Click the Weekly option button, then click Next**
   The next Scheduled Task Wizard dialog box opens, asking you to select the time and day you want the task to start.

5. **In the Start time box, click the minutes in the Start time text box, change the time to one minute ahead of the current time, click the current day of the week check box to select it, then click Next**
   Depending on your Windows setting, the next Scheduled Task Wizard dialog box might ask you to enter the name and password of the current user.

QuickTip
If you are not asked for your password, skip Step 6. If you don't know the password, click Next to continue, then skip Step 7.

6. **If asked to enter your password, type your password in the Enter the password box, press [Tab], type your password in the Confirm password text box, then click Next**

7. **Click Finish**
   The scheduled task appears in the Scheduled Task window, as shown in Figure E-16.

QuickTip
To stop a scheduled task that is running, right-click the task that you want to stop, then click End Task; to modify a scheduled task, right-click the task you want to modify, then click Properties.

8. **Wait for the clean disk operation to begin, then click Cancel in the dialog box**
   If you don't know the password, the scheduled task will not run. To be notified when a scheduled task does not run, click Advanced on the menu bar, then click Notify Me of Missed Tasks to select it.

9. **Right-click the Disk Cleanup icon, click Delete, click Yes to delete the icon to the Recycle Bin, then click the Close button on the Scheduled Tasks window**
   You deleted the scheduled task, and the Scheduled Tasks window closes.

FIGURE E-14: **Scheduled Tasks window**

Double-click icon to add scheduled task

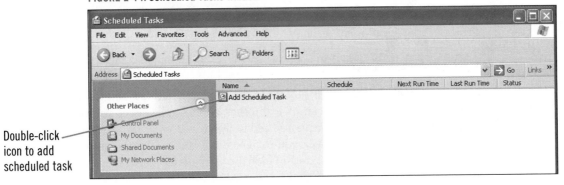

FIGURE E-15: **Scheduled Task Wizard**

Scheduled task name

Scheduled task time interval

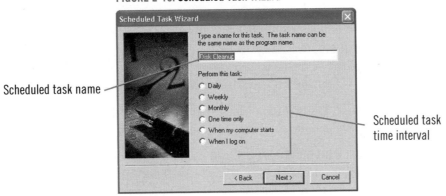

FIGURE E-16: **Task added to Scheduled Tasks window**

Scheduled task

Detailed information about scheduled tasks

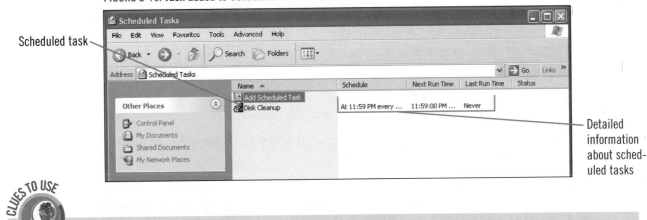

Adding new hardware and software to Windows

You can add new hardware, such as a printer, and add or remove programs by using tools in the Control Panel. The Add Hardware Wizard and Add/Remove Programs dialog box walk you through the necessary steps. To start the add new hardware procedure, double-click the Add Hardware icon 🎤 in the Control Panel, then navigate through the Add Hardware Wizard, making the appropriate selections, and clicking Next to move forward, then clicking Finish when complete. To add or remove a program, double-click the Add or Remove Programs icon 🖭, click Add New Programs in the Add or Remove Programs window, click CD or Floppy, then follow the prompts. In both cases, Windows should recognize that new hardware needs to be added or that an installation file needs to be executed. To install a Windows accessory or feature, such as Character Map or Desktop Wallpaper, click Add/Remove Windows Components in the Add or Remove Programs window, double-click a category if necessary, click the check box next to the accessory or feature you want to install, then click OK (you might be asked to insert your Windows installation CD). When you install a new program on your computer, the Start menu highlights the menus you need to click to start the program.

Customizing the Taskbar

The taskbar is initially located at the bottom of the Windows desktop, and is most often used to switch from one program to another. As with other Windows elements, you can customize the taskbar; for example, you can change its size and location, customize its display, or add or remove toolbars to help you perform the tasks you need to do. If you need more room on the screen to display a window, Auto-hide can be used to hide the taskbar automatically when it's not in use. If icons in the notification area are hidden when you want to see them, you can customize the notification area to always show the icons you want to use. ◢◣ John removes and adds a toolbar to the taskbar, then he learns how to hide the taskbar and show icons in the notification area.

1. **Place the mouse pointer in an empty area of the taskbar, right-click the taskbar, then point to Toolbars**

   The Toolbars submenu appears, as shown in Figure E-17. You can add or remove a variety of existing toolbars to the taskbar or create a new one.

2. **Click Quick Launch to select it if a check mark doesn't appear next to it**

   You added the Quick Launch toolbar to the taskbar.

3. **Right-click an empty area of the taskbar, then click Properties**

   The Taskbar and Start Menu Properties dialog box opens, displaying the Taskbar tab, as shown in Figure E-18. The Taskbar tab allows you to lock and unlock the taskbar, keep the taskbar visible, group similar taskbar buttons together in one button, and show or hide items, such as the Quick Launch toolbar, clock, and notification icons, on the taskbar.

4. **Click the Auto-hide the taskbar check box to select it, click the Show Quick Launch check box to deselect it, then click Apply**

   You hid the taskbar at the bottom of the screen and removed the Quick Launch toolbar from the taskbar.

5. **Click Customize**

   The Customize Notifications dialog box opens.

6. **Click an item in the list, click the list arrow as shown in Figure E-19, click Always show, then click OK**

   The Customize Notifications dialog box closes.

7. **Click Apply, then move the mouse pointer to the bottom of the screen**

   The icon you set to always show appears in the notification area. While the mouse pointer is at the bottom of the screen, the taskbar appears. When you move the mouse pointer up, the taskbar is hidden.

8. **In the Taskbar and Start Menu Properties dialog box, click the Auto-hide the taskbar check box to deselect it**

9. **Click Customize, click the same item in the list you modified earlier, click the list arrow, click Hide when inactive, then click OK twice**

   The Auto-hide feature is turned off and the notification icons are hidden when inactive.

> **QuickTip**
>
> To open the Taskbar and Start Menu Properties dialog box from the Control Panel in Classic View, double-click the Taskbar and Start Menu icon 📑.

> **QuickTip**
>
> To hide the clock in the notification area, click the Show the clock check box to deselect it in the Taskbar and Start Menu Properties dialog box.

FIGURE E-17: **Adding a toolbar to the taskbar**

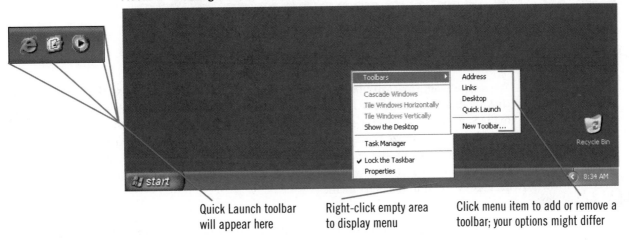

Quick Launch toolbar
will appear here

Right-click empty area
to display menu

Click menu item to add or remove a
toolbar; your options might differ

FIGURE E-18: **The Taskbar and Start Menu Properties dialog box with Taskbar tab**

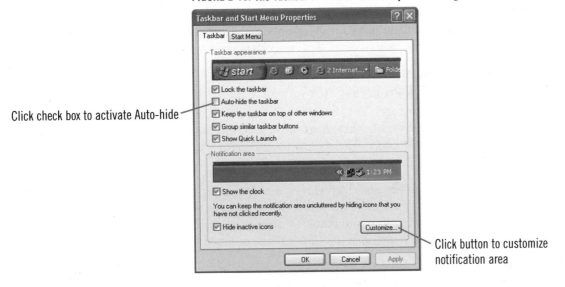

Click check box to activate Auto-hide

Click button to customize
notification area

FIGURE E-19: **Customize Notifications dialog box**

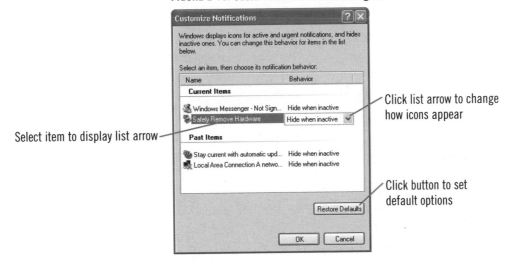

Click list arrow to change
how icons appear

Select item to display list arrow

Click button to set
default options

Customizing the Start Menu

You can add shortcuts to programs, files, or folders to the Start menu so that you can simply click the Start button, then click the item you want on the Start menu. Adding too many items to the Start menu defeats the purpose, so only add icons for your most frequently used programs and files. To customize the Start menu further, you can display additional menu items on the Start menu. You can also extend a submenu from the Control Panel, Printers, or Network Connections menu items. ✏️ Because John works with the Calculator program often, he decides to add it to the Start menu.

1. Click the **Start button** on the taskbar, point to **All Programs**, point to **Accessories**, then point to the **Calculator**, but do not click it
   The Accessories submenu appears with the Calculator program highlighted.

▶

> **QuickTip**
>
> You can also add an item to the Start menu by creating a shortcut to it on the desktop or in Windows Explorer, then dragging the icon anywhere on the All Programs submenu on the Start menu.

2. Right-click the **Calculator program** as shown in Figure E-20, then click **Pin to Start menu**
   The Calculator program appears above the separation line on the Start menu in the permanent menu items section. The menu item stays on the Start menu until you remove it.

3. Click outside the Start menu to close it, right-click the **Start button** on the taskbar, then click **Properties**
   The Taskbar and Start Menu Properties dialog box opens, displaying the Start Menu tab, which allows you to choose the Start menu style you want: either Start menu (for Windows XP) or Classic Start menu. The Start menu option for Windows XP is selected by default.

4. Click the **Start menu option** button if necessary, then next to Start menu, click **Customize**
   The Customize Start Menu dialog box opens, displaying the General tab, which allows you to select an icon size for programs, clear the list of recently used programs on the Start menu, indicate the number of programs you want to see on the list, and specify the Internet and E-mail programs to use when you click Internet or E-mail on the Start menu.

> **QuickTip**
>
> To remove all recently used documents from the My Recent Documents submenu, click the Advanced tab in the Customize Start Menu dialog box, then click Clear List.

5. Click the **Advanced tab**
   The Advanced tab appears, as shown in Figure E-21. The Advanced tab allows you to modify the way menus appear on the Start menu, add and remove Windows commands to and from the Start menu, and select options to access documents you opened most recently.

6. In the Start menu items list, click the **Display as a menu option button** under Control Panel, click **OK**, then click **Apply** in the Taskbar and Start Menu Properties dialog box
   The customized Control Panel option is applied to the Start menu, and the Taskbar and Start Menu Properties dialog box remains open.

7. Click the **Start button** on the taskbar, then point to **Control Panel** to display the submenu of Control Panel options
   The Control Panel menu options correspond to the icons in the Control Panel window.

8. Right-click **Calculator** on the Start menu, then click **Remove from This List**
   The Calculator program is removed from the Start menu.

9. Click **Customize** in the Taskbar and Start Menu Properties dialog box, click the **Advanced tab**, click the **Display as a link option button** under Control Panel in the Start menu items list, then click **OK** twice
   The Taskbar and Start Menu Properties dialog box closes, and the Start menu is restored.

FIGURE E-20: Adding a program to the Start menu

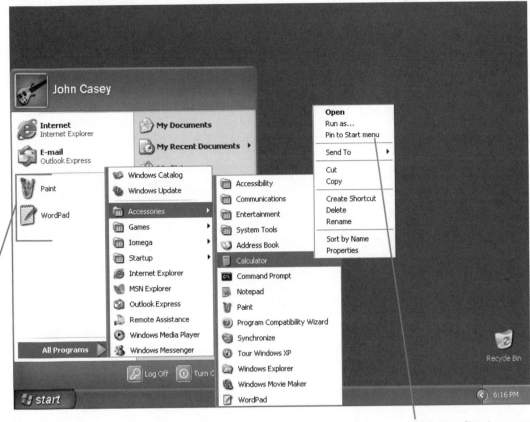

Frequently used programs list

Click menu item to permanently add to the Start menu

FIGURE E-21: Customize Start Menu dialog box with Advanced tab

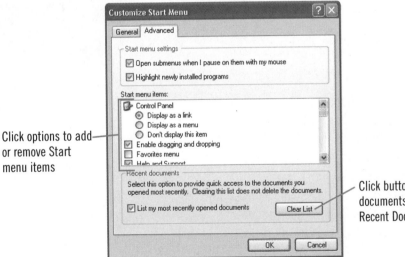

Click options to add or remove Start menu items

Click button to remove all documents listed on My Recent Documents menu

Rearranging Start menu items

If you don't like the location of an item on the Start menu, you can move the item to a different location by dragging it. A thick black line appears as you move the mouse pointer, indicating the new location of the item. For example, to move the Windows Explorer menu item from the Accessories submenu to the Start menu, open the Accessories submenu on the All Programs submenu, then drag the Windows Explorer item to the left column of the Start menu in the pinned section above the separator line.

Practice

► Concepts Review

Label each element of the screen shown in Figure E-22.

FIGURE E-22

1. Which element points to desktop icons?
2. Which element points to the Quick Launch toolbar?
3. Which element points to an expanded menu?
4. Which element points to recently used programs?
5. Which element points to pinned programs?
6. Which element points to Windows customization utilities?
7. Which element points to the desktop background?

Match each term with the statement that describes its function.

8. Background
9. Screen saver
10. Color schemes
11. Control Panel
12. Start menu

a. Preset designs for the desktop
b. Used to start programs and open documents
c. Used to change properties of various elements of a computer
d. Preset combinations of desktop colors
e. Used to prevent damage to the monitor

Select the best answers from the following lists of choices.

13. To customize the desktop, you need to open the:
    a. Desktop Settings dialog box.
    b. Custom Desktop dialog box.
    c. Folder Options dialog box.
    d. Display Properties dialog box.

14. An Internet document or Paint file used as a background is called (a):
    a. Display.
    b. Shortcut.
    c. Web item.
    d. Wallpaper.

15. Which of the following screen resolutions displays screen elements the largest?
    a. 640 by 480 pixels
    b. 1024 by 768 pixels
    c. 1280 by 1024 pixels
    d. 1600 by 1200 pixels

16. Which of the following color quality values displays the smallest number of colors?
    a. 16-bit
    b. 24-bit
    c. 32-bit
    d. All the same

17. Which of the following fonts consists of bitmapped characters?
    a. TrueType
    b. Screen
    c. OpenType
    d. Outline

▶ Skills Review

1. **Change the desktop background.**
   a. Open the Display Properties dialog box.
   b. Change the background to Santa Fe Stucco, then apply the change.

2. **Customize the desktop.**
   a. Open the Desktop Items dialog box.
   b. Display the My Documents, My Computer, and My Network Places icons on the desktop.
   c. Display the Web tab, select a Web item, then apply the desktop changes.
   d. Restore the desktop icons and the Web item to their original state, then apply the changes.

3. **Change the desktop appearance.**
   a. Display the Themes tab in the Display Properties dialog box. Change the theme to Windows Classic.
   b. Display the Appearance tab. Change the color scheme to Windows Classic, then apply the desktop changes.
   c. Save the theme as **Windows Classic 2**.
   d. Change the theme to Windows XP, then apply the desktop change.
   e. Delete the Windows Classic 2 theme (*Hint:* Select the theme from the Theme list, then click Delete).
   f. Display the Desktop tab, change the background to (None) if necessary, then apply the desktop change.

4. **Change desktop screen settings.**
   a. Display the Settings tab.
   b. Change the Screen resolution to a different setting, then apply the change.
   c. Display the Screen Saver tab. Select the 3D Pipes screen saver, then preview it.
   d. Restore the screen resolution and screen saver to their original settings.
   e. Close the Display Properties dialog box.

5. **Set the date and time.**
   a. Open the Date and Time Properties dialog box.
   b. Change the time to three hours ahead, then apply the change.
   c. Display the Internet Time tab, then update the time (only if you have an Internet connection). Otherwise, change the time back three hours. Close the Date and Time Properties dialog box.

6. Work with fonts.

   a. Open the Fonts window.

   b. Double-click a Times New Roman icon. Print the font information.

   c. Close the Times New Roman and Fonts windows.

7. Add a scheduled task.

   a. Open the Scheduled Tasks window. Start the Scheduled Task Wizard.

   b. Schedule a task for Character Map, or another available program, with the One time only option, then continue.

   c. Change the time to one minute ahead, select the current day, then continue.

   d. If necessary, type your password, press [Tab], type your password again, then continue.

   e. Finish creating the task, wait for the task to take place, then close the program window.

   f. Delete the scheduled task, then close the Scheduled Tasks window.

8. Customize the taskbar.

   a. Display the Quick Launch toolbar on the taskbar.

   b. Open the Taskbar and Start Menu Properties dialog box.

   c. Select the Auto-hide feature and hide the Quick Launch toolbar.

   d. Set any notification icon to display all the time, then apply the changes.

   e. Move the mouse pointer to the bottom of the screen.

   f. Deselect the Auto-hide feature, then restore defaults for the notification icon.

   g. Apply the changes, then close the Taskbar and Start Menu Properties dialog box.

9. Customize the Start Menu.

   a. Point to the Paint program on the Accessories submenu on the Start menu.

   b. Pin the Paint program to the Start menu.

   c. Open the Taskbar and Start Menu Properties dialog box, then display the Advanced tab on the Customize Start Menu dialog box. Show the Favorites menu on the Start menu, then apply the change.

   d. Display the Start menu with the changes.

   e. Remove the Paint program from the Start menu, then hide the Favorites menu.

   f. Close the Taskbar and Start Menu Properties dialog box and the Control Panel.

▶ Independent Challenge 1

As owner of a small optical laboratory, you are trying to abide by the Americans with Disabilities Act, which states that employers should make every reasonable effort to accommodate workers with disabilities. One worker is visually impaired. Customize the Windows desktop for this employee so that it is easier to work in, desktop items are easier to see and read, and desktop colors strongly contrast with each other. Save this custom configuration.

   a. Open the Display Properties dialog box from the Control Panel.

   b. Change the background to a dark green color.

   c. Set the screen saver for one minute, so you can show employees how it works without waiting too long.

   d. On the Appearance tab, set the Font size to Extra Large Fonts and the Color scheme to Olive Green.

   e. Set the screen resolution to the lowest setting to make it easier for employees to see.

   f. Save the theme as **Visible**, then apply the changes.

   g. Print the screen. (Press [Print Screen] to make a copy of the screen, open Paint, click Edit on the menu bar, click Paste to paste the screen into Paint, then click Yes to paste the large image, if necessary. Click the Text button on the Toolbox, click a blank area in the Paint work area, then type your name. Click File on the menu bar, click Page Setup, change 100 % normal size to 50% in the Scaling area, then click OK. Click File on the menu bar, click Print, then click Print.)

   h. Delete the scheme Visible, then apply the Windows XP theme.

   i. Set the screen saver for five minutes and restore the screen resolution if necessary.

▶ Independent Challenge 2

You accepted a temporary consulting job in Rome, Italy. After moving into your new home and unpacking your stuff, you decide to set up your computer. Once you set up and turn on the computer, you decide to change the date and time settings and other regional and language options to reflect Rome, Italy.

a. Open the Control Panel, click Switch to Classic View if necessary, then open the Date and Time Properties dialog box.

b. Click the Time Zone tab, then click the Time Zone list arrow.

c. Select Amsterdam, Berlin, Bern, Rome, Stockholm, Vienna from the list (scroll if necessary).

d. Click the Date & Time tab, change the month and year to June 2003, then click Apply.

e. Print the screen. (See Independent Challenge 1, Step g, for screen printing instructions.)

f. Open the Regional and Languages Options dialog box.

g. On the Regional Options tab, set the language formats to Italian (Italy).

h. Print the screen. (See Independent Challenge 1, Step g, for screen printing instructions.)

i. Restore the original date and time zone settings and the regional and language options to English (United States).

j. Close the Control Panel window.

▶ Independent Challenge 3

As system administrator of a small computer network for a chain of specialty book stores, you want to make sure all the computers don't lose important data. To accomplish this goal, you need to set up a scheduled task to backup the hard disk drives of all computers on a weekly basis.

a. Open the Scheduled Tasks window.

b. Schedule the Backup program as a task.

c. Schedule the task for a monthly time period.

d. Set the time one minute ahead of the current time.

e. When the Backup program task appears in the Scheduled Tasks window, print the screen. (See Independent Challenge 1, Step g, for screen printing instructions.)

f. Delete the Backup scheduled task.

▶ Independent Challenge 4

As owner of Holly's Office Supply, you need to make your business computers easier for your employees to use. One way to do that is to add programs to the Start menu. Your employees use WordPad almost exclusively, and they also use the same documents quite often.

a. Create a memo to employees about the upcoming company picnic using WordPad, then save the memo as **Company Picnic Memo** in the drive and folder where your Project Files are located.

b. Close the memo and WordPad.

c. Add the WordPad program to the Start menu as a pinned item.

d. Create a shortcut to the Company Picnic Memo file and add it to the Start menu as a pinned item.

e. Extend the My Computer menu item on the Start menu to display a submenu.

f. Open the Start menu and point to My Computer.

g. Print the screen. (See Independent Challenge 1, Step g, for screen printing instructions.)

h. Open the Company Picnic Memo from the Start menu.

i. Remove all the shortcuts you created on the Start menu and restore the My Computer menu item to its original state.

► Visual Workshop

Re-create the screen shown in Figure E-23, which displays the Windows desktop, then print the screen. Your user name on the Start menu, icons in the Control Panel, and background name (Windows XP Professional) might differ. (See Independent Challenge 1, Step g, for screen printing instructions.)

FIGURE E-23

Maintaining
Your Computer

Objectives

- ▶ **Format a disk**
- ▶ **Copy a disk**
- ▶ **Find and repair disk errors**
- ▶ **Defragment a disk**
- ▶ **Clean up a disk**
- ▶ **Restore computer settings**
- ▶ **Remove a program**
- ▶ **Add a program**
- ▶ **Enter DOS commands**

Windows XP offers a number of useful tools for managing such routine tasks as installing and removing programs, and formatting, copying, and repairing disks. Windows XP also provides tools to find and fix disk problems, speed up disk access, clean up disk space, and restore computer settings when problems occur. By periodically finding and repairing disk errors or restoring computer settings, you can keep your files in good working condition and prevent disk problems that might cause you to lose your work. In addition, you can work with the DOS operating system to enter DOS commands or run older DOS-based programs alongside your Windows operating system. ✎ John Casey, owner of Wired Coffee Company, formats and copies disks, performs several routine disk management tasks, and uses DOS commands to view his hard disk drive directory.

Formatting a Disk

Formatting a disk prepares it so that you can store information on it. Formatting removes all information from the disk, so you should never format a disk that has files you want to keep. Disks are now usually formatted before you buy them, so you no longer need to format a new disk before you can use it; however, formatting is still a quick way to erase old files from a floppy disk and to scan a disk for errors before you reuse it to store files. See Table F-1 for information about disk capacity, file system, and allocation unit size; default settings are strongly recommended. Do not use the disk that stores your Project Files for this lesson; use a disk that does not contain files you want to keep. ◤ John wants to make a copy of the disk that stores his Project Files for safekeeping, but first he needs to format the disk to which he will copy.

Steps

1. Click the **Start button** on the taskbar, point to **All Programs**, point to **Accessories**, then click **Windows Explorer**

2. Insert a floppy disk in the appropriate drive on your computer
   In this example, the floppy disk drive is the 3½ (A:) drive. Make sure the disk you are using does not contain any files you want to keep.

3. In the left pane of Windows Explorer, click the **drive icon** containing your floppy disk
   Disks and drives appear under the My Computer icon in the left pane of Windows Explorer. The icon representing the 3½ (A:) drive is highlighted, and the files on the disk drive appear in the right pane of Windows Explorer. Review the files on your floppy disk to make sure they are not ones you want to keep.

4. Right-click the **drive icon** containing your floppy disk in the left pane of Window Explorer, then click **Format** on the shortcut menu
   The Format dialog box opens, as shown in Figure F-1. The fastest way to format a floppy disk is with the **Quick Format** option. This option simply formats a previously formatted disk, removing all files from it. The **Full Format** option, which you choose by deselecting the Quick Format check box, removes all files from any floppy disk and scans the disk for bad sectors. You should choose Quick Format only if you are sure that your disk is not damaged. Additional format options include Enable Compression and Create an MS-DOS startup disk. The **Enable Compression** option, supported only on NTFS drives, specifies whether to format the drive so that folders and files on it are compressed. The **Create an MS-DOS startup disk** option formats a disk so that you can start up your computer in MS-DOS, a disk-based operating system, to fix a problem, display information, or run an MS-DOS program using MS-DOS commands; experience with MS-DOS is required.

5. In the Format options area, click the **Quick Format check box** to select it

6. Select any text in the **Volume label text box**, then type **Backup**
   After you format the disk, the volume label appears in Windows Explorer and My Computer to make the floppy disk easier to identify.

7. Click **Start**, then click **OK** in the message box
   A progress meter appears at the bottom of the Format dialog box. After a few moments, the Format Complete message box opens.

8. Click **OK** in the Format Complete message box
   The Format Complete message box closes.

9. Click **Close** in the Format dialog box, then remove the formatted disk from the appropriate drive on your computer
   The disk is now formatted. You will use the formatted disk in the next lesson to make a copy of your Project Files.

Trouble?

Formatting removes all the files on your disk, so do not use the disk that contains your Project Files or any disk that has files you want to keep.

QuickTip

If you format a disk with the FAT file system, the label can contain up to 11 characters; all floppy disks use FAT. If you format a disk with NTFS, the limit is 32 characters.

FIGURE F-1: Format dialog box

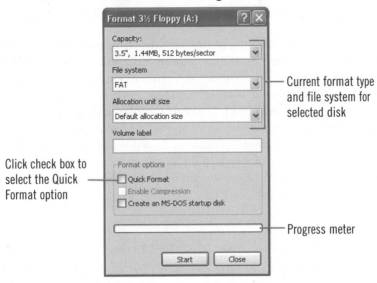

Current format type
and file system for
selected disk

Click check box to
select the Quick
Format option

Progress meter

TABLE F-1: Format dialog box options

option	description
Capacity	Specifies how much data the disk or partition can hold, such as the physical size, storage size, and sector size.
File system	Displays the file system for the disk. A file system is the overall structure in which files are named, stored, and organized. NTFS and FAT are types of file systems.
Allocation unit size	Specifies the disk allocation unit size, or cluster size (a group of sectors on a disk). The operating system assigns a unique number to each cluster and then keeps track of files according to which clusters they use. The default allocation size is typically selected.

CLUES TO USE

Protecting against computer viruses

A computer virus is a program that attaches itself to a file, reproduces itself, and spreads to other files. A virus is typically attached to programs and files downloaded from the Internet, electronic mail attachments, or shareware disks containing free or inexpensive software or illegally obtained pirated software. When you open a program or file with the computer virus, the computer becomes infected with the virus and can corrupt or destroy data, or disrupt program or Windows functionality. For example, the Chernobyl virus attempts to erase a computer's hard drive and damage the computer's system settings, making it impossible to access your data. The virus is called the Chernobyl virus because it is timed to go off on April 26, the anniversary of the 1986 Russian nuclear accident, one of technology's worst disasters. The Chernobyl virus didn't propagate quickly because it required a person to open an infected file to contaminate a computer. Many viruses stay dormant on a computer before doing any damage, so catching and destroying these viruses before they cause damage can prevent computer disaster. Antivirus software, or virus detection software, examines the files stored on a disk to determine whether they are infected with a virus, then destroys or disinfects them. Antivirus software typically starts when you start Windows and watches for viruses whenever your computer is on. Popular antivirus software, which needs to be purchased from a software retailer, includes Norton Anitvirus and MacAfee VirusScan. New viruses appear all the time, so it is important that your antivirus software be kept up-to-date to look for the new viruses. You can easily download updates from the Internet. Typically, you should check for updates every three months, or if you hear about a new virus.

Copying a Disk

One way to protect the information on a disk from possible problems is to copy the disk, placing copies of all the files on it to another disk. Then, if information goes bad on a disk, you still have the copied information. You can use Windows to copy information from one disk to another using the same disk drive. When you copy disks, the disk must be the same type, either 3½", or 5¼", and size (1.44 MB or 1.2 MB), and not write-protected. A floppy disk is not write-protected when the tab in the upper-left corner on the back of the floppy disk is pushed down so that you cannot see through the square hole. 5¼" disk drives are common on older computers, but are not standard on new computers. ✐ John wants to make a copy of the information he has compiled on his floppy disk. He'll copy it to the disk he formatted in the previous lesson.

Steps

Trouble?

If you store your Project Files on a network or hard drive, copy the Project Files to a floppy disk before completing this lesson.

1. Insert the disk that stores your Project Files in the appropriate drive, then right-click the **drive icon** containing your Project Files in the left pane of Windows Explorer
In this example, the icon representing the 3½" disk drive is highlighted, and the shortcut menu for the left pane opens, as shown in Figure F-2.

2. Click **Copy Disk** on the shortcut menu
The Copy Disk dialog box opens, as shown in Figure F-3. On the left side of the dialog box, you select the **source disk** from which you want to copy. On the right side, you select the **destination disk** to which you want to copy. Both the disk you are copying from (the Project Disk) and the disk you are copying to (the disk you formatted in the previous lesson) are 3½" floppy disks, so the drive shown is the same. The 3½ Floppy (A:) or (B:) icons on both sides of the dialog box are selected by default; no additional drives appear because the computer in this example does not contain additional floppy disk drives, although yours might.

3. Click **Start**, then click **OK** in the Copy Disk message box
A progress meter appears in the Copy Disk dialog box with the status message "Reading source disk." After reading the source disk, a Copy Disk message box opens, asking you to insert a destination disk.

4. Remove your Project Disk, label the blank formatted disk from the previous lesson **Copy of Project Disk**, insert it into the same drive, then click **OK** in the Copy Disk message box
In the Copy Disk dialog box the progress meter continues with the status message "Writing to destination disk." Upon completion, the status message "Copy completed successfully" appears.

5. Click **Close** in the Copy Disk dialog box
Now that he has a copy of his disk, John can perform maintenance operations on his disk without worrying about losing any information. Leave the "Copy of Project Disk" disk in the floppy drive for the next lesson.

FIGURE F-2: Windows Explorer with shortcut menu for floppy disk

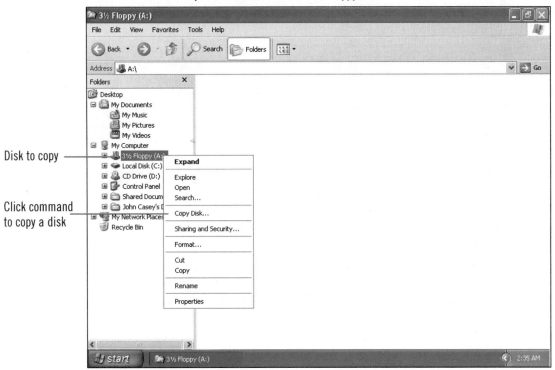

Disk to copy

Click command
to copy a disk

FIGURE F-3: Copy Disk dialog box

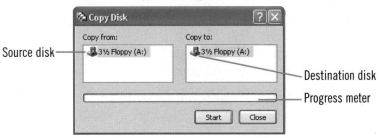

Source disk

Destination disk

Progress meter

Synchronizing files between computers

If you want to work with files that are copied onto two different computers, such as your work computer and your home computer, you can synchronize the files to keep the various copies updated between computers using a Windows feature called Briefcase. Before you can use Briefcase, you need to create one. Open the folder in My Computer where you want the new Briefcase to appear, or display the desktop. Right-click an empty area of the desktop or My Computer, click New, then click Briefcase. To use Briefcase, drag the files you want to copy to your other computer from Windows Explorer to the Briefcase icon. Then, drag the Briefcase icon to the icon for the removable disk drive, and remove the disk. You can now insert the removable disk in a different computer. If you edit the files, you need to synchronize them when you return to your main computer. To synchronize them, reinsert the removable disk, double-click the Briefcase icon, then click Update All on the Briefcase menu to copy the new versions of your files from the removable disk to the hard disk.

Windows XP

Finding and Repairing Disk Errors

Sometimes an unexpected power loss or program error can create inaccessible file segments that take up space on a hard disk or a floppy disk. The **Check Disk** program that comes with Windows helps you find and repair damaged sections of a disk. Check Disk can also be used to find physical disk errors or **bad sectors**. The program doesn't physically repair your media, but it moves data away from any bad sectors it finds. To keep your hard disk drive working properly, you should run Check Disk from time to time. When you run Check Disk, all files must be closed for the process to run. While the Check Disk process is running, your hard disk will not be available to perform any other task. ✐ John wants to make sure his disk has no problems, so he runs Check Disk. For this lesson, use the copy of your Project Disk that you made in the previous lesson.

Steps

1. Close any open files or programs, right-click the **drive icon containing the copy of your Project Disk** in the left pane of Windows Explorer, then click **Properties** on the shortcut menu
   The Properties dialog box opens.

2. Click the **Tools tab**
   The Properties dialog box appears with the Tools tab, as shown in Figure F-4, in which you can start the Check Disk program. The Tools tab also provides you with access to other utilities that can make Windows work more efficiently: defragmentation and backup, which is available only with the Professional version of Windows XP. Defragmentation starts the Disk Defragmenter program and optimizes a disk for better performance, while backup starts the Backup program and copies files and folders to a disk for safe keeping.

   QuickTip

   For Help, click the Help button ? in the title bar, then click any item to display a Help screen.

3. In the Error-checking area, click **Check Now**
   The Check Disk dialog box opens, as shown in Figure F-5.

4. Click the **Automatically fix file system errors check box** to select it
   This option repairs most errors automatically using predetermined settings.

5. Click the **Scan for and attempt recovery of bad sectors check box** to select it
   This option makes corrections for any unreadable or bad sectors on the disk.

6. Click **Start**
   A progress meter appears, displaying scanning status. When the process is complete, the Disk Check Complete message box opens.

7. Click **OK** in the Disk Check Complete message box, then click **OK** to close the Properties dialog box

8. Click the Windows Explorer **Close button**

9. Remove the copy of your Project Disk from the appropriate drive on your computer, then insert your original Project Disk

FIGURE F-4: **Properties dialog box with Tools tab**

Click button to
check the disk

Only available in the
Professional edition

FIGURE F-5: **Check Disk dialog box**

Click check box to
fix file system errors

Click check box to
recover bad sectors

Progress meter

Backing up files

The more you work with a computer, the more files you create. To protect yourself from losing critical information, it's important to back up, or make copies of your files on a separate disk, frequently. If you are using the Windows XP Professional edition, you can click Backup Now on the Tools tab in the disk drive Properties dialog box to open the Backup program and walk you through the Backup or Restore Wizard to help you back up the files on your hard

disk to a floppy or tape drive. You can back up the contents of an entire disk or only certain files. Using the Backup option has several advantages over simply copying files to a floppy, such as compressing files as it copies them so you can fit more onto a floppy disk. It can also split a large file across two or more floppies, something you cannot do with the Copy Disk command.

Unit F

Windows XP

Defragmenting a Disk

When you delete files from a disk, you create empty spaces that might be fragmented over different areas of the disk. When you create a new file on a fragmented disk, parts of the file are stored in these empty spaces, resulting in a single file that is broken into many parts, which takes longer to retrieve or store when you open or save the file. A file broken up in this way is called a **fragmented file**. To retrieve a fragmented file, the computer must search many areas on the disk, which lengthens retrieval time, but the file is otherwise usable, and it is undetectable to the user that the file is fragmented. You can use the **Disk Defragmenter** program to place all of the parts of a file in one **contiguous**, or adjacent, location. This procedure, which efficiently arranges all of the files and unused space, is called **optimization**. Optimization makes your programs run faster and your files open more quickly. For best results, run Check Disk to check for errors on your disk before you start the disk defragmentation process. While Disk Defragmenter works, you can use your computer to carry out other tasks; however, your computer will operate more slowly. John uses Disk Defragmenter to optimize his hard disk; you cannot defragment a floppy disk with Windows XP, although you could with previous Windows versions.

Steps

1. Click the **Start button** on the taskbar, point to **All Programs**, point to **Accessories**, point to **System Tools**, then click **Disk Defragmenter**
   The Disk Defragmenter dialog box opens. You need to choose a hard disk drive, typically, the C: drive.

2. Click the **hard disk drive** if necessary
   Before you perform a complete disk defragmentation, you can analyze the disk to determine the extent of the fragmentation.

QuickTip

To temporarily stop Disk Defragmenter, click Pause, then click Resume when you are ready.

3. Click **Analyze**
   The analyzing process can take a few minutes, depending on the extent of the fragmentation on your disk. You can monitor the process with the progress meter. Upon completion, the Analysis complete message box opens.

4. Click **View Report**
   The Analysis Report dialog box opens, as shown in Figure F-6.

QuickTip

To print the analysis, click Print in the Analysis Report dialog box, then click Print in the Print dialog box.

5. In the Volume information box, click the **down scroll arrow** to display the file fragmentation statistics
   The file fragmentation statistics provide information on the total number of files, average file size, total number of fragmented files and excess file fragments, and average fragments per file.

6. Click **Close** in the Analysis Report dialog box
   The Disk Defragmenter window appears, as shown in Figure F-7. The defragmentation process can take several minutes or more, depending on the extent of the fragmentation on your disk.

Trouble?

If you are working in a lab, check with your instructor or technical support person for authorization to defragment your hard disk drive. If you do not receive authorization, click the Close button in the Defragmentation window and skip Steps 7 and 8.

7. Click **Defragment**
   The Analysis display shows you the defragmentation process. Different colored lines, each representing a disk sector, appear in the Analysis display. The colored lines tell you the defragmentation status of your hard disk drive, and the legend at the bottom of the window explains how to interpret the colors. You can monitor the process with the progress meter. When complete, the Disk Defragmenter window opens, as shown in Figure F-8. The Defragmentation display shows you the result of the defragmentation process.

8. When the defragmentation is complete, click **Close**, then click the **Close button** in the Defragmentation window
   Your disk is now optimized.

FIGURE F-6: **Analysis Report dialog box**

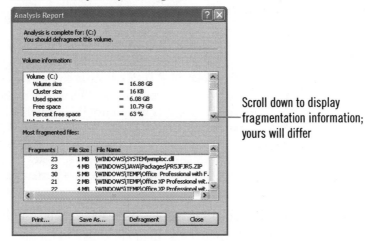

Scroll down to display
fragmentation information;
yours will differ

FIGURE F-7: **Disk Defragmenter window**

Selected volume for
disk defragmentation

Defragmented
files in red

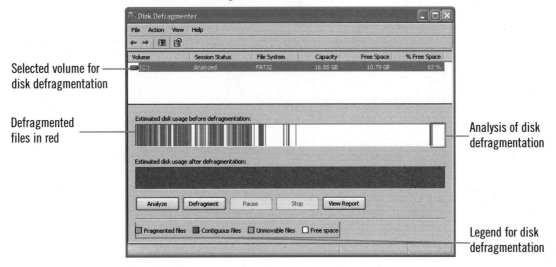

Analysis of disk
defragmentation

Legend for disk
defragmentation

FIGURE F-8: **Disk defragmentation process completed**

Defragmented
disk; no red areas

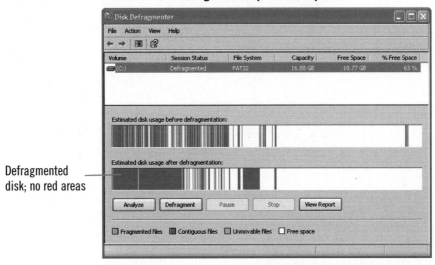

Cleaning Up a Disk

Cleaning up a disk involves removing unneeded files to make room for other files on your computer, which can be difficult if you don't know the significance of each file. You can use a Windows XP program called **Disk Cleanup** to clean up your hard disk drive safely and effectively. You can also empty the Recycle Bin to clear space on the hard disk. Disk Cleanup searches your drive, then lists temporary files, Internet cache files, and unnecessary program files that you can safely delete. You can select the types of files you want Disk Cleanup to delete. Before you select and delete files, make sure you will not need them in the future. Disk Cleanup also gives you the option to remove Windows components and installed programs that you no longer use. John decides to clean up his hard disk.

Steps

1. Click the **Start button** on the taskbar, point to **All Programs**, point to **Accessories**, point to **System Tools**, then click **Disk Cleanup**
   Disk Cleanup selects your hard drive and calculates how much disk space you can free on the drive, then the Disk Cleanup for (C:) dialog box opens (the hard drive is C: in this example), displaying the Disk Cleanup tab with types of files to remove and the amount of disk space taken up by each type of file, as shown in Figure F-9. Your list of files to delete might differ.

2. In the Files to delete list, click **Recycle Bin** (but not the check box), then click **View Files**
   The Recycle Bin window opens, listing the files currently stored in the Recycle Bin.

3. Click the **Close button** in the Recycle Bin window

4. In the Files to delete box, click the **check boxes** next to any item with a check mark to deselect them (be sure to scroll through the entire list)

5. In the Files to delete box, click the **Recycle Bin check box** to select it
   The check mark indicates that you want to delete all the files in the Recycle Bin, as shown in Figure F-10.

6. Click **OK** in the Disk Cleanup dialog box, then click **Yes** in the message box to confirm the deletion
   The Disk Cleanup for (C:) message box opens, and a progress meter appears, displaying deletion status. After a few moments, the message box closes. If you open the Disk Cleanup dialog box after deleting the Recycle Bin files, the amount of disk space taken up by the Recycle Bin will be 0 KB.

FIGURE F-9: **Disk Cleanup for (C:) dialog box**

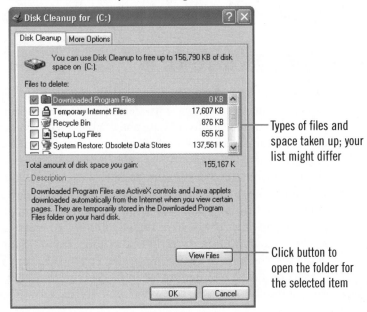

Types of files and
space taken up; your
list might differ

Click button to
open the folder for
the selected item

FIGURE F-10: **Disk Cleanup for (C:) dialog box with
Recycle Bin selected**

Selected item
to be deleted

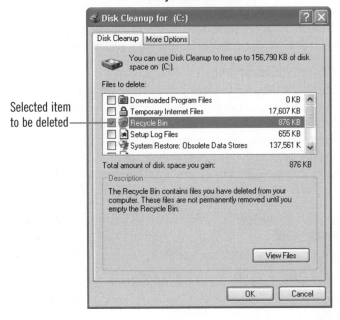

Terminating an inactive program

If a program stops responding to mouse or keyboard commands, you can use the Windows Task Manager to terminate and exit the program, after which you can restart it. To terminate an inactive program, right-click an empty area on the taskbar, then click Task Manager to open the Windows Task Manager window. Click the Applications tab if necessary. Click the program you want to terminate in the task list, then click End Task. Sometimes it takes a few moments to terminate the program. If the program still doesn't terminate, click End Task again. When the program termination process completes, click the Close button in the Windows Task Manager window.

Windows XP

Restoring Computer Settings

Windows XP is a reliable operating system, but anytime you make changes to your computer, such as adding or removing software and hardware, you run the risk of causing problems with your operating system. To alleviate potential problems, you can use **System Restore**, a program installed with Windows XP Professional, to undo harmful changes to your computer and restore its settings. System Restore returns your computer system, but not your personal files, to an earlier time, before the changes were made to your computer, called a **restore point**. As you work with your computer, System Restore monitors your changes and automatically creates restore points on a daily basis or at important system events, but you can also create your own restore point at any time. If you have recently performed a system restoration, you can use System Restore to undo your most recent restoration. System Restore is turned on by default when you install the Windows XP operating system, but you can turn it off or make other System Restore changes on the System Restore tab in the System Properties dialog box. ✎ John wants to make some changes to his computer, so he creates a restore point in case problems arise.

QuickTip

To restore your computer, start the System Restore program, click the Restore my computer to an earlier time option button if necessary, click Next, select a date and a restore point, click Next to restore and reboot the computer, then click OK in the Restoration Complete dialog box.

1. Click the **Start button** on the taskbar, point to **All Programs**, point to **Accessories**, point to **System Tools**, then click **System Restore**

The Welcome to System Restore window opens, as shown in Figure F-11. The window displays an introduction to the process and two or three (or more) options: Restore my computer to an earlier time, Create a restore point, and Undo my last restoration, which will appear only if you have previously performed a restoration.

2. Click **System Restore Settings**

The System Properties dialog box opens, displaying the System Restore tab, as shown in Figure F-12. The System Restore tab allows you to turn off System Restore, which stops the automatic creation of restore points and changes the amount of disk space available for System Restore. Windows needs space on your hard disk to save restore points. When you decrease the available disk space, you reduce the number of restore points. System Restore requires a minimum of 200 MB of available space on your hard disk. If System Restore runs out of disk space, it becomes inactive until sufficient disk space is made available.

Trouble?

Check with your instructor or technical support person for authorization to change the disk space usage; if you do not receive it, skip Step 3, then click Cancel.

3. If your disk space usage is greater than 20%, drag the Disk space to use slider to **20%**, then click **OK**

The Welcome to System Restore window appears.

4. Click the **Create a restore point option button**, then click **Next**

The Create a Restore Point window appears, asking you to type a description for your restore point.

QuickTip

To delete all but the most recent restore point, start the Disk Cleanup program, click the More Options tab, click Clean up under System Restore, then click Yes to confirm the deletion.

5. In the Restore point description text box, type **Default Windows XP installation**, then type **your initials**

The restore point cannot be changed after you create it, so make sure you have the name you want.

6. Click **Create**

Windows creates a restore point, which includes the current date and time. The Restore Point Created window opens, displaying the day, date, time, and name of the new restore point.

7. Click **Close**

The Restore Point Created window closes.

FIGURE F-11: **Welcome to System Restore window**

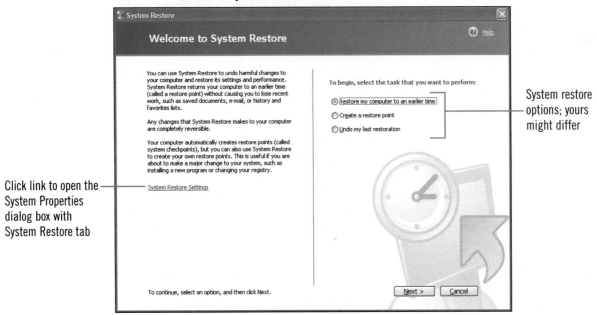

Click link to open the
System Properties
dialog box with
System Restore tab

System restore
options; yours
might differ

FIGURE F-12: **System Properties dialog box with**
System Restore tab

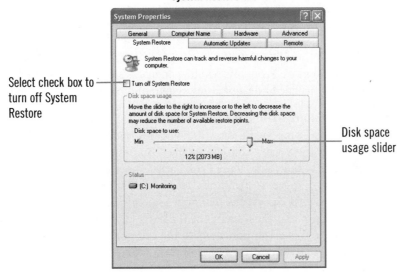

Select check box to
turn off System
Restore

Disk space
usage slider

Recover from a system failure

If your computer doesn't start properly for any reason, known as system failure, System Restore will not help you unless you can start the program. You need an Automated System Recovery (ASR) disk to start and recover your computer. To create an ASR with Windows XP Professional, click the Start button on the taskbar, point to All Programs, point to Accessories, point to System Tools, click Backup to start the program, then click Advanced Mode in the Backup Utility Wizard. Click Tools on the menu bar, click ASR Wizard, and then follow the instructions in the Automated System Recovery Preparation Wizard.

During the process, you'll need a blank 3½" floppy disk to save your system settings. You will also need backup media, such as a floppy disk or tape, to contain the backup files. Only those system files necessary for starting up your system will be backed up; personal files will need to be backed up separately, so you only need to do this once. To recover from a system failure using ASR, insert the original Windows XP installation CD in your CD drive, restart your computer from the CD, press [F2] when prompted during the text-only mode section of Setup, insert the ASR floppy disk when prompted, then follow the recovery instructions.

Windows XP

Removing a Program

Adding and removing programs gives you the flexibility to use the programs you need when you need them and to maximize the free space on your hard drive. If you do not use a program very often and want to free some space, you can remove the program. You can always reinstall it. Windows XP comes with many programs called Windows components. If you want to free space on your hard drive, use Add or Remove Programs to remove a component. If you have installed a program that is not included on the Windows XP installation CD, such as Microsoft Office XP, you should avoid using Windows Explorer to delete the program because program files and other information might be located in other places, and you might not find everything. Also, some programs share files with other programs, so deleting them can cause damage to other programs. The Change or Remove Programs feature in Add or Remove Programs will make sure all of the program files are removed, except those which are shared with other programs. ✎ John needs more space on his hard drive, so he decides to remove some game programs.

Steps

(STOP) **If you do not have the Windows XP installation CD-ROM to reinstall the program in the next lesson, don't remove the program in this lesson and simply read through this lesson and the next without completing the steps.**

Trouble?

Click **Switch to Classic view** if necessary.

1. Click the **Start button** on the taskbar, then click **Control Panel**
   The Control Panel opens in Classic view.

2. Double-click the **Add or Remove Programs icon** 🗊 in the Control Panel
   The Add or Remove Programs window opens, as shown in Figure F-13, and Setup searches for currently installed non-operating system programs on your computer.

3. Click **Add/Remove Windows Components**
   The Windows Components Wizard dialog box opens, and the wizard searches for components installed on your computer. The Components list shows all the components of Windows XP, as shown in Figure F-14. Each component contains one or more parts that you can install or remove. A blank box means that none of the parts of that component are installed; a shaded box means that only some of the parts of the component are installed; and a checked box means that all of the parts of that component are installed. To display what is included in a component, click the component name (but not the check box), then click Details. The Accessories and Utilities component at the top of the list is selected.

4. Click **Details** to display Accessories and Utilities subcomponents, click **Games** in the Subcomponents list, then click **Details**
   The Games dialog box appears, listing the Windows game components. Windows XP comes with five games that you can play over the Internet. The games take up 8.5 MB of hard disk space, so you want to remove them for now and will reinstall them later.

Trouble?

If you are working in a lab, check with your instructor or technical support person for authorization to remove the program or instructions to remove another one. If you do not receive authorization, skip Steps 5, 6, and 7, then click Cancel three times.

5. Click the **Internet Games check box** to deselect it
   The Internet Games check box clears. When you clear a check box, Windows removes the component. Make sure that you do not change any other settings.

6. Click **OK** in the Games dialog box, click **OK** in the Accessories and Utilities dialog box, then click **Next** in the Windows Components Wizard dialog box

7. Click **Finish** in the Windows Components Wizard, then click **Close** in the Add or Remove Programs window
   The Windows Components Wizard removes the software and reconfigures Windows.

FIGURE F-13: **Add or Remove Programs window**

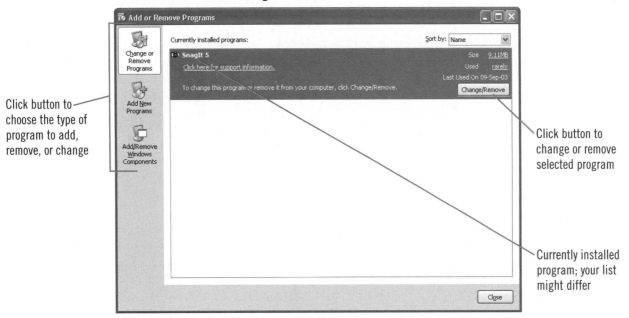

Click button to choose the type of program to add, remove, or change

Click button to change or remove selected program

Currently installed program; your list might differ

FIGURE F-14: **Windows Components Wizard dialog box**

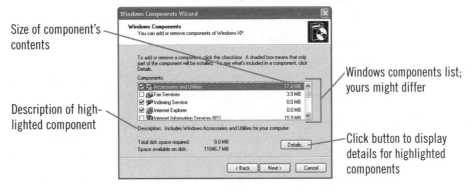

Size of component's contents

Description of high-lighted component

Windows components list; yours might differ

Click button to display details for highlighted components

Updating Windows using the Web

You can use the Windows Update feature to add the latest Windows updates and new features from the Internet to your Windows XP installation. Windows Update is a Microsoft Web site that helps you keep your computer up-to-date. Windows Update provides a central location where you can find and add new Windows features, system updates, and device drivers. To add features from Microsoft Windows Update, connect to the Internet, click the Start button on the taskbar, point to All Programs, click Windows Update, then follow the instructions on the Web site. Windows Update can review device drivers and system software on your computer, compare those findings with a master database on the Web, and then recommend and install updates specifically for your computer. Windows Update indicates the approximate download time and whether an update is already installed on your computer. You can also restore to a previous device driver or system file using the uninstall option. Updates are continually added to the Web site, so it is important to check for important new content on a regular basis. If you want to be notified when updates occur, you can set up Windows XP to let you know when they happen. Double-click the System icon in the Control Panel in Classic view, click the Automatic Updates tab, click the notification setting you want, which includes turning it off, then click OK.

Adding a Program

Windows XP comes with many programs; a typical installation installs only the most common programs, but you can install any additional components as needed. You can use Add or Remove Programs to add Windows components you chose not to include in the original installation or that you removed to free space on a disk. When you install a Windows component, you need the Windows XP installation CD-ROM to complete the process. You can also use the Add New Programs feature in Add or Remove Programs to install programs that are not included on the Windows XP installation CD, such as Microsoft Office XP, or to add the latest Windows updates and new features from the Internet. ✎ John deleted some files to free space on his hard disk, so he can reinstall the Internet games he previously removed.

Steps

 If you did not remove the program in the previous lesson, simply read through this lesson without completing the steps.

1. Double-click the **Add or Remove Programs icon** 🗟 in the Control Panel

The Add/Remove Programs window opens. At the same time, the Setup program searches for currently installed programs on your computer, which may take a few moments.

2. Click **Add/Remove Windows Components**

The Windows Components Wizard dialog box opens, and the wizard searches for components installed on your computer. The Components list shows all the components of Windows XP. The Accessories and Utilities component at the top of the list is selected.

3. Click **Details** to display the Accessories and Utilities subcomponents, click **Games** in the Subcomponents list, then click **Details**

The Games dialog box appears, listing the Windows game components. The check boxes indicate which parts are currently installed on your computer.

4. Click the **Internet Games check box** to select it

The Internet Games check box is selected, as shown in Figure F-15. When you select a check box, Windows installs the component. Make sure that you do not change any other settings.

5. Insert the Windows XP installation CD-ROM in the appropriate drive, if the Welcome to Windows screen appears click **Exit** if necessary, click **OK** in the Games dialog box, click **OK** in the Accessories and Utilities window, then click **Next** in the Windows Components dialog box

A status bar appears, indicating progress as the wizard copies files from the installation CD-ROM to your hard drive.

6. Click **Finish** in the Windows Components Wizard dialog box, click **Close** in the Add or Remove Programs window, then click the **Close button** in the Control Panel

7. Click the **Start button** on the taskbar, point to **All Programs**, then point to **Games**

The Start menu highlights the menus and submenus to indicate where the new programs are located, as shown in Figure F-16.

8. Click an empty area of the desktop to close the Start menu, then remove the Windows XP installation CD-ROM from the appropriate drive

FIGURE F-15: **Windows Components Wizard dialog box for Games**

Selected item to install

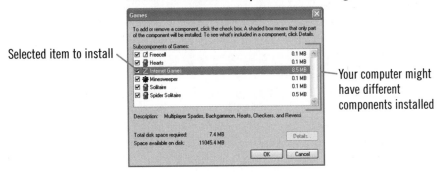

Your computer might have different components installed

FIGURE F-16: **Start menu with a highlighted path**

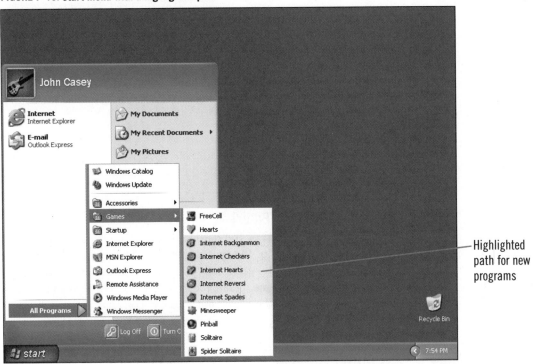

Highlighted path for new programs

Getting older programs to run on Windows XP

If you have an older program, such as a game, that was written for an earlier version of Windows and doesn't run on Windows XP, you can run the Program Compatibility Wizard to help you fix the problem. The wizard steps you through the process of testing your program in different Windows environments, such as Windows 95, and with various settings, such as screen resolution and color quality. To start the Program Compatibility Wizard, click the Start button on the taskbar, point to All Programs, point to Accessories, click

Program Compatibility Wizard, read the introduction, click Next, then follow the step-by-step instructions. If you have problems installing a program on Windows XP, you can run the Program Compatibility Wizard on the setup file, such as Setup.exe, for the program. If you are comfortable working with the compatibility settings, you can manually set the properties. Right-click the program you want to change, click Properties, click the Compatibility tab, change the compatibility settings you want, then click OK.

Unit F
Windows XP

Entering DOS Commands

Besides running Windows XP programs, you can also enter commands and run programs written in Windows 3.1 and MS-DOS. **MS-DOS** stands for Microsoft Disk Operating System. MS-DOS, or DOS, employs a **command-line interface** through which you must type commands at a **command prompt** to run different tasks. A character such as a > or $ appears at the beginning of a command prompt. Each DOS command has a strict set of rules called a **command syntax** that you must follow when expressing a command. Table F-2 lists common DOS commands and their syntax. You can also start Windows XP programs from within DOS; for example, you can type "explorer" after the command prompt to start Windows Explorer. ◢◤ For some tasks, John prefers to enter commands at the DOS prompt. He decides to display the Command Prompt window on his computer and run a few simple commands.

Steps

1. **Click the Start button on the taskbar, point to All Programs, point to Accessories, then click Command Prompt**
   The Command Prompt window opens, displaying the DOS command prompt, as shown in Figure F-17. The command prompt indicates the current directory, in this case the Documents and Settings directory for John Casey. You can view the contents of the current directory using the dir command.

2. **Type cd c:\, then press [Enter]**
   DOS changes from accessing the Documents and Settings directory for John Casey to accessing the hard drive (C:) directory. The command prompt changes from C:\Documents and Settings\John Casey> to C:\>.

Trouble?

If the contents of the directory don't fill the page, type cd c:\ program files, then press [Enter] to change the directory.

3. **Type dir /p, then press [Enter]**
   DOS displays the contents of the hard drive directory. The "/p" part of what you type is called an **argument**, part of the syntax that gives DOS more information about what you want it to do. By adding the optional /p argument to the dir command, DOS displays the contents of the directory one screen at a time. Figure F-18 shows the first screen, also called the **output**, or results, of the command. You can continue viewing the directory listing one page at a time by pressing any key, or you can return to the DOS command prompt at any time by pressing [Ctrl][C].

4. **Press [Ctrl][C] to return to the DOS command prompt**

QuickTip

To view information about a particular DOS command, type the command name, type /?, then press [Enter] at the DOS command prompt.

5. **Type exit, then press [Enter]**
   The Command Prompt window closes, and you return to Windows.

CLUES TO USE

Controlling the appearance of the Command Prompt window

Windows XP gives you several options for controlling the appearance of the Command Prompt window, including a Control Panel program called Console. To open the Console, right-click the Command Prompt window title bar, then click Properties. In the "Command Prompt" Properties dialog box, you can click the Options tab to change the cursor size and display options, click the Font tab to change font sizes and styles, click the Layout tab to change the window size and position and screen buffer size, then click the Colors tab to change screen text, screen background, popup text, and popup background colors.

FIGURE F-17: Command Prompt window

DOS command
prompt

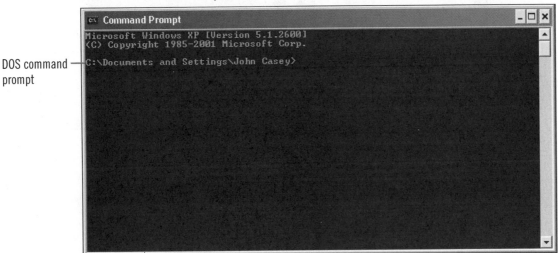

FIGURE F-18: Results of dir /p command

File size

Filename or
directory name

Output of
dir /p com-
mand in C:
directory

Filename
extension

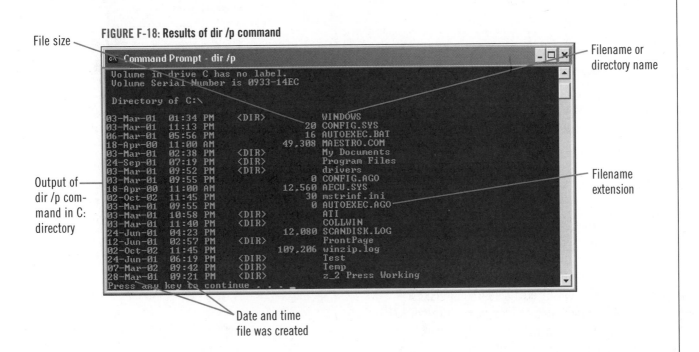

Date and time
file was created

TABLE F-2: Common DOS commands (arguments are in italics)

command	purpose
cd *foldername*	Opens the folder named *foldername*
dir /p	Lists the contents of the current folder, one screen at a time if you use the /p argument
dir at*.doc	The asterisk is a wildcard and represents any number of characters in a filename. The command matches at back.doc, ati.doc, and atlm.doc
exit	Closes the Command Prompt window
more *filename*	Displays the contents of a file, one screen of output at a time
type *filename*	Displays the contents of the text file named filename

Practice

► Concepts Review

Label each element of the screen shown in Figure F-19.

FIGURE F-19

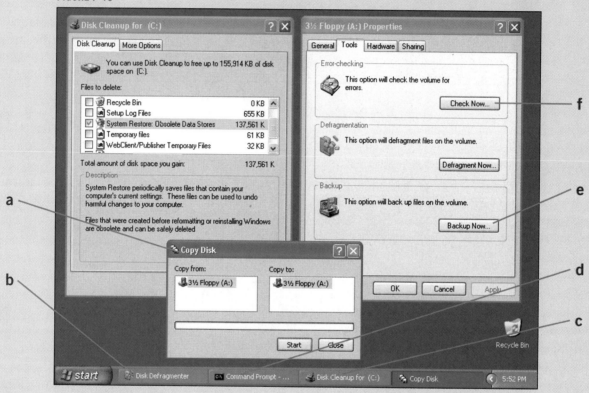

1. Which element optimizes a disk?
2. Which element deletes files from a disk?
3. Which element copies files from disk to disk?
4. Which element fixes and repairs a disk?
5. Which element accepts MS-DOS commands?
6. Which element copies files from disk to tape?

Match each term with the statement that describes its function.

7. **Reinstalls computer files**
8. **Optimizes disk access**
9. **Deletes files**
10. **Stores files**
11. **Finds and repairs disk errors**

a. Disk Cleanup
b. Check Disk
c. Disk Defragmenter
d. System Restore
e. Formatted disk

Select the best answers from the following lists of choices.

12. **Which option performs a disk format that removes all files from a disk and scans the disk for bad sectors?**
   a. Quick Format selected
   b. Quick Format deselected
   c. Full Format selected
   d. Full Format deselected

13. **When copying a floppy disk, the disks that you use do NOT need to be:**
    a. Formatted.
    c. The same type.
    b. The same size.
    d. Non write-protected.

14. **Which of the following locations is NOT a tool on the drive properties dialog box?**
    a. Error checking
    c. Maintenance
    b. Defragmentation
    d. Backup

15. **Which of the following is NOT a Check Disk function?**
    a. Finds damaged sections of a disk
    c. Repairs damaged sections of a disk
    b. Moves data away from damaged sections of a disk
    d. Physically repairs a damaged disk

16. **Disk defragmentation arranges:**
    a. Data files.
    c. System files.
    b. Unused space.
    d. All of the above.

17. **Which of the following is NOT a Disk Cleanup file type?**
    a. Program Files
    c. Temporary files
    b. Recycle Bin
    d. Temporary Internet files

18. **When you type the DOS command *more text.txt*, DOS:**
    a. Displays the contents of the file text.txt.
    c. Displays the contents of the file text.txt one screen at a time.
    b. Finds the file text.txt.
    d. Displays more information about the file text.txt.

▶ Skills Review

 If you are working in a lab, check with your instructor or technical support person for authorization to perform Steps 4-8; if you do not receive authorization, skip Steps 4-8.

1. **Format a disk.**
   a. Start Windows Explorer.
   b. Insert a disk in the floppy drive. (You can reuse the disk "Copy of Project Files Disk" that you created in this unit.)
   c. Right-click the drive icon containing your floppy disk, then click Format.
   d. Click the Quick Format check box to deselect it if necessary, click Start, then click OK in the warning box.
   e. Click OK in the message box, then click Close in the Format dialog box.
   f. Remove the formatted disk from the floppy drive.

2. **Copy a disk.**
   a. Insert the disk with your Project Files in the floppy drive.
   b. In Windows Explorer, right-click the floppy disk drive, then click Copy Disk.
   c. In the Copy Disk dialog box, click the drive containing the disk with your Project Files, click Start, then click OK in the message box.
   d. When prompted, remove the floppy disk with your Project Files, insert the blank disk you just formatted (not the disk with your Project Files) in the floppy drive, then click OK.
   e. Click Close in the Copy Disk dialog box when done and leave the disk in the floppy drive.

3. **Find and repair disk errors.**
   a. In Windows Explorer, right-click the drive icon containing your Project Files, then click Properties.
   b. Click the Tools tab, then click Check Now.
   c. Click the Automatically fix file system errors check box to select it.
   d. Click the Scan for and attempt recovery of bad sectors check box to select it, then click Start.

e. Click OK in the message box, click OK in the Properties dialog box, then click the Close button.

f. Remove the floppy disk, then insert your original disk containing your Project Files.

4. Defragment a disk.

a. Start Disk Defragmenter.

b. Click the hard disk drive (typically, the C: drive), then click Analyze.

c. Click View Report, click Print, then click Print in the Print dialog box.

d. Click Close in the Analysis Report dialog box, then click the Close button.

5. Cleanup a disk.

a. Start Disk Cleanup.

b. If necessary, click the drive list arrow, click the hard disk drive, then click OK.

c. In the Files to delete list, click Temporary Internet Files (but not the check box), then click View Files.

d. Click the Content window Close button.

e. Click the check boxes next to any items with check marks to deselect the items. (Be sure to scroll through the entire list.) Click the Temporary Internet Files check box to select it.

f. Click OK in the Disk Cleanup dialog box, then click Yes in the message box.

6. Restore computer settings.

a. Start System Restore. Create a restore point with your name, then close System Restore.

7. Remove a program.

a. Open the Add or Remove Programs window from the Control Panel.

b. Open the Windows Components Wizard dialog box.

c. Open the details for Accessories and Utilities, then open the details for Accessories.

d. Deselect the Character Map check box if necessary, then complete the wizard to remove the program.

8. Add a program.

a. Open the Add or Remove Programs window from the Control Panel.

b. Open the Windows Components Wizard dialog box.

c. Open the details for Accessories and Utilities, then open the details for Accessories.

d. Select the Character Map check box.

e. Insert a Windows XP installation disk or CD-ROM, then complete the wizard to add the program.

f. Remove the installation CD-ROM, then close the Control Panel.

9. Enter DOS commands.

a. Start Command Prompt.

b. Type **cd c:\program files**, then press [Enter]. Type **dir /w**, then press [Enter].

c. Type **exit**, then press [Enter].

► Independent Challenge 1

You own Wilkenson & Associates, an international public relations firm that specializes in overseas travel. You want to protect important company data from software viruses.

a. Format a blank floppy disk using the Full Format type and the label Backup. You can use the copied disk you made in this unit if you want, but not the disk with your Project Files.

b. Copy the files **2003 Income Projections** and **2003 Expense Budget** from the disk with your Project Files to a blank formatted disk.

c. Scan the floppy disk for errors. Label the disk for easy identification.

▶ Independent Challenge 2

You are the network administrator at Robotz, Inc., a toy company that specializes in the production and distribution of robots. You want employees to update their computer systems with the latest Windows XP components. You check out the Windows Update Web site and determine which components you want the employees to install.

a. Start the Add/Remove Programs utility in the Control Panel. Connect to the Internet as necessary.

b. Click Add New Programs, then click Windows Update to access the Windows Update Web site in your browser.

c. Click the About Windows Update link. If you are starting Windows Update for the first time, you might be prompted to install additional software.

d. Click the Support Information link. Click the Pick updates to install link.

e. Display and print the Critical Updates page and the Windows XP page with the software updates for your Windows system.

f. Close the Add/Remove Programs window and the Control Panel.

g. Close your Web browser and disconnect from the Internet.

▶ Independent Challenge 3

You are a course developer at EZSoft Inc., a computer training company that specializes in training beginner- to expert-level software users. You are developing a new course on maintaining a computer. You are currently working on a lesson to teach students how to speed up disks by using the Windows system tools Check Disk and Disk Defragmenter.

a. Open WordPad, then create a document called **Win Tools Training** on the drive and folder where your Project Files are located that instructs students on how to use the Check Disk and Disk Defragmenter system tools.

b. Follow the steps in the WordPad document to check and defragment the hard disk drive (see your instructor or technical support person for authorization to defragment your hard disk), and take at least one print screen of the Check Disk and Disk Defragmenter window as you go through the material, and insert the picture in the WordPad document. To take a print screen of the current window and then insert it into the WordPad document, press [Alt][Print Screen] to copy the picture to the Clipboard, switch to the WordPad document, place the insertion point where you want the picture, then click the Paste button on the WordPad toolbar.

c. Save the document, print it, then close WordPad.

▶ Independent Challenge 4

You are an employee at an insurance firm. Since installing Windows XP, one of your DOS programs has been behaving erratically. To help figure out the problem, you need to display the autoexec.bat or config.sys file in DOS.

a. Click the Start button on the taskbar, point to All Programs, point to Accessories, then click Command Prompt.

b. Type **cd c:\Windows** at the DOS prompt, then press [Enter].

c. Type **More win.ini** at the DOS prompt, then press [Enter].

d. Press [Enter] to step through the file. (*Hint:* press [Ctrl] [C] to cancel at any time.)

e. Print the screen. (Press [Alt][Print Scrn] to make a copy of the window, open Paint, click Edit on the menu bar, click Paste to paste the screen into Paint, then click Yes to paste the large image, if necessary. Click the Text button on the Toolbox, click a blank area in the Paint work area, then type your name. Click File on the menu bar, click Page Setup, change 100 % normal size to 50% in the Scaling area, then click OK. Click File on the menu bar, click Print, then click Print.)

f. Press [Spacebar] to advance to the next screen if necessary, then type **exit** to return to Windows.

► Visual Workshop

Re-create the screen shown in Figure F-20, which shows the results of using the Disk Cleanup for (C:) dialog box. Print the screen. (See Independent Challenge 4, Step e for screen printing instructions.) If you are working in a lab, check with your instructor or technical support person for authorization to delete all the files in the Disk Cleanup for (C:) dialog box.

FIGURE F-20

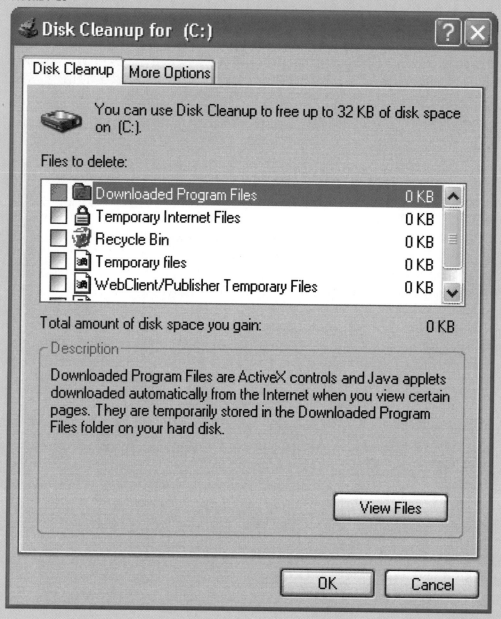

Exploring

the Internet with Microsoft Internet Explorer

Objectives

► **Understand the Internet and Web browsers**
► **Connect to the Internet**
► **Start Internet Explorer**
► **Open a Web page and follow links**
► **Add a Web page to the Favorites list**
► **Make a Web page available offline**
► **Change your home page and add a link button**
► **Search the Web**
► **Preview and Print a Web page**

Microsoft Internet Explorer 6, a component included with Windows XP, is a software program that helps you access the World Wide Web. In this unit, you learn about the benefits of the World Wide Web, examine the basic features of Internet Explorer 6, connect to the Internet, and access Web pages. Before you begin the lesson, check with your instructor or technical support person to see if it's possible for you to connect to the Internet. If not, simply read the lessons to learn about using Internet Explorer. ✏ Wired Coffee Company is a growing business that wants to take advantage of Internet technology. John uses Internet Explorer to open the company Web page and find information related to the coffee business.

Understanding the Internet and Web Browsers

The **Internet** is a global collection of more than 75 million computers (and growing) linked together to share information. The Internet's physical structure includes telephone lines, cables, satellites, and other telecommunications media, as depicted in Figure G-1. Using the Internet, computer users can share many types of information, including text, graphics, sounds, videos, and computer programs. The **World Wide Web** (also known as the Web or WWW) is a part of the Internet that consists of Web sites located on different computers around the world. A **Web site** contains Web pages linked together to make searching for information on the Internet easier. **Web pages** are documents that contain highlighted words, phrases, and graphics, called **hyperlinks** (or simply **links**) that open other Web pages when you click them. Some Web pages contain frames. A frame is a separate window within a Web page. Frames let you see more than one Web page at a time. Figure G-2 shows a sample Web page. **Web browsers** are software programs that you use to "browse the Web," or access and display Web pages. Browsers make the Web easy to navigate by providing a graphical, point-and-click environment. This unit features Internet Explorer 6, a popular browser from Microsoft that comes with Windows XP. Netscape (formally Netscape Navigator and Netscape Communicator) is another popular browser. John realizes that there are many uses for Internet Explorer in his company.

Internet Explorer will allow John to do the following:

► **Display Web pages from all over the world**
John can look at Web pages for business purposes, such as checking the pages of other coffee companies to see how they market their products.

► **Display Web content on his desktop**
John can make his desktop look and work like a Web page. John can display Web content, such as the Microsoft Investor Ticker, ESPN SportsZone, Expedia Maps Address Finder, or MSNBC Weather Map, directly on his desktop and have the content updated automatically.

► **Use links to move from one Web page to another**
John can click text or graphical links (which appear either as underlined text or as graphics) to move from one Web page to another, investigating different sources for information. Because a Web page can contain links to any location on the Internet, he can jump to Web pages all over the world.

► **Play audio and video clips**
John can click links that play audio and video clips, such as the sound of coffee grinding or a video of workers picking coffee beans. He can also play continuous audio and video broadcasts through radio and television stations over the Internet.

► **Search the Web for information**
John can use search programs that allow him to look for information about any topic throughout the world.

► **Make favorite Web pages available offline**
John can create a list of his favorite Web pages to make it easy for him to return to them at a later time. He can also make a Web page available offline. When he makes a Web page available offline, he can read its content when his computer is not connected to the Internet.

► **Print the text and graphics on Web pages**
If John finds some information or images that he wants to print, he can easily print all or part of the Web page, including the graphics.

FIGURE G-1: **Structure of the Internet**

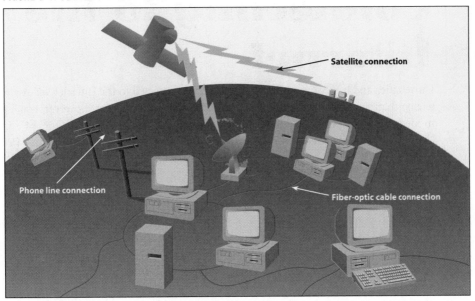

FIGURE G-2: **Sample World Wide Web page**

Web page title
and browser
name

Graphic hyperlink   Text hyperlink

The history of the Internet and World Wide Web

The Internet has its roots in the Advanced Research Projects Agency Network (ARPANET), which the United States Department of Defense started in 1969. In 1986, the National Science Foundation formed NSFNET, which replaced ARPANET. NSFNET expanded the foundation of the U.S. portion of the Internet with high-speed, long-distance data lines. In 1991, the U.S. Congress expanded the capacity and speed of the Internet further and opened it to commercial use.

The Internet is now accessible in over 300 countries. The World Wide Web was developed in Switzerland in 1991 to make finding documents on the Internet easier. Software programs designed to access the Web, known as Web browsers, use point-and-click interfaces. The first such Web browser, Mosaic, was introduced at the University of Illinois in 1993. Since the release of Mosaic, Microsoft Internet Explorer and Netscape have become the two most popular Web browsers.

Connecting to the Internet

Universities and large companies are most likely connected to the Internet via expensive, high-speed wiring that transmits data very quickly. Home computer owners, however, usually must rely on a modem and the phone lines already in place, as shown in Figure G-3. In some areas, **ISDN** (Integrated Services Digital Network) or **DSL** (Digital Subscriber Lines) **lines**, wires that provide a completely digital connection, or **cable modems**, which use cable television lines, are becoming available and affordable. DSL and cable modems, also known as **broadband** connections, are continually turned on and connected and use a network setup, so you don't need to establish a connection using a dial-up modem. Data travels slower over phone wires than over digital lines and cable modems. Whether you use a phone line or an ISDN or DSL line or cable modem, Windows can help you establish a connection between your computer and the Internet using the New Connection Wizard. First, you need to select an **ISP** (Internet Service Provider), which is a company that sets up an **Internet account** for you and provides Internet access. ISPs maintain servers connected directly to the Internet 24 hours a day. You pay a fee, sometimes by the hour, but more often a flat monthly rate. To connect to the Internet, you need to obtain an Internet account and connection information from your ISP or your system administrator. John has signed up with an ISP. He uses the New Connection Wizard to set up the service.

Trouble?

If the vocation information dislog box opens, enter the necessary user information, then click OK.

1. Click the **Start button**, point to **All Programs**, point to **Accessories**, point to **Communications**, then click **New Connection Wizard**
   The New Connection Wizard dialog box opens, displaying a welcome message. If your ISP provides you with an installation program that sets up the connection for you, install and run that program and skip this lesson.

2. Read the introduction, then click **Next**
   The next wizard dialog box asks you to choose a network connection type. You can choose to connect to the Internet (which is the default), the network at my workplace, an existing home or small office network, or another computer directly.

3. Click the **Connect to the Internet Option button** if necessary, then click **Next**
   The next wizard dialog box asks you to choose how you want to connect to the Internet. You can select from a list of ISPs, set up the connection manually, or use the CD from your ISP.

Trouble?

If you connect to the Internet through a network, follow your instructor's or technical support person's directions to establish your connection.

4. Click the **Set up my connection manually option button**, then click **Next**
   The next wizard dialog box asks you to choose how to connect to the Internet, as shown in Figure G-4. The first option helps you connect to the Internet using a dial-up modem, while the next two options help you connect using a broadband connection.

5. Click the **Connect using a dial-up modem option button**, then click **Next**

6. In the next wizard dialog box, type the name of your ISP in the text box, click **Next**, type the area code and telephone number of your ISP in the text box, then click **Next**
   Your ISP documentation provides the numbers you should use.

7. Type your **user name** in the User name text box, press **[Tab]**, type your **password**, press **[Tab]**, then type your **password** again
   Your ISP documentation provides you with the user name and password you should use. As you type the password, bullets appear instead of characters.

8. Click **Next**, then click **Finish** to complete the Internet connection

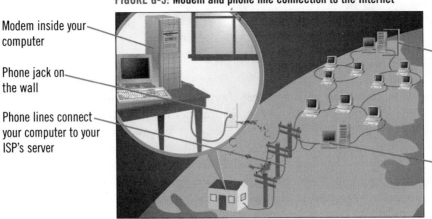

FIGURE G-3: Modem and phone line connection to the Internet

Modem inside your computer

Phone jack on the wall

Phone lines connect your computer to your ISP's server

Computers and networks on the Internet

Your ISP maintains a server directly connected to the Internet

FIGURE G-4: Selecting an Internet connection option

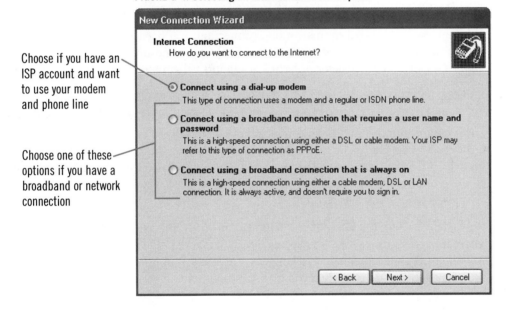

Choose if you have an ISP account and want to use your modem and phone line

Choose one of these options if you have a broadband or network connection

Sharing an Internet connection

If you have a home or small office network using Windows XP Professional, you can use Internet Connection Sharing (ICS) to connect all the computers on the network to the Internet using one connection, which saves you money on multiple connections. To enable ICS, click the Start button on the taskbar, point to All Programs, point to Accessories, point to Communications, click Network Setup Wizard to start the Network Setup Wizard, then follow the step-by-step wizard instructions.

Starting Internet Explorer

Internet Explorer is a Web browser that you use to search the World Wide Web. You can start Internet Explorer using the Start menu, the Internet Explorer icon on the desktop, or the button on the Quick Launch toolbar on the taskbar. After you start Internet Explorer, you might need to connect to the Internet by selecting a dial-up or broadband service and entering a user name and password. The elements of the Internet Explorer window allow you to view, print, and search for information on the Internet. Table G-1 describes the various elements of the Internet Explorer window. You can have more than one Internet service connection. One connection might provide your business Internet service, another might be for home or family use, and another might access a university or institutional account. Once you establish a connection to the Internet, you are ready to explorer Web pages on the Internet. ⬧⬧⬧ Before John can take advantage of the many features of the World Wide Web, he must start Internet Explorer.

Steps

Trouble?

If Internet Explorer doesn't appear on the left column of the Start menu, it's available on the All Programs submenu.

1. Click the **Start button** on the taskbar, then click **Internet** (with Internet Explorer in gray below it) in the left column of the Start menu
Internet Explorer opens. If you connect to the Internet through a network, follow your instructor's or technical support person's directions to log on. If you connect to the Internet by telephone using a dial-up networking connection, you need to select a connection and enter your user name and password in the Dial-up Connection dialog box, as shown in Figure G-5. See your instructor or technical support person for this information.

Trouble?

If your computer is not connected to the Internet, check with your instructor or technical person to see if it's possible for you to connect.

2. If necessary, click the **Connect to list arrow**, select the name of your ISP from the previous lesson, type your **user name**, press **[Tab]**, type your **password**, then click **Connect**
Upon completion of the dial-up connection, you are connected to the Internet (unless an error message appears; if so, search for the Modem Troubleshooter in the Help and Support Center). A Connection icon 🖳 appears in the notification area on the taskbar to indicate you are connected. You can now view Web pages, check your e-mail, or use any other Windows communications features.

3. If necessary, click the **Maximize button** to maximize the Internet Explorer window
Internet Explorer displays a Web page, as shown in Figure G-6. The Web page on your screen will differ from the one shown in Figure G-6. Later in this unit, you will learn how to change the Web page that appears when you first start Internet Explorer.

CLUES TO USE

Getting help with Internet Explorer

If you want information on a general topic or a specific task, you can find the information you are looking for in Microsoft Internet Explorer Help. To access Help, click Help on the menu bar, then click Contents and Index. The Microsoft Internet Explorer Help window appears and works in the same way Windows Help does. You can find help information you need by using a table of contents, index, or keyword search. If you need more help with Internet Explorer on the Web, you can click Help on the menu bar, then click Online Support. You can also get tips on how to use Internet Explorer more effectively. To display a tip, click Help on the menu bar, then click Tip of the Day. A Tip pane appears at the bottom of the Internet Explorer window. Read the tip, then click the Next tip link to display another tip. Click the Close button in the Tip pane to close the pane.

FIGURE G-5: Dial-up Connection dialog box

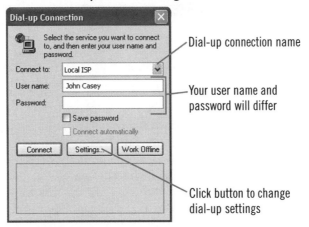

Dial-up connection name

Your user name and password will differ

Click button to change dial-up settings

FIGURE G-6: Elements of Internet Explorer window

Title bar

Menu bar

Address bar

Web page window; yours will differ

Status bar

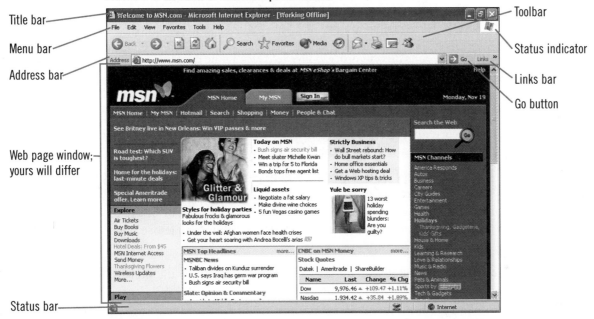

Toolbar

Status indicator

Links bar

Go button

TABLE G-1: Elements of the Internet Explorer window

option	description
Title bar	Displays the name of the Web page and the name of the browser you are using at the top of the window
Menu bar	Provides access to a variety of commands, much like other Windows programs
Toolbar	Provides buttons for easy access to the most commonly used commands in Internet Explorer
Address bar	Displays the address of the current Web page or the contents of a local or network computer drive; you can also type the address of a site you want to visit in the Address bar, then press [Enter]
Go button	Displays the current Web address or Web search information about a particular topic in the Address bar
Links bar	Displays link buttons to Web pages on the Internet or to documents on a local or network drive
Status indicator	Located below the Close button; waves the Windows logo to indicate a new Web page is loading
Web page window	Displays the current Web page or the contents of a local or network computer drive; you may need to scroll down the page to view its entire contents
Status bar	Displays information about your connection progress with new Web pages that you open, including notification that you have connected to another site, the percentage of information transferred from that site, and locations of the links in the document window as you move your mouse pointer over them

Windows XP

Opening a Web Page and Following Links

You can open a Web page quickly and easily by entering a Web address in the Address bar. A **Web address** is a unique place on the Internet where you can locate a Web page. A Web address is also called a **URL**, which stands for **Uniform Resource Locator**. If you change your mind, or the Web page takes too long to **download**, or open on the screen, you can click the Stop button on the toolbar. If you stop a Web page while it is downloading, and the page doesn't completely open, you can click the Refresh button on the toolbar to update the screen. Often, Web pages connect to each other through links that you can follow to obtain more information about a topic, as shown in Figure G-7. A link can move you to another location on the same Web page, or it can open a different Web page altogether. To follow a link, simply click the highlighted word, phrase, or graphic. The mouse pointer changes to ⬆ when it is over a link. If you open a Web page written in different languages, Internet Explorer asks you to update your computer with character sets you need to view the page correctly. ✎ John contracts with a Web development company to create a Web site for Wired Coffee. He wants to access the Web site and follow some of its links in order to give feedback to the developer. John knows that the URL for the Web page is www.course.com/illustrated/wired/.

Steps 1 2 3 4

1. Click anywhere in the Address bar

The current address is highlighted, and any text you type replaces the current address. If the current address isn't highlighted, select the entire address.

Trouble?

If you receive an error message, type one of the URLs listed in Table G-2 instead to open a Web page, then follow a link found on the Web page.

2. Type www.course.com/downloads/illustrated/wired/, then press [Enter]

Be sure to type the address exactly as it appears. When you enter a Web address, Internet Explorer automatically inserts "http://" in the Address bar before the URL. The status bar displays the connection process. After downloading for a few seconds, the Web page appears in the document window.

3. Locate the menu link on the main page, then move the mouse pointer over the link, as shown in Figure G-8

When you move the mouse pointer over a link, the mouse pointer changes to ⬆. This indicates that the text or graphic is a link. The address of the link appears in the Status bar.

QuickTip

To listen to media files and Internet radio stations using the Media bar while you browse the Web, click the Media button 🔘 Media on the toolbar.

4. Click the menu link

The status indicator waves as you access and open the new Web page. The menu Web page appears in the document window.

5. Move the mouse pointer over the Wired Coffee logo in the upper-left corner, then click the logo

The Wired Coffee Company page appears in the document window.

6. Click the Back button ⬅ Back on the toolbar

The previous Web page, menu, appears in the document window.

QuickTip

To expand the document window to fill the screen, click View on the menu bar, then click Full Screen. Press [F11] to return to the normal view.

7. Click the Forward button ➡ on the toolbar

The Wired Coffee Company page appears in the document window again. You also could have clicked the Wired Coffee logo link to return to the Wired Coffee Company page.

8. Click the Back button list arrow ⬅ Back ▾ on the toolbar, then click Home Page

The Wired Coffee Home Page appears in the document window. Notice that when you have already visited a link, the color of the link changes.

FIGURE G-7: **Web pages connected through links**

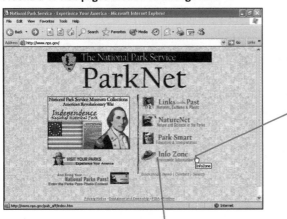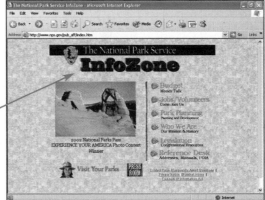

Graphic link; click to jump
to InfoZone Web page

FIGURE G-8: **Wired Coffee Company Web page**

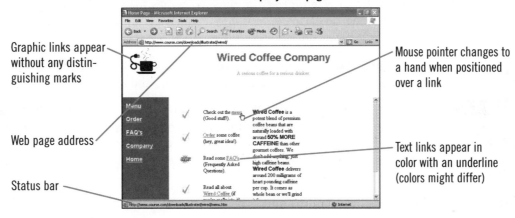

Graphic links appear
without any distin-
guishing marks

Web page address

Status bar

Mouse pointer changes to
a hand when positioned
over a link

Text links appear in
color with an underline
(colors might differ)

TABLE G-2: **URLs of coffee companies' Web sites**

company name	URL
Peet's Coffee & Tea	www.peets.com
Seattle's Best Coffee	www.seabest.com
Starbucks Coffee	www.starbucks.com

CLUES TO USE

Understanding a Web address

The address for a Web page is called a URL. Each Web page has a unique URL that is typically composed of four parts: the protocol (a set of rules that allows computers to exchange information), the location of the Web site, the name that maintains the Web site, and a suffix that identifies the type of site. A URL begins with a protocol, followed by a colon, two slashes, location of the Web site, a dot, name of the Web site, a dot, and a suffix. The Web site is the computer where the Web pages are located. At the end of the Web site name, another slash may appear, followed by one or more folder names and a filename. For example, in the address, http://www.course.com/ downloads/illustrated/wired/main.htm, the protocol is *http* (HyperText Transfer Protocol), the location of the Web site is *www* (World Wide Web), the name of the Web site is *course*, and the suffix is *com* (a commercial organization); folders at that site are called */downloads/illustrated/wired*; and within the wired folder is a file called *main.htm*.

Windows XP

Adding a Web Page to the Favorites List

Rather than memorizing URLs or keeping a handwritten list of Web pages you want to visit, you can use a Favorites list to store and organize the addresses. When you display a Web page in your document window that you want to display again at a later time, you can add the Web page to your Favorites list. You add Web pages in the Internet Explorer window to your Favorites list in the same way you add folders in the My Computer or Windows Explorer window to the list. Once you add the Web page to the Favorites list, you can return to the page by opening your Favorites list and selecting the link to the page you want. John wants to add the Wired Coffee Web page to his Favorites list.

Steps

1. Click Favorites on the menu bar, then click Add to Favorites

The Add Favorite dialog box opens, as shown in Figure G-9. You have the option to make the Web page available for offline viewing. When you make a Web page available for **offline viewing**, the pages are copied to your computer for viewing after you disconnect your Internet connection. This is helpful when you want to read a Web page without worrying about how long you are connected to the Internet.

2. In the Name text box, select the current text, type Wired Coffee Company, then click OK

You name the Web page "Wired Coffee Company" and add it to your Favorites list.

QuickTip

You can browse folders on your hard disk drive and run programs from the Address bar. Click anywhere in the Address bar, then type the location of the folder or program. For example, typing "C:\Windows\" opens the Windows folder.

3. Click anywhere in the Address bar, type www.course.com, then press [Enter]

When you type a Web address in the Address bar, a feature called **AutoComplete** suggests possible matches from previous entries you made for Web addresses. If a suggestion in the list matches the Web address you want to enter, click the suggestion from the Address bar list, then press [Enter].

4. Click the Favorites button ☆ on the toolbar

The Explorer bar opens on the left side of the document window and displays the Favorites list. The Favorites list contains several folders, including a Links folder and individual favorite Web pages that come with Internet Explorer.

QuickTip

You can import favorites, known as bookmarks, from Netscape or another browser by clicking File on the menu bar, clicking Import and Export, then following the steps in the Import/Export wizard.

5. Click Wired Coffee Company in the Favorites list

The Wired Coffee Company Web page appears in the document window, as shown in Figure G-10. The Favorites list also includes folders to help you organize your Favorites list. You can click a folder icon in the Favorites list to display its contents.

6. Click the Links folder in the Favorites list

The Favorites list in the Links folder expands and appears in the Explorer bar, as shown in Figure G-11. To open a favorite in the Links folder, position the 🖑 pointer over the favorite you want to open, then click the mouse button.

7. Click the Links folder in the Favorites list again

The Favorites list in the Links folder collapses to display the Links folder icon only. If you no longer use a favorite, you can delete it from the Favorites list, as described in the Clues to Use "Organizing favorites."

FIGURE G-9: Add Favorite dialog box

Click check box to make Web page available offline

Displays the name of the Web page as it will appear in your Favorites list

Click button to save the current page in another folder

FIGURE G-10: Internet Explorer window with Favorites list

Explorer bar displays Favorites list

Folder to help organize your favorites

Individual favorites; your list might differ

Click button to close Explorer bar

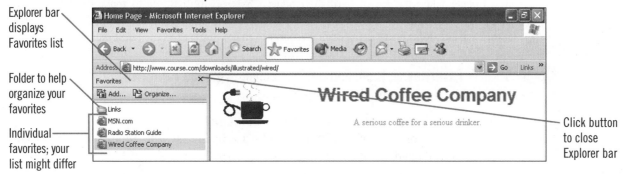

FIGURE G-11: Links folder in Favorites list

Click folder to display or hide the Favorites list in the Links folder

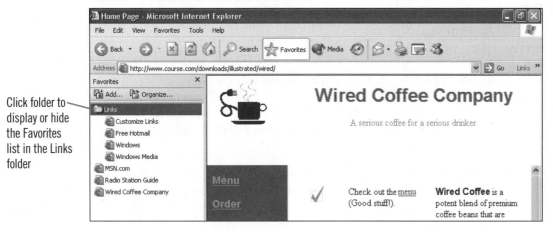

CLUES TO USE

Organizing favorites

If your list of favorites grows long, you can delete favorites you don't visit anymore or move favorites into folders. To delete and move your favorites, click Favorites on the menu bar, then click Organize Favorites. In the Organize Favorites dialog box, select one or more files from the Favorites list, then click the Delete button or the Move to Folder button. If you want to add a new folder to your Favorites list, click the Create Folder button, type the new folder name, then press [Enter]. If you prefer to use another name for a favorite, you can select the favorite you want to rename, click the Rename button, type the new name, then press [Enter]. When you finish making changes, click Close to exit.

Making a Web Page Available Offline

When you make a Web page available offline, you can read its content when your computer is not connected to the Internet or network. For example, you can view Web pages on your laptop computer when you have no Internet or network connection. Or, you might want to read Web pages at home but not want to tie up a phone line. When you make a Web page available offline, you save, or **synchronize**, the latest online version of your Web page on your hard disk drive for offline viewing. You can specify how much content you want available, such as an individual Web page or a Web page and all of its linked Web pages, and choose how you want to update that content on your computer. When you choose to view a Web page and all its linked pages offline, be aware that the additional linked pages take up a lot of hard drive space. John wants to make the Wired Coffee Company Web site on the Favorites list available for offline viewing. After viewing the offline version of the Web site, John updates the offline version to make sure he has the latest data.

Steps

QuickTip

To make the current Web page available offline, click Favorites on the menu bar, click Add to Favorites, click the Make available offline check box to select it, click Customize, follow the Offline Favorite Wizard instructions, click Finish, then click OK.

1. Click **Favorites** on the menu bar, then click **Organize Favorites**
   The Organize Favorites dialog box opens.

2. In the Favorites list, click **Wired Coffee Company**
   Status information about the Wired Coffee Company favorite appears in the Organize Favorites dialog box, as shown in Figure G-12.

3. Click the **Make available offline check box** to select it, then click **Close**
   The Synchronizing dialog box opens and synchronizes the Wired Coffee Company Web page, then the dialog box closes. The latest version of your Web page is now saved on your hard disk drive for offline viewing.

QuickTip

When you choose to work offline, Internet Explorer starts in offline mode until you click File on the menu bar, then click Work Offline again to clear the check mark.

4. Click the **Home button** on the toolbar, click **File** on the menu bar, then click **Work Offline**
   You disconnect Internet Explorer from the Internet or network.

5. In the Favorites list, click **Wired Coffee Company**
   When you access the Wired Coffee Company Web site in offline mode, Internet Explorer displays the offline version of the Web page that is on your hard disk drive. You can view any offline Web page, but if you click a link to a Web page not available offline, Internet Explorer asks you to reconnect to the Internet or network.

6. Click **File** on the menu bar, then click **Work Offline** to deselect it
   When you re-establish the connection to the Internet or network, you can synchronize with the latest online version of the Wired Coffee Web page to update the offline version on your hard disk drive.

QuickTip

To specify a schedule for updating that page and how much content to download, select the link, then click Properties, then click the Schedule tab. You can also click Setup to schedule updating when you log on or log off your computer and when your computer becomes idle.

7. Click **Tools** on the menu bar, then click **Synchronize**
   The Items to Synchronize dialog box opens, as shown in Figure G-13. You can select which Web pages or files you want to synchronize and specify when and how you want them updated.

8. Click the **Wired Coffee Company check box** to select it if necessary, deselect all other check boxes if necessary, then click **Synchronize**
   The Synchronizing dialog box opens, then closes when the download is complete. The Wired Coffee Company Web page is resynchronized, with the latest online version of the Web page on your hard disk drive and ready for offline viewing.

9. Right-click **Wired Coffee Company** in the Favorites list, click **Delete**, click **Yes** to confirm the deletion to the recycle bin, then click the **Close button** in the Explorer bar

FIGURE G-12: **Organize Favorites dialog box**

Selected favorite

Status information about the selected favorite

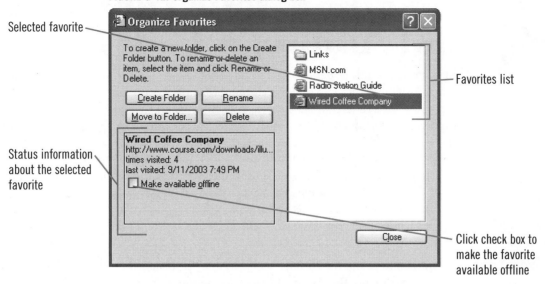

Favorites list

Click check box to make the favorite available offline

FIGURE G-13: **Items to Synchronize dialog box**

Select the items you want to synchronize

Click button to synchronize selected Web pages

Click button to change offline synchronize settings

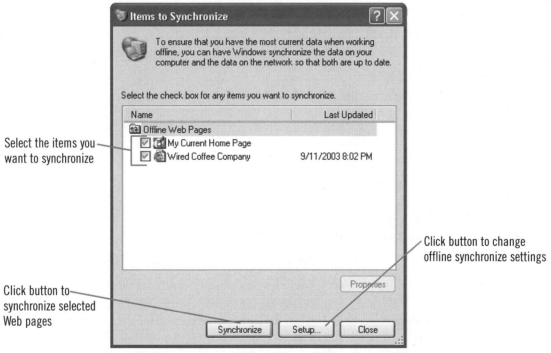

Saving a Web page and a Web graphic

If you want to view a Web page offline, but you don't ever need to update its content, such as a published article whose content will not change, you can save the page on your computer. There are several ways you can save the Web page, from just saving the text to saving all of the graphics and text needed to display that page as it appears on the Web. To save a Web page, click File on the menu bar, then click Save As. In the Save Web Page dialog box, specify the drive and folder in which you want to save the file, type the name you want for the file, click the Save as type list

arrow, select the file format type you want, then click Save. When you save a complete Web page, Internet Explorer saves all the graphic and text elements in a folder. If you want to save an individual graphic on a Web page, point to the graphic you want to save to display a toolbar on the graphic, then click the Save this image button. If the toolbar doesn't appear, right-click the graphic, then click Save Picture As. You can also use the toolbar on a graphic to print or e-mail the graphic and open the My Pictures folder.

Windows XP

Changing Your Home Page and Adding a Link Button

Your **home page** in Internet Explorer is the page that opens when you start the program. When you first install Internet Explorer, the default home page is the Microsoft Network (MSN) Web site. If you want a different page to appear when you start Internet Explorer and whenever you click the Home button, you can change your home page. You can choose one of the millions of Web pages available through the Internet, or you can select a particular file on your hard drive. The Links bar, located to the right of the Address bar, provides easy access buttons to display Web pages. The Links bar comes with predefined buttons to Microsoft-related Web pages, but you can add or remove buttons, or change the Web pages associated with the buttons on the Links bar to customize it to meet your needs. *John* decides to change his home page to the Wired Coffee Company Web page and add a link button to the Links bar.

Steps

QuickTip

You change your home page back to www.msn.com in the Skills Review exercise at the end of this unit. If you want to change it back at any other time, type "www.msn.com" in the Address bar, press [Enter], then complete Steps 1 through 3 of this lesson.

1. Click **Tools** on the menu bar, click **Internet Options**, the Internet Options dialog box opens, then click the **General tab** if necessary
   The Internet Options dialog box, as shown in Figure G-14, allows you to change a variety of Internet Explorer settings and preferences. See Table G-3 for a description of each tab.

2. In the Home page section, click **Use Current**
   The address of the Wired Coffee Company Web page appears in the Address text box.

3. Click **OK**
   You associate the Home button on the toolbar with the current Web page, Wired Coffee Company.

4. Click the **FAQ's link**, then click the **Home button** 🏠 on the toolbar
   The home page appears in the document window.

Trouble?

If the Links bar doesn't move, you need to unlock it. Click View on the menu bar, point to Toolbars, then click Lock the Toolbars to deselect it.

5. Double-click the word **Links** on the Links bar
   The Links bar opens and may hide the Address bar. The Links bar contains buttons with links to Web pages. You can drag a link on a page or a Web site address in the Address bar to a blank area on the Links bar to create a new Links button.

6. Place 👆 over the **Order link**, click the **left mouse button**, then drag the **Order link** on the main page to the left of the first button on the Links bar, the mouse pointer changes to a black bar ⌐ to indicate the placement of the button, then release the mouse button
   A new link button appears on the Links bar with the name associated with the Web site, as shown in Figure G-15. You can delete or change the properties of a links button. Simply right-click the link button you want to change, then click the Delete or Properties command on the shortcut menu.

7. Click the **Order button** on the Links bar, then click the **Back button** ⬅ Back on the toolbar

8. Right-click the **Order button** on the Links bar, click **Delete**, then click **Yes** to confirm the deletion to the Recycle Bin
   The home page appears in the document window.

QuickTip

To display buttons on a hidden toolbar, click ⊗ on the right side of the toolbar.

9. Position the ⇖ pointer over the word **Links**, click the **Links bar**, the mouse pointer changes to ✛, drag the **Links bar** to the right to hide it, then relock the toolbars if previously locked

FIGURE G-14: **Internet Options dialog box**

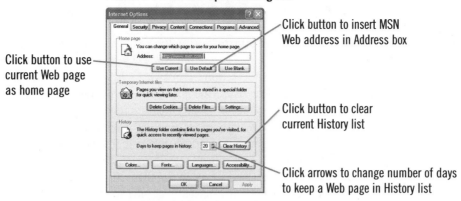

Click button to use current Web page as home page

Click button to insert MSN Web address in Address box

Click button to clear current History list

Click arrows to change number of days to keep a Web page in History list

FIGURE G-15: **New button on Links bar**

Drag link to Links bar

New link button

TABLE G-3: **Internet Options dialog box tabs**

tab	allows you to
General	Change your home page, temporary file settings, and history settings
Security	Select security levels for different parts of the Internet
Privacy	Select privacy levels for cookie usage on your computer; a **cookie** is a file created by a Web site that stores information on your computer, such as your preferences, when visiting that site
Content	Set up a rating system for Internet content and personal information for typing Web addresses and buying items over the Internet
Connections	Change connection settings (phone and network)
Programs	Choose which programs (Mail, News, and Internet call) you want to use with Internet Explorer
Advanced	Change individual settings for browsing, multimedia, security, printing, and searching

CLUES TO USE

Viewing and maintaining a History list

Sometimes you run across a great Web site and simply forget to add it to your Favorites list. With Internet Explorer there's no need to try to remember all the sites you visit. The History feature keeps track of where you've been by date, site, most visited, or order visited today. To view the History list, click the History button ⌚ on the toolbar, then click a day or week in the Explorer Bar to expand the list of Web sites visited. Because the History list can grow to occupy a large amount of space on your hard drive, it's important that you control the length of time you retain Web sites in the list. Internet Explorer deletes the History list periodically, based on the settings you specify in the General tab of the Internet Options dialog box, as shown in Figure G-14.

Windows XP

Searching the Web

You can find all kinds of information on the Web. The best way to find information is to use a search engine. A **search engine** is a program you access through a Web site and use to search through a collection of Internet information to find what you want. Many search engines are available on the Web, such as MSN, AltaVista, Google, AOL Search, and Excite. When performing a search, the search engine compares the words or phrases, known as **keywords**, you submit that best describe what you want to retrieve, with words the search engine finds on various Web sites on the Internet. If it finds your keywords in the stored database, it lists the matched sites on a Web page. These matched sites are sometimes called **hits**. The company that manages the search engine determines what information its database stores, so search results of different search engines vary. John wants to search for other coffee-related Web sites to check out the competition.

QuickTip

To customize search options, click Change preferences in the Search Companion, click the options you want, then click OK if necessary.

1. Click the **Search button** 🔍 on the toolbar

The Search Companion appears in the Explorer bar, as shown in Figure G-16. You can select search options to find a personal or business address, display a list of links to previous searches, and find a map for a specific address. Each search option requires different search criteria, which is information related to what you want to find. To search for a Web page containing the information you want, you need to enter a keyword or words in the search text box. The more specific your search criteria, the better list of matches you receive from the search engine. You can also search directly from the Address bar. Type keywords in the Address bar, press [Enter], and Internet Explorer displays a list of sites that match what you are searching for.

QuickTip

To search for other items using a search engine, such as a file, computer, or person, click Search this computer for files in the Search Companion, then click the type of items in which you want to search.

2. In the text box, type **find coffee imports**

Now you're ready to start the search.

3. Click **Search** in the Search Companion

The search engine, in this case MSN, retrieves and displays a list of Web sites that match your criteria, as shown in Figure G-17. The total number of Web sites found is listed at the top. The search results appear in order of decreasing relevance. If the search results return too many hits, you should narrow the search by adding more keywords. As you add more keywords, the search engine finds fewer Web pages that contain all of those words. See Table G-4 for other techniques to narrow a search.

QuickTip

To perform a new search, click Start a new search at the bottom of the Search Companion.

4. Click any **link** to a Web site in the list of matches

The Web site that you open appears in the right pane of the document window. You can follow links to other pages on this Web site or jump to other Web sites. When you finish, close the Search Companion.

5. Click **Close button** in the Search Companion

The Search Companion closes.

6. Click the **Home button** 🏠 on the toolbar

You return to the Wired Coffee Company home page.

Searching for people on the Web

Internet Explorer includes several directory services to help you find people you know who may have access to the Internet. To find a person on the Internet, click the Start button, click Search, click Computers or people, then click People in your address book to open the Find People dialog box, which shows a directory service, WhoWhere? in the Find People dialog box. Select the directory service you want to use, type the person's name, then click Find Now. Each directory service accesses different databases on the Internet, so if you don't find the person using the first service, try a different directory service.

FIGURE G-16: Explorer Bar with Search Companion

Type search criteria here

Click to search for other items

Click to change search options

Search animation character

Click button to retrieve Web site matches

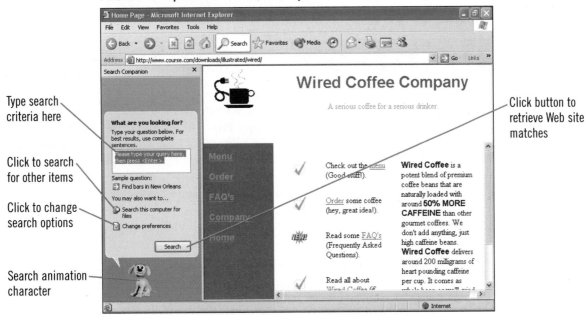

FIGURE G-17: Search results

Additional search options; yours might differ

Search results; your list might differ (scroll down to see entire list)

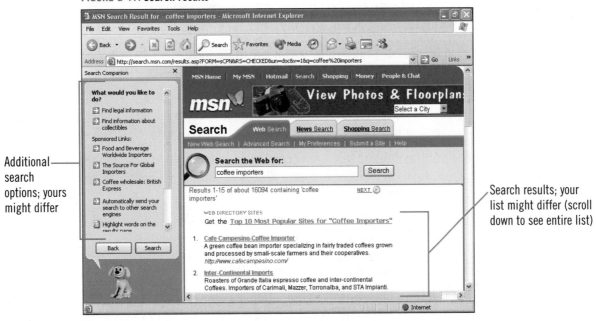

TABLE G-4: Techniques to narrow a search

technique	example
Use descriptive, specific words	Beaches surfing Pacific
Use plain English phrases	Surfing beaches on the Pacific Ocean
Place exact phrases and proper names in quotes	"Sunset Beach"
Use a + sign between words your results must contain	Surf + beach
Use a - sign between words your results should not contain	Surf + beach - Atlantic
Use AND to find results containing all words	Surf AND sea AND sand
Use OR to find results containing at least one word	Surf OR beach

Windows XP

Previewing and Printing a Web Page

Web pages are designed for viewing on a computer screen, but you can also print all or part of one. Before you print, you should verify that the page looks the way you want. You save time, money, and paper by avoiding duplicate or wasteful printing. Print Preview shows you exactly how your Web page will look on the printed page. This is especially helpful when you have multiple pages to print. When you are ready to print, Internet Explorer provides many options for printing Web pages. For Web pages with frames, you can print the page just as you see it, or you can elect to print a particular frame or all frames. You can even use special Page Setup options to include the date, time, or window title on the printed page. You can also choose to print the Web addresses from the links contained on a Web page. John previews and prints a Web page, then exits Internet Explorer.

1. Click **File** on the menu bar, then click **Print Preview**
   The Print Preview window opens, as shown in Figure G-18.

2. Click the **Zoom Out button** on the Print Preview toolbar
   The entire page appears in the Print Preview window.

QuickTip

You can also click the Print button on the Internet Explorer toolbar to print the current page directly or click File on the menu bar, then click Print to open the Print dialog box.

3. Click the **Print button** on the Print Preview toolbar
   The Print dialog box opens, displaying the General tab, as shown in Figure G-19.

4. In the Select Printer box, select the printer you want to use

5. Click the **Pages option button**
   This option prints the pages specified, in this case, pages 1 to 1. The Print dialog box also gives you several options to print the frames. You can print the Web page as laid out on the screen, only the selected frame, or all frames individually.

6. Click the **Options** tab, then click the **As laid out on screen option button** if necessary
   Instead of handwriting links to a Web page, you can automatically print a list of the Web site addresses for each link.

7. Click the **Print table of links check box** to select it, then click **Print**
   The Print Preview window closes, and the Web page prints on the selected printer. You do not need to save the page before you exit because you only view documents with Internet Explorer; you do not create or change documents.

Trouble?

If you connect by telephone, you can right-click the Connect icon in the notification area of the taskbar, then click Disconnect.

8. Click the **Close button** in the Internet Explorer window
   The Internet Explorer window closes. If you connected to the Internet by telephone, a disconnect dialog box opens. If you connected to the Internet through a network, follow your instructor's or technical support person's directions to close your connection.

9. If the disconnect dialog box opens, click **Disconnect**

FIGURE G-18: **Preview a Web page**

Click button to
print Web page

Click buttons to zoom
in or zoom out

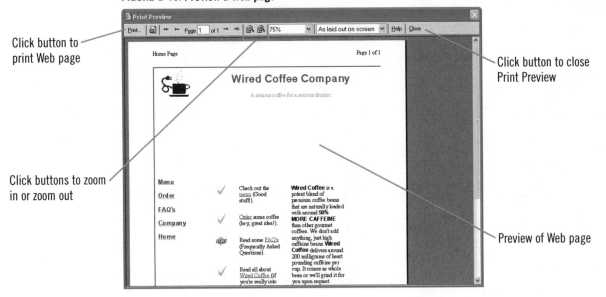

Click button to close
Print Preview

Preview of Web page

FIGURE G-19: **Print dialog box**

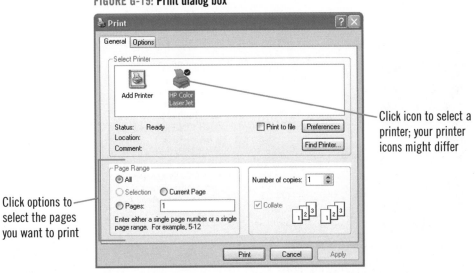

Click icon to select a
printer; your printer
icons might differ

Click options to
select the pages
you want to print

CLUES TO USE

Setting up the page format

When you print a Web page, you can use the Page Setup
dialog box to control the printing of text and graphics on
a page. The Page Setup dialog box, shown in Figure G-20,
specifies the printer properties for page size, orientation,
and paper source; in most cases, you won't want to
change them. From the Page Setup dialog box, you can
also change header and footer information. In the
Headers and Footers text boxes, you can type text to
appear as a header and footer of a Web page you print. In
these text boxes, you can also use variables to substitute
information about the current page, and you can combine text and codes. For example, if you type "Page &p of
&P" in the Header text box, the current page number
and the total number of pages print at the top of each
printed page. Check Internet Explorer Help for a complete list of header and footer codes.

FIGURE G-20: **Page Setup dialog box**

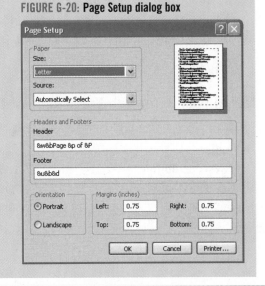

Practice

► Concepts Review

Label each element of the screen shown in Figure G-21.

FIGURE G-21

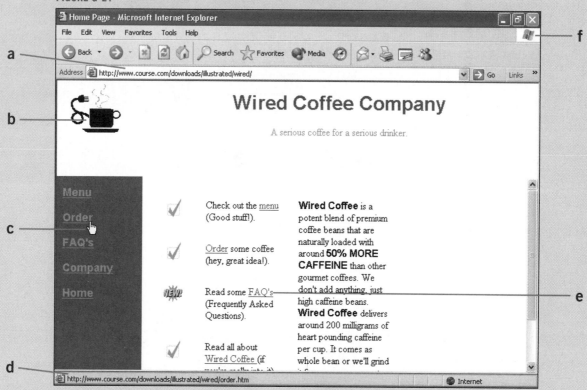

1. Which element displays status information?
2. Which element indicates a Web page is loading?
3. Which element represents a graphic link?
4. Which element represents a text link?
5. Which element displays the address of the current Web page?
6. Which element indicates the position of a link?

Match each term with the statement that describes its function.

7. Address bar
8. Toolbar
9. Favorites button
10. Status indicator
11. Back button

a. Spins as Internet Explorer loads a page
b. Displays the URL for the current page
c. Provides shortcuts for options on the menu bar
d. Displays a list of selected Web pages and folders to organize them
e. Displays the previously viewed page

Select the best answers from the following lists of choices.

12. **Software programs used to access and display Web pages are called:**
    a. Web sites.
    c. Web utilities.
    b. Search engines.
    d. Web browsers.

13. **If you want to save the name and URL of a Web page in Internet Explorer and return to it later, you can add it to a list called:**
    a. Favorites.
    c. Home pages.
    b. Bookmarks.
    d. Preferences.

14. **The international telecommunications network that consists of linked documents is called the:**
    a. NSFNET.
    c. Internet Explorer.
    b. Netscape Communicator.
    d. World Wide Web.

15. **In Internet Explorer, where are the buttons that perform common functions, such as moving to a previous Web page?**
    a. Address bar
    c. Status bar
    b. Toolbar
    d. Menu bar

16. **Which of the following is a valid URL?**
    a. http:/www.usf.edu/
    c. htp:/ww.usf.edu/
    b. htp://www.usf.edu/
    d. http//www.usf.edu/

17. **Underlined words that you click to jump to another Web page are called:**
    a. Explorers.
    c. Web browsers.
    b. Favorites.
    d. Hyperlinks.

18. **The URL of the current Web page appears in the:**
    a. Title bar.
    c. Address bar.
    b. Document window.
    d. Status bar.

▶ Skills Review

1. **Connect to the Internet.**
   a. Create a dial-up Internet connection using the New Connection Wizard.

2. **Start Internet Explorer.**
   a. Start Internet Explorer.
   b. Identify the toolbar, menu bar, Address bar, Links bar, status bar, status indicator, URL, document window, and scroll bars.
   c. In the toolbar, identify icons for searching, viewing favorites, viewing history, and moving to the previous page.

3. **Open a Web page and follow links.**
   a. Click in the Address bar, type **www.cnet.com**, then press [Enter].
   b. Explore the Web site by using the scroll bars, toolbar, and hyperlinks.
   c. Click in the Address bar, type **www.sportsline.com**, then press [Enter].
   d. Follow the links to investigate the content.

4. **Add a Web page to the Favorites list.**
   a. Click in the Address bar, type **www.loc.gov**, then press [Enter].
   b. Click Favorites on the menu bar, then click Add to Favorites.
   c. Click OK.
   d. Click the Favorites button.
   e. Click the Home button.
   f. Click the Library of Congress Home Page link in the Favorites list.

5. **Make a Web page available offline.**
   a. Click Favorites on the menu bar, then click Organize Favorites.
   b. In the Favorites list, click Library of Congress.
   c. Click the Make available offline check box to select it, then click Close.
   d. Click the Home button.
   e. Click File on the menu bar, then click Work Offline to select it. Click Stay Offline in the Message box if necessary.
   f. Click Library of Congress Home Page in the Favorites list.
   g. Click File on the menu bar, then click Work Offline to deselect it.
   h. Click Tools on the menu bar, then click Synchronize.
   i. Click the Library of Congress Home Page check to select it if necessary, then deselect all other check boxes if necessary.
   j. Click Synchronize.
   k. Right-click Library of Congress Home Page in the Favorites list, click Delete, then click Yes.
   l. Click the Close button in the Favorites list.

6. **Change your home page and add a link button.**
   a. Click in the Address bar, type www.msn.com (or your home page), then press [Enter].
   b. Click Tools on the menu bar, then click Internet Options.
   c. Click the General tab if necessary.
   d. Click Use Current.
   e. Click OK.
   f. Click the Back button.
   g. Click the Home button.

7. **Search the Web.**
   a. Click the Search button.
   b. Type job computer training in the text box.
   c. Click the Search button.
   d. Click a link to a Web site from the matches list.
   e. Click the Close button in the Search Companion.
   f. Click the Home button.

8. **Preview and print a Web page.**
   a. Click File on the menu bar, then click Print Preview.
   b. Click the Zoom Out button on the Print Preview toolbar.
   c. Click the Print button on the Print Preview toolbar.
   d. In the Select Printer box, click a printer.
   e. Click the Pages option button. Use the range 1-1.
   f. Click Print.
   g. Click the Close button to exit Internet Explorer.
   h. Click Yes to disconnect if necessary.

▶ Independent Challenge 1

You will soon graduate from college with a degree in business management. Before entering the workforce, you want to make sure that you are up-to-date on all advances in the field. You decide that checking the Web would provide the most current information. In addition, you can look for companies with employment opportunities.

a. Use Internet Explorer to investigate one or two of the business related sites from Table G-5, or search for other business sites if these are not available.

b. Click the necessary links on the page to locate information about employment opportunities that sound interesting to you.

c. When you find a promising page, print the page.

TABLE G-5: Business related sites

Career Builder	www.careerbuilder.com
College Grad	www.collegegrad.com
Small Business Solutions	www.bcentral.com

▶ Independent Challenge 2

You leave tomorrow for a business trip to France. You want to make sure that you take the right clothes for the weather and decide that the best place to check France's weather might be the Web.

a. Use Internet Explorer to access one or two of the weather sites from Table G-6, or search for other weather sites if these are not available.

b. Click the necessary links on the page to locate information about the weather in Paris.

c. Print at least two reports on the Paris weather.

TABLE G-6: Weather sites

The Weather Channel	www.weather.com
National Weather Service	www.nws.noaa.gov
CNN Weather	www.cnn.com/WEATHER

▶ Independent Challenge 3

Your boss wants to buy a new desktop computer (as opposed to a laptop). He assigns you the task of investigating the options. You decide that looking on the Web would be more expedient than visiting computer stores in the area.

a. Use Internet Explorer to visit two of the Web sites from Table G-7, or search for other computer company sites if these are not available.

b. Click the necessary links to find a page from each of the two that you think offer the best deal.

c. Add the pages to your favorites.

d. Make the pages available offline and synchronize them.

e. Print a page from each of the two that you think offer the best deal.

f. Delete the two favorites.

TABLE G-7: Computer companies' Web sites

IBM	www.ibm.com
Apple	www.apple.com
Dell	www.dell.com
Gateway	www.gateway.com

▶ Independent Challenge 4

During the summer, you want to travel to national parks in the United States. Use one of the Search Companions through your Web browser to find Web sites with maps of the national parks. Visit four or five sites from the match list, and print a page from the one that you think offers the best maps and related information for park visitors.

▶ Visual Workshop

Re-create the screen shown in Figure G-24, which displays the Internet Explorer window with the Favorites list and a Web site. Print the Web page, then print the screen. (Press [Print Screen] to make a copy of the screen, open Paint, click Edit on the menu bar, click Paste to paste the screen into Paint, then click Yes to paste the large image, if prompted. Click the Text button on the Toolbox, click a blank area in the Paint work area, then type your name. Click File on the menu bar, click Page Setup, change 100% normal size to 50% in the Scaling area, then click OK. Click File on the menu bar, click Print, then click Print.)

FIGURE G-22

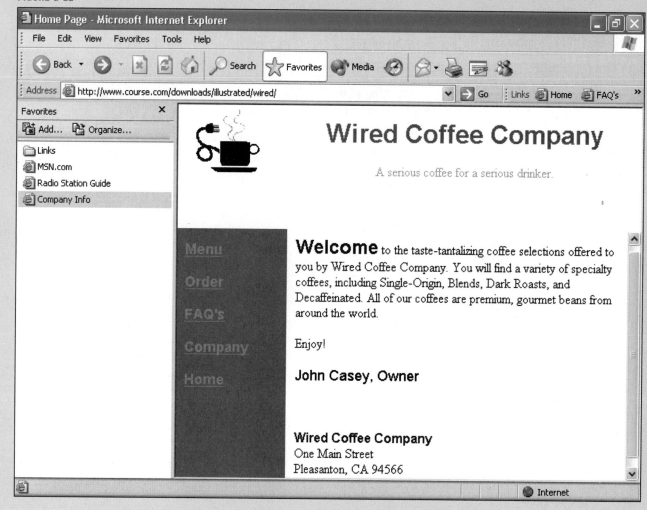

Exchanging
Mail and News

 Objectives

- ► **Start Outlook Express**
- ► **Explore the Outlook Express window**
- ► **Add a contact to the Address Book**
- ► **Compose and send e-mail**
- ► **Retrieve, read, and respond to e-mail**
- ► **Manage e-mail messages**
- ► **Select a news server**
- ► **View and subscribe to a newsgroup**
- ► **Read and post a news message**

STOP *If you are not connected to the Internet and do not have an e-mail account, you cannot work through the steps in this unit; however, you can read the lessons without completing the steps to learn what you can accomplish using Outlook Express.*

Windows XP includes Microsoft Outlook Express 6, a powerful program for managing **electronic mail**, known as e-mail. With an Internet connection and Microsoft Outlook Express, you can exchange e-mail messages with anyone on the Internet and join any number of **newsgroups**, collections of e-mail messages on related topics posted by individuals to specified Internet locations. John Casey, owner of the Wired Coffee Company, uses Outlook Express to send and receive e-mail messages and join a newsgroup about the coffee industry.

Windows XP

Starting Outlook Express

Whether you want to exchange e-mail with colleagues and friends or join newsgroups to trade ideas and information, Outlook Express provides you with the tools you need. When you install Windows XP, a menu item for Outlook Express appears on the left column of the Start menu and the All Programs submenu. If your computer is not connected to the Internet or you do not have an e-mail account, check with your instructor or technical support person to see if it's possible for you to connect or set up an e-mail account. Otherwise, read through the lessons in this unit without completing the steps. ✒ John wants to use Outlook Express to exchange e-mail with his employees.

Steps 1 2 3 4

1. **If necessary, establish a connection to the Internet via the network or telephone**
If you connect to the Internet through a network, follow your instructor's or technical support person's directions to establish your connection. If you connect by telephone, create a new connection using the New Connection Wizard to establish your connection or use an existing dial-up networking connection. To start the New Connection Wizard, click the Start button on the taskbar, point to All Programs, point to Accessories, point to Communications, then click New Connection Wizard.

Trouble?

If Outlook Express doesn't appear on the left column of the Start menu, it's available on the All Programs submenu.

2. **Click the Start button on the taskbar, then click E-mail (with Outlook Express in gray below it) in the left column of the Start menu**
The Outlook Express window opens and displays the Outlook Express Start Page, as shown in Figure H-1. Depending on past use, your folders and contacts may differ. If you connect to the Internet through a network, follow your instructor's or technical support person's directions to log on. If you connect to the Internet by telephone using a dial-up networking connection, you might need to enter your user name and password. See your instructor or technical support person for this information.

Trouble?

If the Internet Connection Wizard opens, follow the step-by-step instructions to setup your e-mail account.

3. **If necessary, click the Connect to list arrow, select the name of your ISP, type your user name, press [Tab], type your password, then click Connect**
Upon completion of the dial-up connection, you are connected to the Internet (unless an error message appears; if so, search for the Modem Troubleshooter in the Help and Support Center). When you start Outlook Express for the first time, you need to use the Set up a Mail account link on the Start Page to start the Internet Connection Wizard and enter your e-mail account set-up information. See your instructor or technical support person for this information.

QuickTip

To modify or add an account, click Tools on the menu bar, click Accounts, click an account, then click Properties, or click Add, click an account type, then follow the wizard instructions.

4. **If available, click the Set up a Mail account link on the Start Page, in the Internet Connection Wizard dialog box type your name, click Next, type your e-mail address, click Next, select an incoming mail server type, type the name of the incoming mail server, type the name of the outgoing server, click Next, type your e-mail account name, type your password, click Next, then click Finish**
Your mail account is set up. The Set up a Mail account link is replaced on the Start Page in the E-mail area with the Read Mail and new Mail message links.

5. **If necessary, click the Maximize button to maximize the Outlook Express window**

FIGURE H-1: **Outlook Express window with Start Page**

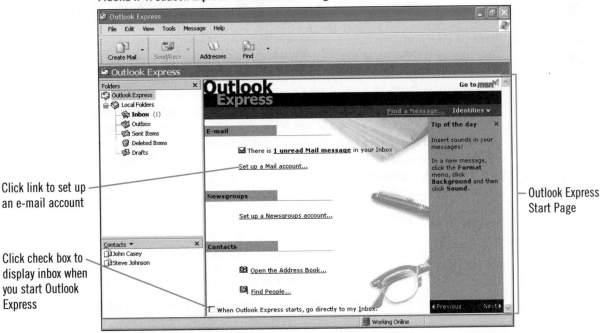

Click link to set up an e-mail account

Click check box to display inbox when you start Outlook Express

Outlook Express Start Page

Understanding e-mail account information

Before you can set up an e-mail account, you need your account name, password, e-mail server type, and the names of your incoming and outgoing e-mail servers from your ISP or network administrator. The Internet Connection Wizard helps you connect to one or more e-mail servers. Outlook Express allows you to send and retrieve e-mail messages from different types of **e-mail servers,** which are the locations where your e-mail is stored before you access it. Outlook Express supports three types of incoming e-mail servers: **POP3** (Post Office Protocol), **IMAP** (Internet Message Access Protocol), and **HTTP** (Hypertext Transfer Protocol). A **Protocol** is a set of

rules and standards that control the transmission of content, format, sequencing, and error management for information over the Internet or network like rules of the road govern the way you drive. POP3 servers allow you to access e-mail messages from a single Inbox folder, while IMAP servers allow you to access multiple folders. HTTP servers are used on Web sites, such as Hotmail, and allow you to send and receive e-mail messages in Outlook Express or on a Web site. When you use POP3 or IMAP e-mail servers, you also need to provide an outgoing e-mail server. **SMTP** (Simple Mail Transfer Protocol) is generally used to send messages between e-mail servers.

Starting Outlook Express from your Web browser

You can set Outlook Express as your default e-mail program, so that whenever you click an e-mail link on a Web page or choose the mail command in your Web browser, Outlook Express opens. You can also set Outlook Express as your default news reader, so that when you click a newsgroup link on a Web page or choose the news reader command in your Web browser, Outlook Express opens. To set Outlook Express as your default e-mail or newsgroup

program, start Internet Explorer, click Tools on the menu bar, click Internet Options, click the Programs tab, click either the E-mail or Newsgroups list arrow, click Outlook Express, then click OK. In Internet Explorer, you can click the Mail button ✉ on the toolbar, then click Read Mail to check your e-mail or click Read News to check your newsgroup messages in Outlook Express.

Exploring the Outlook Express Window

Windows XP

After you start Outlook Express, the Outlook Express window displays the Outlook Express Start Page, as shown in Figure H-2. The **Outlook Express Start Page** displays tools that you can use to read e-mail, set up a newsgroup account, read newsgroup messages, compose e-mail messages, enter and edit Address Book information, and find people on the Internet. Before reading his e-mail, John decides to familiarize himself with the components of the Outlook Express window.

He notes the following features:

▶ The **title bar** at the top of the window displays the name of the program.

▶ The **menu bar** provides access to a variety of commands, much like other Windows programs.

▶ The **Toolbar** provides icons, or buttons, for easy access to the most commonly used commands. See Table H-1 for a description of each toolbar button. These commands are also available on menus.

▶ The **Go to MSN link** opens your default Web browser program and displays the MSN Web page.

▶ The **Folders list** displays folders where Outlook Express stores e-mail messages. You can also use folders to organize your e-mail messages.

▶ The **Contacts list** displays the contact names in the Address Book.

▶ The **new Mail message link** opens the New Message dialog box, where you can compose and send e-mail messages.

▶ The **Read Mail link** jumps to the Inbox, where you can read and reply to incoming e-mail messages.

▶ The **Set up a Newsgroups account link** creates a newsgroup account and appears instead of the Read News link if you have not set up a newsgroup account using the Internet Connection Wizard.

▶ The **Read News link** connects to newsgroups that you can view and subscribe to, and appears instead of the Set up a Newsgroup account link if you have already set up a newsgroup account.

▶ The **Open the Address Book link** opens the Address Book, where you can enter and edit your contacts list.

▶ The **Find People link** opens the Find People dialog box, where you can search for people on the Internet or in your Address Book.

▶ The **Tip of the day** pane appears on the right side of the window and displays an Outlook Express tip; click Next and Previous at the bottom of the pane to move between the tips.

▶ The **status bar** displays information about your Internet connection with a mail or news group server.

FIGURE H-2: Outlook Express window with Start Page

Title bar

Menu bar

Toolbar

Folders list; your list might differ

Contacts list; your list might differ

Go to MSN link

Outlook Express Start Page links

Click links to display an Outlook Express tip

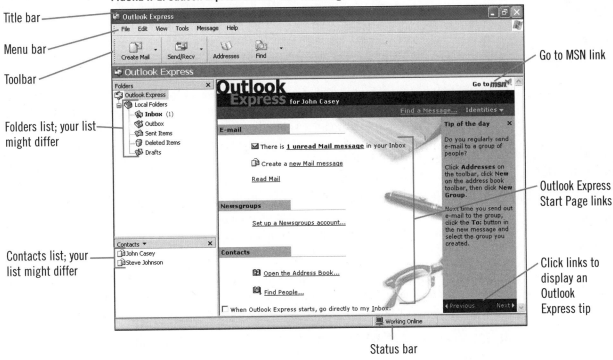

Status bar

TABLE H-1: Outlook Express Start Page toolbar buttons

button	name	description
	Create Mail	Opens the e-mail message composition window
	Send/Recv	Sends e-mail messages and checks for new messages
	Addresses	Opens the Address Book
	Find	Finds e-mail messages, text in an e-mail message, or people on the Internet

Getting help in Outlook Express

If you need help connecting to the Internet to get mail or learning how to use Outlook Express features, you can get help from several different sources. To get Outlook Express Help, you can use the Help system that comes with the program or view Outlook Express Web sites on the Internet. To open Outlook Express Help, click Help on the menu bar, then click Contents and Index. To learn more about Outlook Express from Web sites on the Internet, click Help on the menu bar, point to Microsoft on the Web, then click Product News. Your browser starts and displays the Outlook Express Web site.

Unit H

Windows XP

Adding a Contact to the Address Book

A **contact** is a person or company that you communicate with. You can store a contact's information, such as the contact's title, street address, phone number, and personal Web page address, in the **Address Book**. You can organize your contacts into **contact groups**, which are groups of related people with whom you communicate regularly, or into folders. ✎ John wants to add a new employee to his Address Book.

Steps 1 2 3 4

QuickTip
You can also click the Addresses button 📖 on the toolbar to open the Address Book.

1. Click the Open the Address Book link on the Outlook Express Start Page

The Address Book window opens, as shown in Figure H-3, displaying the current contacts in the Address Book. The Address Book toolbar is above the list of contacts. See Table H-2 for a description of each toolbar button. These commands are also available on the menu bar.

2. Click the New button 📇▾ on the Address Book toolbar, then click New Contact

The Properties dialog box opens, displaying the Name tab. On the Name tab, you enter name and e-mail information. You can use other tabs to enter additional information.

3. Type Shawn in the First text box, press [Tab] twice, then type Brooks in the Last name text box

The name of the new contact appears in the Display text box as it will appear in the contacts list, unless you click the Display list arrow and choose a different name.

QuickTip
Once you add an e-mail address to the Address Book, click Edit to modify it. If an e-mail address is no longer in use, click Remove to delete it.

4. Click in the E-Mail Addresses text box, type shawnbrooks@course.com, then click Add

The e-mail address appears in the box below the E-Mail Addresses text box, as shown in Figure H-4. E-mail addresses are not case-sensitive, so capitalization doesn't matter, and they cannot contain spaces. The e-mail address includes the text "(Default E-Mail)," which indicates this e-mail address is the one used if a contact has multiple e-mail addresses.

5. Click OK

The Properties dialog box closes, and you return to the Address Book.

QuickTip
To create a contact group, click the New button on the Address Book toolbar, click New Group, type a group name, click Select Members, double-click names from the Address Book, click OK, then click OK again.

6. Click any contact in the right pane, then position the mouse pointer over Shawn Brooks in the Address Book to display a ScreenTip

To remove the ScreenTip, move the mouse pointer, or wait a moment and it will close on its own. To edit a contact, double-click anywhere on the contact's entry in the Address Book.

7. Double-click Shawn Brooks in the Address Book

The Shawn Brooks Properties dialog box opens and displays the selected contact's information.

8. Click the Business tab, click in the Phone text box, type 925-555-3084, then click OK

Shawn's business phone number appears in the Address Book. Scroll, if necessary, to view it.

9. Click the Close button in the Address Book window

FIGURE H-3: **Address Book window**

Address Book toolbar

Folders and groups of contacts for use on a shared computer

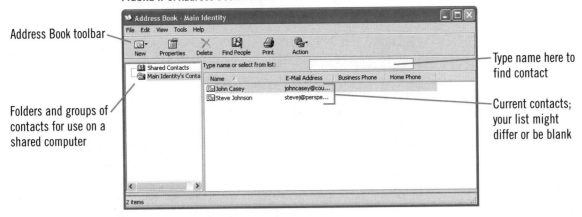

Type name here to find contact

Current contacts; your list might differ or be blank

FIGURE H-4: **Properties dialog box with new contact**

Enter e-mail address here

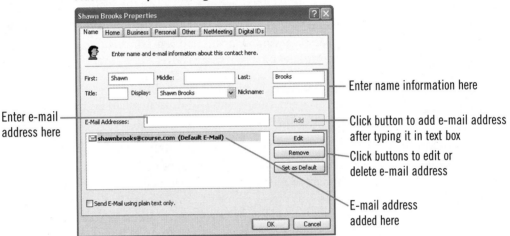

Enter name information here

Click button to add e-mail address after typing it in text box

Click buttons to edit or delete e-mail address

E-mail address added here

TABLE H-2: **Address Book toolbar buttons**

button	name	description
	New	Creates a new contact, group, or folder
	Properties	Opens property information for the selected contact
	Delete	Deletes the selected contact
	Find People	Finds people in the Address Book or on the Internet
	Print	Opens the Print dialog box
	Action	Sends mail, dials a connection, or places an Internet call

Printing contacts from the Address Book

You can print your contact information in a variety of formats, such as Memo, Business Card, and Phone List. The Memo style prints all the information you have for a contact with descriptive titles. The Business Card style prints the contact information without descriptive titles. The Phone List style prints all the phone numbers for a contact or for all your contacts. To print contact information, open the Address Book, select a specific contact (if desired), click the Print button 🖨 on the toolbar, select a print range, print style, and the number of copies you want to print, then click Print in the Print dialog box.

Composing and Sending E-mail

E-mail is becoming the primary form of written communication for many people. E-mail messages follow a standard memo format, with fields for the sender, recipient, date, and subject of the message. To send an e-mail message, you need to enter the recipient's e-mail address, type a subject, then type the message itself. You can send the same message to more than one individual, to a contact group, or to a combination of individuals and groups. You can personalize your e-mail messages and newsgroup messages with stationery templates, or you can design your own stationery. ◣ John wants to send an e-mail message to the new employee whose contact information he added to the Address Book in the previous lesson.

Steps 123 4

QuickTip

To create a new message without stationery, you can click the New Mail button on the toolbar, click the new Mail message link in the Outlook Express window, or double-click a name in the Contacts list.

1. **Click the Create Mail list arrow** 📇 **on the toolbar, click Clear Day or another available stationery, then click the Maximize button in the message window if necessary**
   The New Message window opens and is maximized, as shown in Figure H-5, displaying the Clear Day stationery in the message box.

2. **Click the To button** 📖 **next to the To text box**
   The Select Recipients dialog box opens, as shown in Figure H-6, displaying the contacts from the Address Book.

QuickTip

To remove a name from the Message recipients list, click the person's name in the Message recipients list box, then press [Delete].

3. **Scroll in the list of contacts if necessary, click Shawn Brooks, then click To**
   The contact's name, Shawn Brooks, appears in the Message recipients To box. You can also add additional recipients to this list, select another recipient and click the **Cc (carbon copy)** button to send a copy of your e-mail message to that person, or click the **Bcc (blind carbon copy)** button to send a copy of your e-mail message to another person whose name will not appear in the e-mail message. Bcc is useful when sending e-mails to a large group of unrelated people, and allows for privacy for the recipients.

4. **Click OK**
   Shawn's name appears in the To text box. Shawn's e-mail address is associated with the name selected even though it does not appear. You include a subject title.

5. **Click in the Subject text box, then type Welcome aboard!**
   The message title bar changes from New Message to the subject text "Welcome aboard!" Since the subject text is the first information the recipient sees about the e-mail, it should provide a short, concise summary of the message contents.

QuickTip

To save an incomplete message, click File on the Menu bar, then click Save. The e-mail message is saved with the name of the subject and placed in the Drafts folder.

6. **Click the first line in the text box at the bottom of the message window**
   The Formatting toolbar is now activated and appears just below the Subject text box.

7. **Type Dear Shawn:, press [Enter] twice, type I would like to welcome you to the Wired Coffee Company. We are excited that you have joined our team. Wired Coffee is a growing company, and I believe your contributions will make a big difference. Please come to a luncheon for new employees this Thursday at 12:30 in the company cafe., press [Enter] twice, then type John**

8. **Click the Send button** 📧 **on the toolbar, then click OK in the information box if necessary**
   The New Message window closes. The e-mail message is placed temporarily in the Outbox, a folder for storing outgoing messages, then it is sent automatically to the recipient. A copy of the outgoing message remains in the Sent Items folder so that you can reference the message later. To send a message later, click File on the menu bar, then click Send Later. To send, open the Outbox, then click 📧.

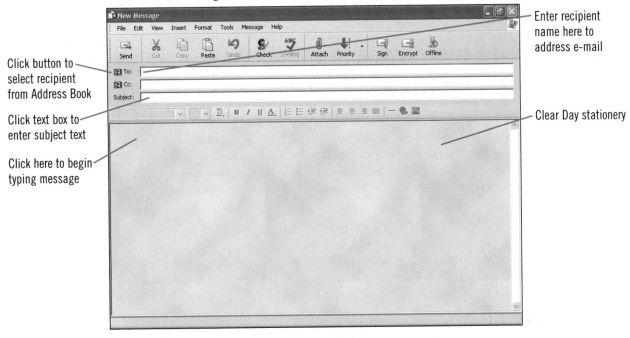
FIGURE H-5: New Message window with Clear Day stationery

Enter recipient name here to address e-mail

Click button to select recipient from Address Book

Click text box to enter subject text

Click here to begin typing message

Clear Day stationery

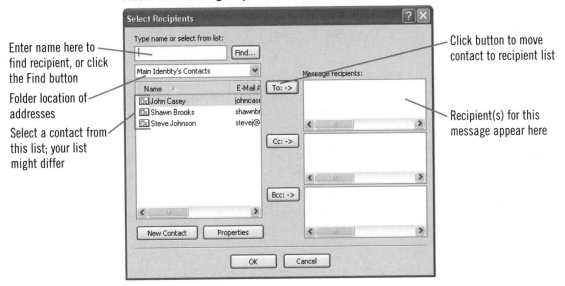

FIGURE H-6: Selecting recipients for e-mail message

Enter name here to find recipient, or click the Find button

Folder location of addresses

Select a contact from this list; your list might differ

Click button to move contact to recipient list

Recipient(s) for this message appear here

Attaching a file to an e-mail message

You can easily share a file, such as a picture or a document, using e-mail by attaching it to an e-mail message. Upon receiving the e-mail, the recipient can open the file in the program that created it or save it on disk. For example, suppose that you are working on a report that you created using WordPad and that a colleague working in another part of the country needs to present the report today. After you finish the report, you can attach the report file to an e-mail message and send the message to your colleague, who can then open, edit, and print the report. To attach a file to an e-mail message, create the message, click the Attach button 📎 on the toolbar in the Insert Attachment dialog box, navigate to the drive and folder location of the file you want to attach, select the file, then click Attach.

Windows XP

Retrieving, Reading, and Responding to E-mail

You can retrieve your e-mail manually or set Outlook Express to do so automatically. New messages appear in the Inbox along with any messages you haven't stored elsewhere or deleted. **Message flags** may appear next to a message. See Table H-3 for common message flags. You can respond to a message in two ways: either reply to it, which creates a new message addressed to the sender(s) and other recipients, or forward it, which creates a new message you can send to someone else. In either case, the original message appears in the message response. ✒️ John forwards an e-mail message he received from Shawn Brooks to another person at the company.

Steps

1. Click the **Send/Recv button** 📧 on the toolbar
An information box displays as Outlook Express sends and receives your e-mail messages. When you receive new e-mail, the Inbox folder name in the Folders list is boldfaced, indicating that it contains unread messages, and a number in parentheses indicates the number of newly received e-mail messages.

QuickTip

To display the Inbox when you start Outlook Express, click the When Outlook Express starts, go directly to my Inbox check box on the Outlook Express Start Page.

2. In the Folders list, click **Inbox**
The Inbox folder opens. The **preview pane** displays the messages in your Inbox. The **display pane** displays the e-mail message selected in the preview pane. E-mail messages that appear with boldfaced subject or heading text are ones you have not opened.

3. Click the **message** you received from Shawn Brooks, as shown in Figure H-7
The display pane displays the e-mail message from Shawn Brooks selected in the preview pane.

Trouble?

If you didn't receive a message from Shawn Brooks, click the Send/Recv button on the toolbar again. It may take a few minutes for the message to arrive.

4. Double-click the **message** you received from Shawn Brooks in the preview pane, then click the **Maximize button** in the message window if necessary
When you receive a short message, you can quickly read it by clicking the message and then reading the text in the display pane. Longer messages are easier to read in a full window instead of in the display pane. You can reply to the author, reply to all recipients, forward the message, or simply close or delete the message.

QuickTip

To print an e-mail message, open the message, then click the Print button 🖨️ on the message window toolbar.

5. Click the **Forward button** 📧 on the message toolbar, then click the **Maximize button** in the message window if necessary
The Forward Message window opens, as shown in Figure H-8, displaying the original e-mail subject title in the Subject text box with the prefix "Fw:" (short for Forward) and the original message you sent in the message box. You can add additional text to the message.

6. Click in the upper-left corner of the message box, then type **Please add Shawn Brooks to Thursday's luncheon guest list.**

Trouble?

If you don't know an e-mail address to send the forwarded message to, click the Close button in the message window, then continue to the next lesson.

7. Click the **To text box**, type the e-mail address of your instructor, technical support person, or someone else you know, then click the **Send button** 📧 on the toolbar
You send the e-mail message. To verify that your message was sent, view the Sent Items folder. If the recipient of the e-mail message is a contact in the Contacts list, you can type the name of the recipient instead of the e-mail address in the To text box. As you type a recipient name, **AutoComplete** suggests possible matches from the Contacts list. Click the suggestion from the list that matches the contact you want.

8. In the Folders list, click **Sent Items** to display e-mail messages you have sent

9. In the Contacts list, right-click **Shawn Brooks**, click **Delete**, then click **Yes**

FIGURE H-7: **Outlook Express window with Inbox**

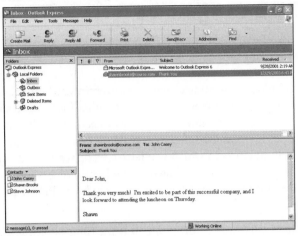

FIGURE H-8: **Forward Message window**

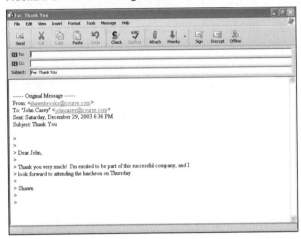

TABLE H-3: **Mail message flag icons**

icon	description	icon	description
✉	Unread message; message heading text appears bold	📎	One or more files attached to message
📨	Read message	!	Sender marked message as high priority
📨	Replied to message	↓	Sender marked message as low priority
📨	Forwarded message		

Checking the spelling and content in e-mail messages

Before you send an e-mail message, you should spell check the text and read through the content to make sure your spelling is accurate and your content conveys the message you want to the recipient(s). If you have Microsoft Word, Microsoft Excel, or Microsoft PowerPoint installed on your computer, Outlook Express uses the spelling checker from the program to spell check your e-mail messages. If you do not have one of these programs installed, the Spelling command is not available, and you need to check spelling manually. To start the spell checker, type your e-mail message, click Tools on the menu bar, then click Spelling. To have Outlook Express automatically check all of your e-mail messages before sending them, display the Outlook window, click Tools on the menu bar, click Options, click the Spelling tab in the Options dialog box, click the Always check spelling before sending check box to select it, then click OK.

Managing E-mail Messages

A common problem with using e-mail is an overcrowded Inbox. To keep your Inbox organized, you should move messages you want to save to other folders and subfolders, delete messages you no longer want, and create new folders as you need them. Storing incoming messages in other folders and deleting unwanted messages makes it easier to see the new messages you receive and to keep track of messages to which you have already responded.　John wants to create a new folder for his important messages in the Local Folders location, move a message from the Inbox to the new folder, then delete the messages he no longer needs.

Steps

1. Click **File** on the menu bar, point to **New**, then click **Folder**

The Create Folder dialog box opens, displaying the list of folders contained in the Outlook Express folder, as shown in Figure H-9.

2. Click in the **Folder name text box**, type **Important**, then click **Local Folders** in the Folders list

You name the new folder Important, and it will appear in the Folders list under Local Folders. To create a **subfolder** (a folder in a folder), you select one of the folders in the Folders list under Local Folders. The Folders list works like the left pane of Windows Explorer. When you create a subfolder, the Expand Indicator ⊞ appears next to the name of the folder that contains the subfolder.

3. Click **OK**

The new folder, Important, appears in the Folders list under Local Folders at the bottom of the list.

4. Click **Inbox** in the Folders list, then right-click the **message you received from Shawn Brooks** in the preview pane of the Inbox

A shortcut menu appears, displaying commands, such as Move to Folder, Copy to Folder, Delete, Print, and Add Sender to Address Book, to help you manage your e-mail messages.

5. Click **Move to Folder** on the shortcut menu

The Move dialog box opens, allowing you to specify the folder where you want to move the selected message.

6. Click the **Important folder**, then click **OK**

7. In the Folders list, click the **Important folder**

The e-mail message you just moved appears in the preview and display panes, as shown in Figure H-10.

8. In the Folders list, right-click the **Important folder**, click **Delete**, then click **Yes** to confirm the deletion

You place the Important folder in the Deleted Items folder. The Deleted Items folder works just like the Recycle Bin. The folder temporarily stores deleted messages until you automatically or manually delete them.

9. In the Folders list, right-click the **Deleted Items folder**, click **Empty 'Deleted Items' Folder**, then click **Yes** to confirm the deletion

You permanently delete the Important folder and all of its contents.

FIGURE H-9: Create Folder dialog box

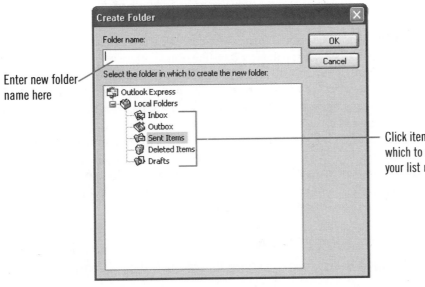

Enter new folder name here

Click item to select folder in which to create a new folder; your list might differ

FIGURE H-10: Important folder

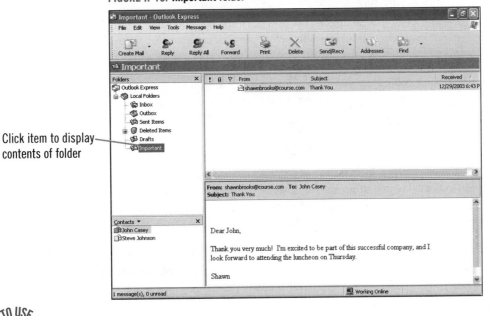

Click item to display contents of folder

Diverting incoming e-mail to folders

Outlook Express can direct incoming messages that meet criteria to other folders in the Folders list rather than to your Inbox. For example, your friend loves sending you funny e-mail, but you often don't have time to read it right away. You can set message rules to store any messages you receive from your friend in a different folder so they won't clutter your Inbox. When you are ready to read the messages, you simply open the folder and access the messages just as you would messages in the Inbox. To set criteria for incoming messages, click Tools on the menu bar, point to Message Rules, then click Mail. If the New Mail Rule dialog box opens, no previous message rules exist. Otherwise, the Message Rules dialog box opens, and you click New to create a new message rule. In the New Mail Rule dialog box, select the conditions for your rule, select the actions for your rule, click any undefined value (such as the e-mail address you want to divert and the folder where you want to store the diverted messages) and provide information. Type a name to identify the rule, then click OK. If you receive unwanted e-mail from a specific address, you can block all messages from that sender. To block all messages from a sender, click the message from the sender, click Message on the menu bar, then click Block Sender.

Selecting a News Server

A newsgroup is an electronic forum where people from around the world with a common interest can share ideas, ask and answer questions, and comment on and discuss any subject. You can find newsgroups on almost any topic. Before you can participate in a newsgroup, you must select a news server. A **news server** is a computer located on the Internet, which stores newsgroup messages, also called **articles**, on different topics. Each news server contains several newsgroups from which to choose. The Internet Connection Wizard walks you through the process of selecting a news server. This wizard also appears the first time you use Outlook Express News. To complete the wizard process and the steps in this lesson, you need to get the name of the news server you want to use from your instructor, technical support person, or Internet service provider (ISP), and possibly an account name and password. John wants to add a news server account so he can access coffee-related newsgroups.

Steps

1. In the Folders list, click **Outlook Express**, then click the **Read News link** or click the **Set up a Newsgroups account link** in the Outlook Express Start Page

2. Click **Tools** on the menu bar, click **Accounts**, then click the **News tab** in the Internet Accounts dialog box
   The Internet Accounts dialog box opens, as shown in Figure H-11, displaying the News tab with your list of available news servers. Using the Internet Accounts dialog box, you can add, remove, and view properties for news servers, mail servers, and directory services.

3. Click **Add**, then click **News** on the shortcut menu
   The Internet Connection Wizard dialog box opens.

4. Type your **name** if necessary, then click **Next**
   The name you enter appears in messages you post to a newsgroup.

5. Type your **e-mail address** if necessary, then click **Next**
   Individuals participating in the newsgroup need to know your e-mail address so they can reply to your news messages, either by posting another news message or by sending you an e-mail message.

6. Type the **name of the news server** provided by your instructor, technical support person, or ISP, as shown in Figure H-12, click the **My news server requires me to log on** check box to select it if required by your ISP, then click **Next**

7. If you selected the My news server requires me to log on check box in the previous step, type **your user name** and **your password** in the appropriate text boxes, then click **Next**

8. Click **Finish**, click **Close** if the Internet Accounts dialog box is still open, then click **No** when prompted to download a list of available newsgroups
   The news server name appears in the Folders list, as shown in Figure H-13. You view a list of available newsgroups in the next lesson.

FIGURE H-11: Internet Accounts dialog box

Click tab to select server type

Available news server

Click button to add server

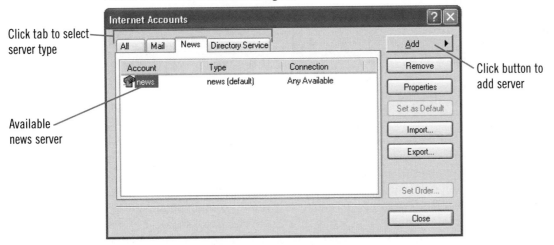

FIGURE H-12: Internet Connection Wizard dialog box

Enter new server here; your news server might differ

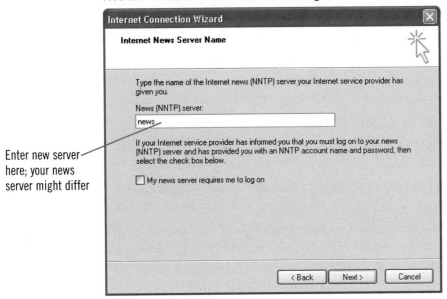

FIGURE H-13: Outlook Express window with news server

News server; your news server name might differ

Newsgroup links on Outlook Express Start Page

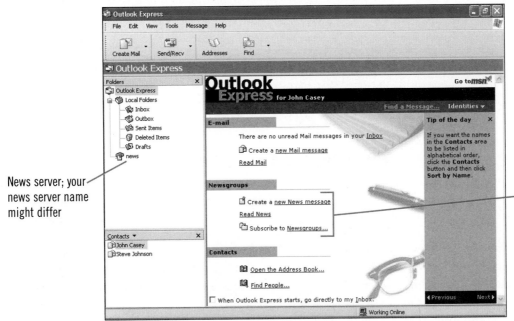

Windows XP

Viewing and Subscribing to a Newsgroup

When you add a news server account to Outlook Express, it retrieves a list of newsgroups available on that server. Often this list is quite lengthy. Rather than scroll through the entire list looking for a particular topic, you can have Outlook Express search the list for that topic. Similarly, you can search all the messages you retrieve from a newsgroup for a particular message. Once you select a newsgroup, you can merely view its contents, or, if you expect to return to the newsgroup often, you can subscribe to it. Subscribing to a newsgroup places a link to the group in the news server folder in your Outlook Express Folders list, providing easy access to the newsgroup. John wants to find and subscribe to a newsgroup for coffee drinkers, so he can keep track of what people want from a coffee company.

Trouble?

If a log in message appears, click OK.

1. Click the **Read News link** in the Outlook Express Start Page, then click **Yes** if necessary, to view a list of available newsgroups
   The Newsgroup Subscriptions dialog box opens, as shown in Figure H-14, displaying news servers on the left (if more than one exists) and related newsgroups on the right.

2. In the News server list, click the **news server** you added in the previous lesson if necessary
   A list of the newsgroups you subscribe to appears in the preview pane. Your list might be empty.

QuickTip

To download new newsgroup messages, click the news server in the Folders list, click the newsgroup in the right pane, click Settings, click New Messages Only on the shortcut menu, then click Synchronize Account.

3. Type **coffee** in the Display newsgroups which contain text box
   Newsgroups related to coffee appear in the Newsgroup list box, as shown in Figure H-15.

4. Scroll if necessary, click any newsgroup from your list, then click **Go to**
   The newsgroup name you choose appears selected in the Folders list, and the newsgroup messages appear in the preview pane of the Outlook Express window, as shown in Figure H-16. You think this newsgroup looks promising, so you decide to subscribe to it.

5. Right-click the **newsgroup name** in the Folders list, then click **Subscribe**
   The number of newsgroup messages appears next to the newsgroup name in the Folders list. The icon next to the newsgroup changes from gray to color to indicate the subscription is complete.

CLUES TO USE

Filtering unwanted newsgroup messages

After you become familiar with a newsgroup, you might decide that you don't want to retrieve messages from a particular person, about a specific subject, of a certain length, or older than a certain number of days. This is called filtering newsgroup messages. To filter unwanted messages, click Tools on the menu bar, point to Message Rules, then click News. If the New News Rule dialog box opens, no previous message rules exist. Otherwise, the Message Rules dialog box opens, and you click New to create a new message rule. In the New Mail Rule dialog box, select the conditions for your rule, select the actions for your rule, click any undefined value (such as the e-mail address you want to divert and the folder where you want to store the unwanted messages) and provide information, type a name to identify the rule, then click OK.

FIGURE H-14: **Newsgroup dialog box**

Click icon to select a new server; your list of news servers might differ

Click button to view selected newsgroup

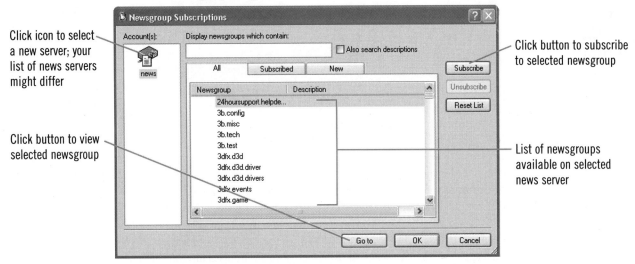

Click button to subscribe to selected newsgroup

List of newsgroups available on selected news server

FIGURE H-15: **List of newsgroups relating to coffee**

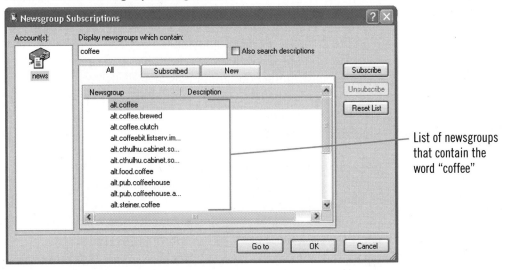

List of newsgroups that contain the word "coffee"

FIGURE H-16: **Outlook Express window with newsgroup**

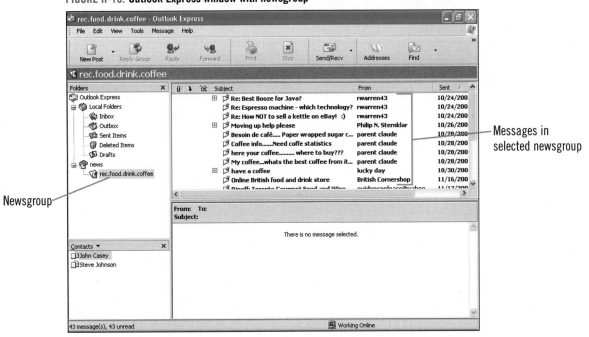

Newsgroup

Messages in selected newsgroup

Reading and Posting a News Message

After retrieving new newsgroup messages, you can read them. Newsgroup messages appear in the preview pane, just as e-mail messages do. To view a newsgroup message in the display pane, click the title of the message in the preview pane. If the Expand Indicator ⊞ appears to the left of a newsgroup message, then the message contains a conversation thread. A **conversation thread** consists of the original message on a particular topic along with any responses that include the original message. To read the responses, click ⊞ to display the message titles, then click the title of the message you want to read. To hide all the responses to a conversation thread, click the Collapse Indicator ⊟ to the left of a newsgroup message. Icons appear next to the news messages to indicate whether a conversation thread is expanded or collapsed, and whether or not it has been read. See Table H-4 for a description of common message icons. ✎ John decides to read some of the messages in the newsgroup. When he finishes, he restores his news server settings by unsubscribing from this newsgroup and removing the news server from the Folders list.

Steps

Trouble?

If a newsgroup message has no ⊞, click a message without a ⊞, then skip to Step 3.

1. **Click a newsgroup message in the preview pane with ⊞ to the left of the title, then read the message in the display pane**
   The newsgroup message appears in the display pane.

2. **Click ⊞ next to the newsgroup message**
   The titles of the responses to the original message appear under the original newsgroup message, as shown in Figure H-17.

QuickTip

To view only unread messages, click View on the menu bar, point to Current View, then click Hide Read Messages.

3. **Click each reply message under the original message, then read the reply**
   As you read each message, you can choose to compose a new message, send a reply message to everyone viewing the newsgroup (known as **posting**), send a reply message to the author's private e-mail address (rather than posting it on the newsgroup), or forward the message to another person.

4. **After reading the last reply message, click the Reply Group button 📝 on the toolbar, then click the Maximize button if necessary**

5. **Type a response to the newsgroup message, as shown in Figure H-18**
   To see the exchange of messages and replies, click a message in the thread, click Message on the menu bar, then click Watch Conversation.

6. **Click the Send button 📮 on the toolbar, then click OK**
   Your reply message appears in the preview pane along with the other replies to the original message. Everyone viewing the newsgroup can download and read your response.

Trouble?

If another warning message appears, click No to subscribe to the Newsgroup, then click No to view a list of newsgroups.

7. **Right-click the newsgroup in the Folders list, click Unsubscribe, then click OK**

8. **Right-click the news server in the Folders list, click Remove Account, then click Yes**

9. **Click File on the menu bar, click Exit, then click Yes if necessary to disconnect from the Internet**

TABLE H-4: Newsgroup message icons

icon	description	icon	description
📝	Unopened message; message heading text appears in bold	📋	Message unavailable on server
📝	Read message	📝	Replied to message
📋	Read message and stored on your computer	📋	Forwarded message
📋	Unopened message and stored on your computer	❋	Newsgroup new on server

FIGURE H-17: Reading a newsgroup message

Click button to create a new message

Click Collapse Indicator to hide replies to messages

Click Expand Indicator to display replies to messages

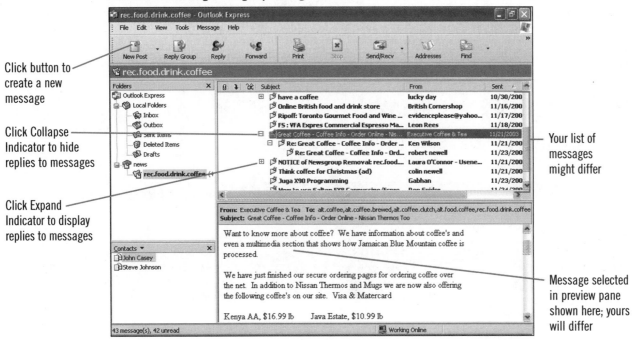

Your list of messages might differ

Message selected in preview pane shown here; yours will differ

FIGURE H-18: Posting a newsgroup message

Click button to post message to newsgroup

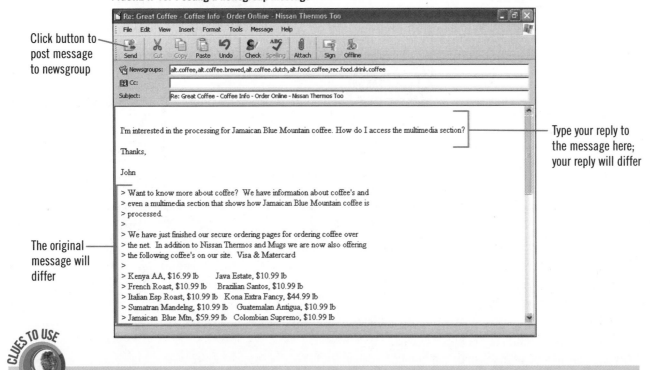

Type your reply to the message here; your reply will differ

The original message will differ

Deleting old news messages

Newsgroup messages are stored on your hard drive, so you should delete unneeded messages to free disk space. Outlook Express gives several clean-up options to help you optimize your hard drive space. You can delete entire messages (titles and bodies), compress messages, remove just the message bodies (leaving the title headers), or reset the information stored for selected messages, which allows you to refresh messages (download again). To clean up files on your local hard drive, select a news server in the Folders list, click Tools on the menu bar, click Options, then click the Maintenance tab. You can select any of the clean-up options to delete or compress news messages at a specified time, or click Clean Up Now, then click the button for the clean-up option you want to perform.

Practice

► Concepts Review

Label each element of the screen shown in Figure H-19.

FIGURE H-19

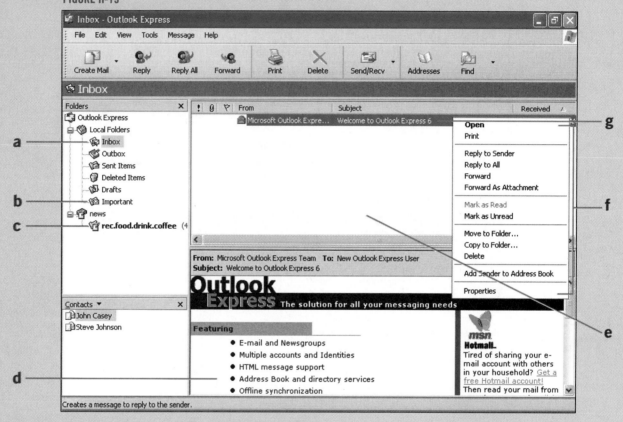

1. Which element displays new e-mail messages?
2. Which element points to an e-mail message?
3. Which element points to a newsgroup?
4. Which element points to the display pane?
5. Which element displays the contents of a folder?
6. Which element points to the preview pane?
7. Which element displays e-mail commands?

Match each term with the statement that describes its function.

8. Message flag   **a.** A computer on the Internet that stores articles
9. Outlook Express   **b.** Displays e-mail, contacts, and newsgroups
10. Message Rules   **c.** An icon that indicates e-mail priority
11. Outlook Express window   **d.** Diverts selected incoming e-mail folders
12. News server   **e.** A program that exchanges e-mail on the Internet
13. Newsgroup   **f.** A collection of articles on related topics

Select the best answers from the following lists of choices.

14. **The location that allows you to jump to folders and open tools is called the:**
    a. Outlook Express window.
    b. Outlook Express Start Page.
    c. Folders list.
    d. Outlook Express Link Page.

15. **To compose a message, you can:**
    a. Click the new Mail message link.
    b. Click Create Mail button on the toolbar.
    c. Click Message on the menu bar, then click New Message.
    d. All of the above

16. **A contact is a:**
    a. Person with whom you communicate.
    b. Mailing address.
    c. Newsgroup.
    d. Program.

17. **When you click the Send button on the toolbar in the New Message window, you first send an e-mail message to the:**
    a. E-mail address.
    b. Outbox.
    c. Internet.
    d. Cc and Bcc addresses.

18. **✉ indicates that the message has:**
    a. Not been read.
    b. Been read.
    c. One or more files attached to it.
    d. Been marked as low priority by the sender.

▶ Skills Review

1. **Start Outlook Express and explore the Outlook Express window.**
   a. Connect to the Internet.
   b. Start Outlook Express.
   c. Identify the title bar, menu bar, toolbar, Internet Explorer link, Folders list, Read Mail link, Read News link, new Mail message link, Open the Address Book link, Find People link, and status bar.
   d. On the toolbar, identify icons for opening the Address Book, sending and receiving e-mail messages, composing a message, and finding a message.
   e. If necessary, enter your user name and password, then click Connect.

2. **Add a contact to the Address Book.**
   a. Click the Address Book button.
   b. Click the New button, then click New Contact.
   c. Type **John** in the First name text box, press [Tab] twice, then type **Asher**.
   d. Click in the E-Mail Addresses text box, then type **johna@course.com**.
   e. Click Add, then click OK. Click the Address Book Close button.

3. **Compose and send e-mail.**
   a. Click the New Mail button, then click the Maximize button if necessary.
   b. Click the To button.
   c. Click the name John Asher.
   d. Click To, then click OK.
   e. Click the Subject text box, then type **Financial Update Request**.
   f. Press [Tab] to move to the message window, then type **John: Please send year-end financial report ASAP. Thanks**.
   g. Click the Send button.

4. **Retrieve, read, and respond to e-mail.**
   a. Click the Send/Recv button. It may take a few minutes before you receive a message from John Asher.
   b. In the Folders list, click Inbox. Click the message you just received from John Asher.
   c. Click the Forward Message button, then click the Maximize button if necessary.

d. Click the To text box, then enter your e-mail address. Enter a response in the message window.

e. Click the Send button.

5. Manage e-mail messages.

a. Click File on the menu bar, point to New, then click Folder.

b. Type **Archive**. Click Local Folders in the Folders list, then click OK.

c. Right-click the message received from John Asher, then click Move To Folder on the shortcut menu.

d. Click Archive, then click OK.

e. In the Folders list, click the Archive folder.

f. Right-click the message received from John Asher, then click Delete on the shortcut menu.

g. Right-click the Archive folder, click Delete, then click Yes.

h. Click the Address Book button.

i. Click John Asher, click the Delete button, then click Yes. Click the Close button.

6. Select a news server.

a. In the Folders list, click Outlook Express.

b. Click the Read News link or the Set up a Newsgroup account link.

c. If the Internet Connection Wizard appears, skip to Step e. Otherwise, click Tools on the menu bar, click Accounts, then click the News tab.

d. Click Add, then click News.

e. Type your name, then click Next. Type your e-mail address, then click Next.

f. Type the name of a news server (see your instructor, technical support person, or ISP for a name), then click Next.

g. Click Finish, click Close if necessary, then click No.

7. View and subscribe to a newsgroup.

a. Click the Read News link, then click Yes if necessary.

b. In the News server list, click the news server you just added (if available).

c. Type **caffeine**. (If no items appear, type **tea** or **chocolate**.)

d. Click a newsgroup. Click Go To.

e. Right-click the newsgroup in the Folders list, then click Subscribe.

8. Read and post a news message.

a. Click a newsgroup message with a ⊞.

b. Click ⊞ next to the newsgroup message.

c. Click and read each reply.

d. Click the Reply Group button, then type a response.

e. Click the Send button, then click OK.

f. Right-click the newsgroup in the Folders list, click Unsubscribe, then click OK.

g. Right-click the news server in the Folders list, click Remove Account, then click Yes.

h. Click File on the menu bar, click Exit, then click Yes if necessary to disconnect.

▶ Independent Challenge 1

You are a new lawyer at Bellig & Associates. You have a home computer with Windows XP and Outlook Express that you often use to do work on while you are at home. Because e-mail is an important method of communication at the law firm, you want to use the Outlook Express Address Book to enter e-mail addresses of colleagues with whom you need to communicate while working out of the office.

a. Start Outlook Express, then open the Address Book.

b. Enter the following names and e-mail addresses:

Greg Bellig   gregb@bellig_law.com

Jacob Bellig   jacobb@bellig_law.com

Derek Quan   derekq@bellig_law.com

c. Print the Address Book in both the Business Card and Memo styles.

d. Delete the names and e-mail addresses you just entered in the Address Book.

▶ Independent Challenge 2

As president of Auto Metals, you just negotiated a deal to export metal auto parts to an assembly plant in China. Your lawyer, Josh Higgins, drew up a preliminary contract. You want to send Josh an e-mail indicating the terms of the deal so he can finish the contract. When Josh responds, move the e-mail into the Legal folder. If you do not have a connection to the Internet, ask your instructor or technical support person for help completing this challenge.

    a. Open a New Message window using the stationery called Technical, or another option.

    b. Type **jhiggins@course.com** in the To text box in the message window, then type **China Deal Contract** in the Subject text box.

    c. Enter the following message:

    Dear Josh,

    I have completed the negotiations with the assembly plant. Please modify the following terms in the contract:

    1. All parts shall be inspected before shipping.

    2. Ship 20,000 units a month for 3 years with an option for 2 more years.

    Sincerely yours,

    [your name]

    d. Send the e-mail.

    e. Print the e-mail you receive from Josh Higgins.

    f. Create a new folder called Legal, then move the e-mail message you received from Josh Higgins to the new folder.

    g. Delete the Legal folder.

▶ Independent Challenge 3

You are a legal assistant at a law firm specializing in international law. Your boss asks you to research international contracts with China. You decide to start your research with newsgroups on the Internet.

    a. Select a news server. (See your instructor, technical support person, or ISP to obtain a news server.)

    b. Subscribe to a newsgroup about China, then read several newsgroup messages and replies.

    c. Reply to a message, then post a new message.

    d. Print the newsgroup messages, including the original message and replies.

    e. Unsubscribe to the newsgroup, then remove the newsgroup server.

▶ Independent Challenge 4

You like to play sports, watch sports, read about sports, and talk about sports all the time, so you decide to join a sports newsgroup.

    a. Select a news server. (See your instructor, technical support person, or ISP to obtain a news server.)

    b. Subscribe to a newsgroup about sports, then read several newsgroup messages and replies.

    c. Reply to a message, then post a new message.

    d. Print the newsgroup messages, including the original message and replies.

    e. Unsubscribe to the newsgroup, then remove the newsgroup server.

▶ Visual Workshop

Re-create the screen shown in Figure H-20, which displays the Outlook Express window with a message that has been sent. Print the Outlook Express window. (Press [Print Screen] to make a copy of the screen, open Paint, click Edit on the menu bar, click Paste to paste the screen into Paint, then click Yes to paste the large image if necessary. Click the Text button on the Toolbox, click a blank area in the Paint work area, then type your name. Click File on the menu bar, click Page Setup, change 100% normal size to 50% in the Scaling area, then click OK. Click File on the menu bar, click Print, then click Print.)

FIGURE H-20

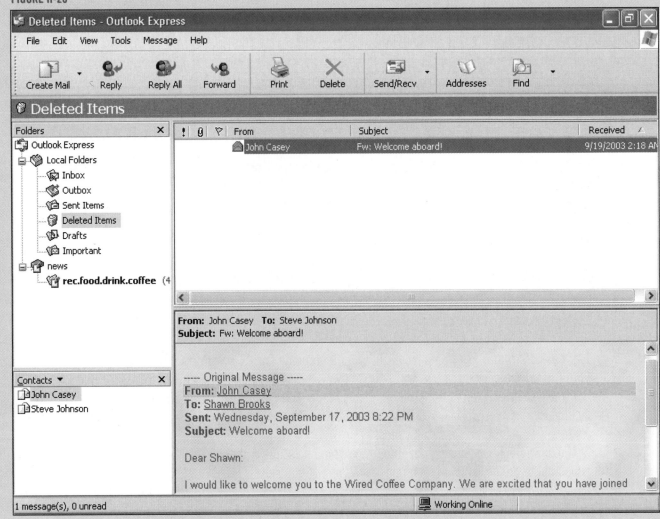

Appendix

Objectives

► **Identify New Features in Windows XP**
► **Identify Differences between Windows XP Home and Professional**
► **Prepare to Install Windows XP**
► **Install Windows XP**
► **Set Up a Computer for Multiple Users**
► **Manage Power Options on Portable Computers**
► **Improve the Font Display on Portable Computers**

This appendix provides information about new features in Windows XP, the differences between Windows XP Home and Windows XP Professional, and how to prepare and install the operating system software. For those users who want to share a computer at home or the office, you'll learn how to set up and use a computer for multiple users. If you use a portable computer, also known as a **laptop** or **notebook**, you can change computer power options to reduce the power consumption of your entire system or a specific device, and smooth out the edges of fonts on the screen to improve the font display.

Windows XP

Identifying New Features in Windows XP

Windows XP comes with new features that make your computer significantly easier and faster to use than earlier versions of Windows. Windows XP makes it easier to open files and programs, find information, and accomplish other common tasks, such as send e-mail, browse the Internet, scan and view pictures, play music and videos, and change Windows XP settings. Windows XP design improvements include a two-column Start menu with frequently-used programs and files, similar windows grouped on the taskbar, a task pane with common commands that correspond to the current task, and Control Panel icons organized by category. If you share a computer with family and friends, Windows XP makes it easy to create individual accounts with customized settings for each user and provides a Welcome screen that allows you to switch between multiple accounts without having to exit programs and log off completely. Some of the main new features in Windows XP are shown in Figure AP-1 and are listed below.

Details

▶ **Welcome screen and Fast User Switching**

With the Welcome screen, you can share the same computer with family and friends and still maintain privacy and control over your personal files. You can use Fast User Switching to switch between users without having to close each other's programs.

▶ **Enhanced Start menu and taskbar grouping**

The Start menu organizes programs and frequently-used tasks. If you have many open files, programs, and windows, they are grouped together on the taskbar according to the program type.

▶ **Task-focused design**

The My Computer, My Documents, and other windows display a task pane on the left side of the window with commands and options associated with your current task or selection. The Control Panel also displays options by category in addition to the Classic view.

▶ **Help and Support Center**

Allows you to search multiple sources including the Microsoft Knowledge Base on the Internet, to print from the online documentation, and to access frequently-used help topics.

▶ **System Restore**

System Restore allows you to restore your computer to a previous version of the system.

▶ **Search Companion**

The Search Companion identifies the kind of help needed and retrieves relevant information.

▶ **Windows Messenger**

An easy way to communicate with your buddies, a list of contacts with whom you interact regularly, in real time using text, voice, and video.

▶ **Remote Assistance**

Gives a friend permission to connect to your computer over the Internet, observe your screen, and control your computer.

▶ **Home Networking**

You can set up a home network and share an Internet connection and other computer resources, such as a printer or fax.

▶ **CD burning**

With a CD recording device installed on your computer, you can create your own CDs by dragging a folder with the files and folders you want to save to the CD-R or CD-RW device icon.

► Enhanced Windows Media Player

You can play DVDs, create your own music CDs, and export videos to portable devices.

► Enhanced My Pictures and My Music folders

With My Pictures, you can order prints, view pictures, publish pictures to the Internet, and compress pictures. With My Music, you can view a list of music files, play music files, shop for music online, and perform file management tasks.

► Scanner and Camera Wizard

Walks you through scanning a single image, collection of images, and multi-page documents.

FIGURE AP-1: **Main new features in Windows XP**

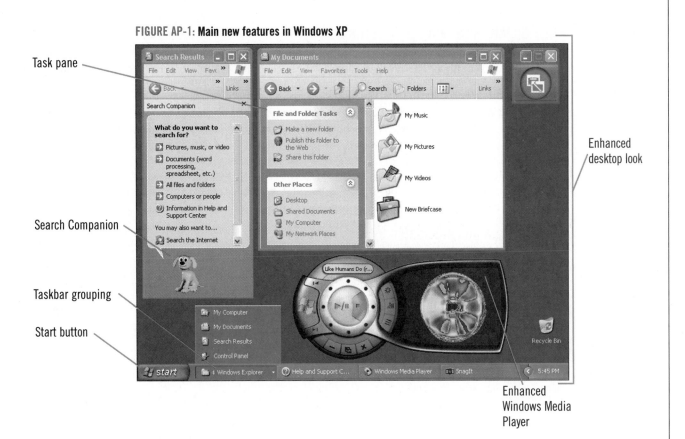

Task pane

Search Companion

Taskbar grouping

Start button

Enhanced desktop look

Enhanced Windows Media Player

Windows XP

Identifying Differences between Windows XP Home and Professional

Windows XP comes in three editions: the Home Edition for consumers, the Professional Edition for business and power users, and a 64-bit version for Intel Itanium processor-based systems, called Windows XP 64-Bit Edition. The Home Edition is a subset of the Professional Edition. In other words, the Home Edition contains all the same features contained in the Professional Edition. However, the Professional Edition also contains additional features, some of which are shown in Figure AP-2, that are geared toward the business world. Each edition allows users to install an upgrade version for those who already have Windows 98 or later installed on their computer, or a full version for those who have Windows 95 or Windows NT 3.51 or earlier or no operating system installed on their computer.

Windows XP Professional features not found in the Home Edition:

► **Slightly different user interface**
Windows XP Professional comes with a few user interface default settings that are different from those in Windows XP Home. See Table AP-1 for a list and description of the user interface differences.

► **Access a remote desktop**
You can access a Windows XP Professional remote desktop from any operating system that supports a Terminal Services client, such as Windows 98 or Me, and Windows XP Home.

► **Supports more than one microprocessor**
Windows XP Professional supports up to two microprocessors, while the Windows XP Home supports only one. This allows you to perform multiple tasks at the same time, such as printing large documents and calculating large amounts of numbers, more quickly.

► **Backup and Automated System Recovery**
With the Backup utility program, you can back up files to a disk or tape and create an Automated System Recovery disk to help you recover a system from a serious error, such as a system crash.

► **Internet Information Service**
You can set up a personal Web server using the Internet Information Services Web server software to use to publish Web pages.

FIGURE AP-2: Windows XP Professional desktop

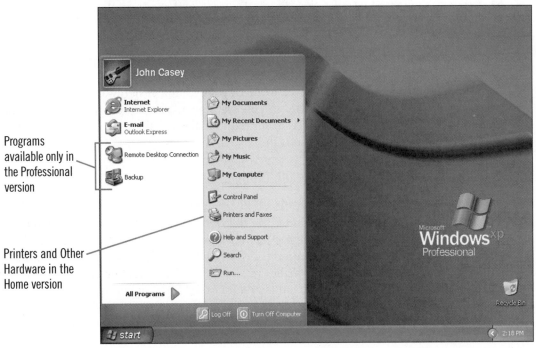

Programs available only in the Professional version

Printers and Other Hardware in the Home version

TABLE AP-1: User interface differences

user interface item	Windows XP Home	Windows XP Professional
Start menu	Printers and Other Hardware (not available unless enabled)	Printers and Faxes; My Recent Documents
Fax functionality	Not available unless you install it	Available
Guest account	Activated	Deactivated
Check box option on Screen Saver tab in the Display Properties dialog box	On resume, display Welcome screen	On resume, password protect

Preparing to Install Windows XP

Before you install Windows XP, you need to check your computer hardware and software and make several setup decisions that relate to your computer. The Windows XP Setup Wizard guides you through many of the choices you need to make, but there are some decisions and actions you need to make before you start the wizard.

To ensure a successful installation, do the following:

► **Make sure your hardware components meet the minimum requirements**

Your computer hardware needs to meet the following minimum hardware requirements: 300 megahertz (MHz) Pentium or higher microprocessor or equivalent recommended (233 MHz minimum), 128 MB of RAM recommended (64 MB minimum), 1.5 GB of free space on hard disk, Super VGA (800 × 600) or higher resolution video adapter and monitor, keyboard, mouse or compatible pointing device, and CD-ROM or DVD drive. Beyond the basic requirements, some software and hardware services, such as Internet access, networking, instant messaging, voice and video conferencing, and sound playback, call for you to meet additional requirements; see Windows XP documentation for specific details.

► **Make sure your hardware and software are compatible**

The Windows XP Setup Wizard automatically checks your hardware and software and reports any potential conflicts, but it is always a good idea to determine whether your computer hardware is compatible before you start the wizard. You can view the Hardware Compatibility List (HCL) at the Microsoft Web site at www.microsoft.com/hcl/, shown in Figure AP-3.

► **Back up your files in case you need to restore your current operating system**

If you're upgrading from an earlier version of Windows, you should back up your current files, so you can correct any problems that might arise during the installation. You can back up files to a disk, a tape drive, or another computer on your network. Check your current operating system help for instructions to back up your files.

► **Make sure you have required network information**

If you are connecting to a network, you need the following information from your network administrator: name of your computer, name of the workgroup or domain, and a TCP/IP address if your network doesn't use a DHCP (Dynamic Host Configuration Protocol) server. If you are not sure whether you are connecting to a workgroup or a domain, select the workgroup option. You can always connect to a domain after you install Windows XP Professional.

► **Determine whether you want to perform an upgrade or install a new copy of Windows XP**

After you start the Windows XP Setup Wizard, you need to decide whether to upgrade your current operating system, as shown in Figure AP-4, or to perform an entirely new installation, known as a **clean install**. You can upgrade from Windows 98, 98 SE, and Me to Windows XP Home Edition or Professional, and you can upgrade only from Windows 2000 Professional and Windows NT 4.0 Workstation to Windows Professional, but not to the Home Edition. Windows 98, 98 SE, and Me users can uninstall Windows XP, but this capability is not available to Windows NT 4.0 and Windows 2000 upgraders. Windows 95 and Windows NT 3.51 or earlier are not supported for upgrading, so those users will need to perform a clean install.

► **Make sure you have the required product key information**

On the back of the Windows XP CD-ROM packaging is a unique 25-character product key, such as KFEPC-12345-MHORY-12345-IROFE, that you need to enter during the Windows XP Setup Wizard installation to complete the process. Keep the product key in a safe place and do not share it with others. The unique product key allows you to activate and use Windows. Without the product key and activation, Windows XP will not work.

FIGURE AP-3: **Microsoft Hardware Compatibility List Web site**

Click button to
check hardware
compatibility

Your Web page
might differ

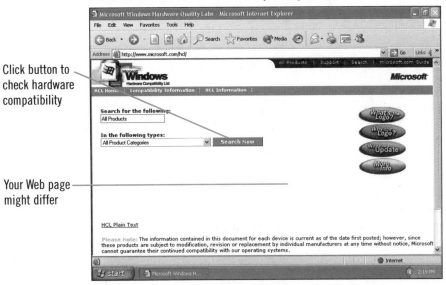

FIGURE AP-4: **Selecting Windows XP installation type**

Click list arrow to
select installation
type

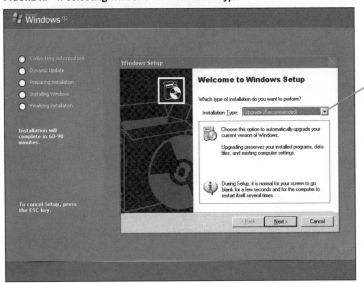

 CLUES TO USE

Understanding activation and registration

When you install Windows XP, you are prompted to activate and register the product. Product activation and product registration are not the same. Product activation is required and ensures that each Windows product is not installed on more than the limited number of computers allowed in the software's end user license agreement. Activation is completely anonymous and requires no personal identification information to complete. To complete the activation process, you enter a unique 25-character product key, usually located on the back of the Windows XP CD-ROM packaging, during the Windows XP Setup Wizard installation process or when using the Activate Windows program located

on the Start menu. You have a 30-day grace period in which to activate your Windows product installation. If the grace period expires, and you have not completed activation, all features will stop working except the product activation feature. In other words, you cannot perform any tasks on your computer, such as display the desktop, access any files on your hard disk, or send and retrieve e-mail. During the activation process, you can also register your copy of Windows XP. Product registration is not required, but completing the process, which includes providing contact information, ensures that you receive product update and support information from Microsoft.

App
Windows XP

Installing Windows XP

The Windows XP Setup Wizard guides you step-by-step through the process of installing Windows XP. When the installation is finished, you are ready to log on to Windows XP. Be aware that your computer restarts several times during the installation process. Depending on the type of installation you need to perform, either upgrade or clean, you start the Windows XP Setup Wizard in different ways. If you perform an upgrade or clean install on a Windows version, you simply start your computer and insert the Windows XP installation CD to start the Windows XP Setup Wizard. However, if you perform a clean install on a nonsupported operating system or a blank hard disk, you need to start your computer by inserting the Windows XP installation CD into the CD-ROM drive, which starts the Windows XP Setup Wizard. A clean install requires you to select additional options as you step through the wizard, but the steps are basically the same. The following procedure performs a Windows XP upgrade installation and is provided as a general guide; your installation steps might differ.

 Steps

(STOP) *If you do not wish to change your current setup, read this lesson without completing the steps. If you are in a lab, see your instructor or technical support person.*

Trouble?

If Windows doesn't automatically detect the CD, click the Start button, click Run, in the Run dialog box click Browse, navigate to the CD-ROM drive, click Setup, click Open, then click OK.

1. Start your computer, then insert the **Windows XP CD** into your CD-ROM drive
   If Windows automatically detects the Windows XP CD, the Welcome to Microsoft Windows XP setup screen opens, as shown in Figure AP-5.

2. Click **Install Windows XP**
   The next setup screen asks you to select the type of installation.

3. Click the **Installation Type list arrow**, select an installation type, then click **Next**
   The steps to upgrade are different than a new installation. In this example, you perform an upgrade. The next setup screen asks you to read and accept the **End User License Agreement** (EULA), a contract that gives you permission to use Windows XP and imposes certain restrictions, such as copying the software.

4. Click the **I accept this agreement option button**, click **Next**, enter the 25-character product key as shown in Figure AP-6, then click **Next**
   The next screen asks if you want to check system compatibility and get an upgrade report.

5. Click the **Show me hardware issues and a limited set of software issues (Recommended) option button**, click **Next** to display an upgrade report screen if issues arise, resolve any issues as directed, then click **Next** if necessary
   The next setup screen appears, asking if you want to download the updated Setup files.

Trouble?

If there is a connection problem accessing the Setup files, click the option button to skip the process to get the updated setup file, then click Next.

6. Click the **Yes, download the updated Setup files (Recommended) option button**, click **Next**; select a network type, then click **Next** if necessary

7. When the Welcome to Microsoft Windows setup screen appears, click **Next** to activate Windows, click an activation option button, then click **Next**
   When the activation process is complete, the Ready to register with Microsoft? screen appears.

8. Click a registration option button, click **Next**, then complete the registration, if necessary
   When the registration process is complete, the User Accounts screen appears, where you can enter names for those who want to share the computer and personalize each user's settings.

9. Enter other user names to share the computer, click **Next**, assign account passwords and customize each user's desktop settings, click **Next**, then click **Finish**
   The Welcome screen opens, where you can select a user account and password.

FIGURE AP-5: Welcome to Microsoft Windows XP setup screen

Click button to start the Windows XP Setup Wizard

Click buttons to perform other setup tasks; your options might differ

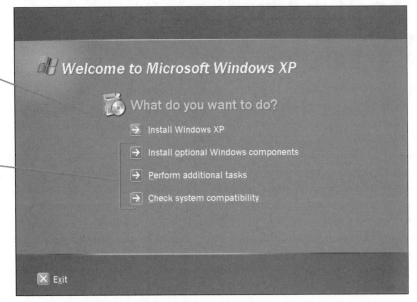

FIGURE AP-6: Product key setup screen

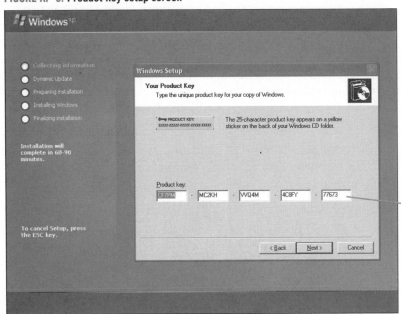

Your product key will differ

Transferring files and settings from another computer

Instead of trying to re-create Windows settings manually from an old computer on a new Windows XP computer, you can use the Files and Settings Transfer Wizard. If you are connected to a computer over a network or a direct cable connection and want to transfer files and settings from that computer to your new Windows XP computer, you can use the Files and Settings Transfer Wizard to transfer settings for Windows, such as folder and taskbar options, desktop and display properties, and Internet Explorer browser and Outlook Express mail setup options, and files or entire folders, such as My Documents and Favorites. To start the Files and Settings Transfer Wizard, click the Start button on the taskbar, point to All Programs, point to Accessories, point to System Tools, then click Files and Settings Transfer Wizard. When the wizard dialog box opens, click Next, click the option button to identify this computer as new or old, click Next, then follow the instructions for the computer type selected.

Windows XP

Setting Up a Computer for Multiple Users

Windows XP allows you to share a computer at home or at the office without sacrificing privacy or control. You can use the User Accounts feature to store personalized settings for multiple users. Each person who uses a shared computer can customize the desktop, protect computer settings, and secure files, without affecting other users. You can set up a computer for multiple users by creating user accounts for each person. There are four types of user accounts: Computer Administrator, Standard, Limited, and Guest. The Computer Administrator account allows you to change all computer settings, such as install programs, make operating system changes, and create and modify user accounts. The Standard account, available only for users of Windows XP Professional in a network environment, allows you to install and uninstall programs and change your account picture and password. The Limited account allows you to change only your account picture and password. The Guest account allows nonregular users to access one account on your computer, so you don't have to create a new account every time you have a visitor. When you create more than one user account, a Welcome screen appears when you start Windows XP where you select the user account to open. Unless you protect a user account with a password, anyone can open it from the Welcome screen. A password helps you make sure your computer files stay private and secure. Once you create multiple accounts, you can use Fast User Switching when you choose the Log Off command on the Start menu to switch between users quickly, without having to close each other's programs each time you switch.

Steps

1. Click the **Start button** on the taskbar, click **Control Panel**, click **Switch to Classic View** if necessary, then double-click the **User Accounts icon** 🖳 in the Control Panel window
   The User Accounts window opens, as shown in Figure AP-7.

QuickTip

To change options for the Welcome screen or Fast User Switching, open User Accounts in the Control Panel, click Change the way users log on or off, select the options you want, then click Apply Options.

2. Under Pick a task, click **Create a new account**, type a name for the new account on the Name the new account page, then click **Next**
   The Pick an account type page opens.

3. Click the option button for the type of account you want, then click **Create Account**
   The new account appears in the User Accounts window.

4. Click the new user account you just created
   The Change account page opens, as shown in Figure AP-8.

5. Click **Create a Password**, type a new password, press **[Tab]**, type the new password again, press **[Tab]**, type a password hint, click **Create Password**, then click the **Close button** in the User Accounts window
   The new user account with a password is setup, and the User Accounts window closes.

QuickTip

To switch between users and still maintain open programs and settings quickly, click the Start button, click Log Off, then click Switch User.

6. Click the **Start button** on the taskbar, click **Log Off**, then click the **Log Off button** in the Log Off Windows dialog box
   Windows XP logs off, saves your settings, and displays the Welcome screen with the user accounts.

7. Click the Computer Administrator user account, type the password if necessary, then click the **Go button** 🠒 to display the desktop for the administrator

8. Click the **Start button** on the taskbar, click **Control Panel**, click **Switch to Classic View** if necessary, double-click 🖳, click the new user account you just created, click **Delete the account**, click **Delete Files**, click **Delete Account**, then click the **Close button** in all the open windows

FIGURE AP-7: User Accounts window

User account help

User account tasks

Current accounts

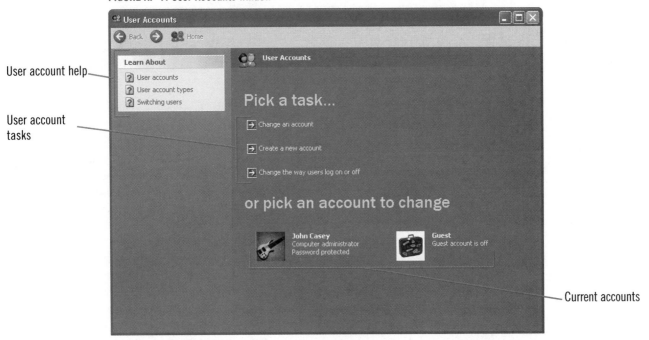

FIGURE AP-8: Changing a user account

Click button to return to the main User Accounts window

Change user account options

User account information

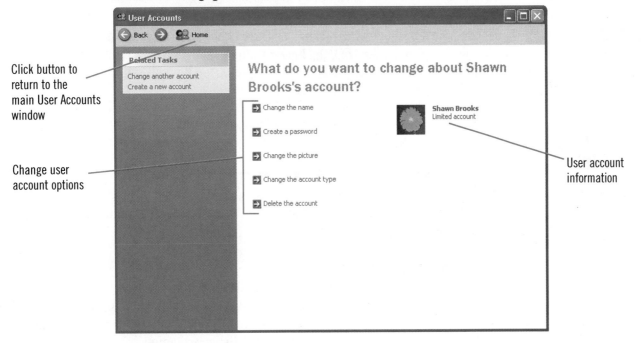

Using the guest account

The Guest account makes it easy for visitors to use a shared computer to create and print documents and graphics, check e-mail, and browse the Internet without making changes to other users' preferences and settings. The Guest account doesn't use a password and works like a Limited account. Before you can use the Guest account in Windows XP Professional, you need to activate it; the account is deactivated by default. To activate the Guest account, you need to log on as the computer administrator. In the User Accounts window, click the Guest account, then click Turn On the Guest Account. In Windows XP Home, the Guest account is active by default.

Managing Power Options on Portable Computers

You can change power options properties on your computer to reduce the power consumption of your entire system or of a specific device. For example, if you often leave your computer for a short time while working, you can set your computer to go into **standby**, a state in which your monitor and hard disks turn off after being idle for a set time. On standby, your entire computer switches to a low power state in which devices, such as the monitor and hard disks, turn off and your computer uses less power. When you bring the computer out of standby, your desktop appears exactly as you left it. Because standby does not save your desktop settings on disk, if a power failure occurs while your computer is on standby, you can lose unsaved information. If you are often away from your computer for an extended time or overnight but like to leave the computer on, you can set it to go into **hibernation**, a state in which your computer first saves everything in memory on your hard disk and then shuts down. When you restart the computer, your desktop appears exactly as you left it. Table AP-2 lists common tabs in the Power Options Properties dialog box and describes the power options each offers. This procedure modifies the power scheme for a portable or laptop computer to maximize battery life. However, you can perform these steps on any type of computer to conserve energy.

Steps

1. Click the **Start button** on the taskbar, click **Control Panel**, click **Switch to Classic View** if necessary, then double-click the **Power Options icon** in the Control Panel window
   The Power Options Properties dialog box opens with the Power Schemes tab in front, as shown in Figure AP-9. A **power scheme** is a predefined collection of power usage settings. You can choose one of the power schemes included with Windows or modify one to suit your needs. The Power Options you see vary depending on your computer's hardware configuration. The Power Options feature automatically detects what is available on your computer and shows you only the options that you can control.

2. Click the **Power schemes list arrow**, then click **Portable/Laptop**
   Settings for the Portable/Laptop power scheme appear in the bottom section.

3. Click the **Turn off monitor list arrow**, click **After 1 min**, click **Apply**, then wait one minute without moving the mouse or pressing a key
   After a minute, the screen goes on standby and the screen is blank.

4. Move the mouse to restore the desktop
   The computer comes out of standby, and your desktop appears exactly as you left it.

5. Click the **Power schemes list arrow**, click **Always On**, then click **Apply**
   The Turn off monitor and Turn off hard disks options change to reflect power settings for this scheme. The power settings change to Never, the preset option.

6. Click the **Advanced tab**
   The Advanced tab appears, displaying settings to always display the Power Options icon on the taskbar and prompt for a password when your computer resumes from standby.

7. Click the **Always show icon on the taskbar check box** to select it, then click **OK**
   The Power Options icon appears in the notification area.

8. Double-click the **Power Options icon** in the notification area (your icon might differ), then click the **Advanced tab** in the Power Options Properties dialog box

9. Click the **Always show icon on the taskbar check box** to deselect it, click **OK**, then click the **Close button** in the Control Panel window

FIGURE AP-9: Power Options Properties dialog box

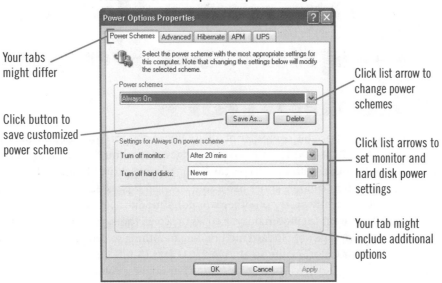

Your tabs might differ

Click button to save customized power scheme

Click list arrow to change power schemes

Click list arrows to set monitor and hard disk power settings

Your tab might include additional options

TABLE AP-2: Common Power Options Properties tabs

tab	allows you to
Power Schemes	Change power settings for your monitor and hard disks
Advanced	Change user power options
Hibernate	Turn on and off hibernation; when the Hibernation option is turned on, you can select it when you shut down your computer
APM	Turn on or turn off Advanced Power Management (APM) support to reduce overall power consumption (available on most laptop and some desktop computers)
UPS	Select and configure an Uninterruptible Power Supply (UPS) device (available depending on the specific UPS hardware installed on your computer)
Alarms	Change settings for low battery notification alarms (available on most laptop computers)
Power Meter	Display power usage details for each battery in your computer (available on most laptop computers)

CLUES TO USE

Adding a secondary monitor to a portable computer

If you have a docked or undocked portable computer or desktop computer with two video ports on one video card, you can use DualView to add a secondary monitor and expand the size of your desktop. DualView is similar to the multiple monitor feature, but you cannot select the primary display, which is always the LCD display screen on a portable computer and the monitor attached to the first video out port on a desktop computer, and you don't need to purchase and install another video adapter on your computer. To install and use the secondary monitor using DualView, turn off your computer, plug the secondary monitor according to the manufacturer's instructions into the video out port on a portable computer or the second video out port on a desktop computer, turn on your computer (Windows detects the new hardware and installs necessary software), double-click the Display icon in the Control Panel, click the Settings tab, click the secondary monitor, click the Extend my Windows desktop onto this monitor check box to select it, then click OK.

App

Windows XP

Improving the Font Display on Portable Computers

If you have a portable computer or a flat screen monitor, you can improve the font display using ClearType. **ClearType** smoothes out the edges of fonts on the screen to look the same as fonts on the printed page. With ClearType, the letter "o" looks more like an oval, while without ClearType, the same letter "o" looks more like a square. ClearType is designed for flat screen monitors, so it might look slightly blurry on other computer monitors. If you are not using a flat screen monitor and still want to smooth out the edges of screen fonts, you can use the Standard option. When you use ClearType or Standard method for smoothing screen fonts, you need to set the video card and monitor Color quality to at least 256 colors (8-bit). For better results, select a higher Color quality setting, such as High color (24-bit) or Highest color (32-bit).

Steps

1. Click the **Start button** on the taskbar, click **Control Panel**, click **Switch to Classic View** if necessary, then double-click the **Display icon** 🖫 in the Control Panel window
   The Display Properties dialog box opens.

2. Click the **Settings tab**
   Settings for screen resolution and color quality appear.

3. Click the **Color quality list arrow**, then click your highest color setting, which must be a color quality setting of at least 256 colors

4. Click the **Appearance tab**, then click **Effects**
   The Effects dialog box opens.

5. Click the **Use the following method to smooth edges of screen fonts check box** to select it
   A list box below the check box is activated.

6. Click the **list arrow** below the check box, then click **ClearType**
   The ClearType feature is selected, as shown in Figure AP-10.

7. Click **OK** to close the Effects dialog box

8. Click **OK** to apply the display property changes
   The screen fonts appear with smooth edges using ClearType, as shown in Figure AP-11.

9. Click the **Close button** in the Control Panel window
   The screen fonts appear with smooth edges using ClearType.

FIGURE AP-10: Effects dialog box with ClearType option selected

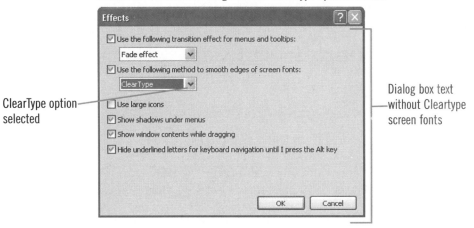

ClearType option selected

Dialog box text without Cleartype screen fonts

FIGURE AP-11: Control Panel window using ClearType screen fonts

Smooth edges on the screen font using Cleartype

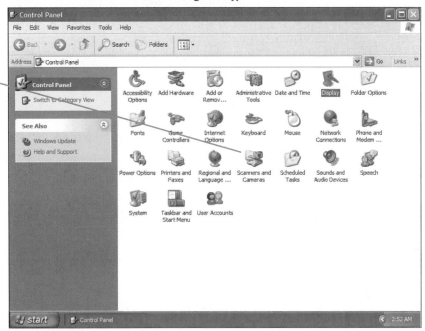

Changing Windows visual effects

Windows XP adds visual effects, such as a transition or shadow, to menus, windows, and other screen items by default to enhance the way they appear on the screen. For example, some of the visual effects include adding a transition effect, such as Fade or Scroll, when displaying menus and ScreenTips, showing shadows under menus or the mouse pointer, animating windows when minimizing and maximizing, or showing a translucent selection rectangle while you drag to select files and folders. If a visual effect doesn't appeal to you or slows your computer down, you can change or turn off the effect. You can change some visual effect options using Display Properties and others using System Properties in the Control Panel. To change

visual effects in Display Properties, double-click the Display icon in the Control Panel, click the Appearance tab, click Effects to display the Effects dialog box, select or deselect the options you want to turn on or off, then click OK twice. To change visual effects in System Properties, double-click the System icon in the Control Panel, click the Advanced tab, click Settings in the Performance area, click the Visual Effects tab, click the Custom option button, select or deselect the options you want to turn on or off, then click OK. Some visual effects options appear in both Display Properties and System Properties with slightly different names; you can change the common options in either place.

Project Files List

Read the following information carefully!!

1. **Find out from your instructor the location of the Project Files you need and the location where you will store your files.**

   - To complete many of the units in this book, you need to use Project Files. Your instructor will either provide you with a copy of the Project Files or ask you to make your own copy.

   - If you need to make a copy of the Project Files, you will need to copy a set of files from a file server, standalone computer, or the Web to the drive and location where you will be storing your Project Files.

   - Your instructor will tell you which computer, drive letter, and folders contain the files you need, and where you will store your files.

   - You can also download the files by going to www.course.com. See the inside back cover of the book for instructions to download your files.

2. **Copy and organize your Project Files.**

   ## Floppy disk users

   - If you are using floppy disks to store your Project Files, this list shows which files you'll need to copy onto your disk(s).

   - Unless noted in the Project Files list, you will need one formatted, high-density disk for each unit. For each unit you are assigned, copy the files listed in the **Project File Supplied column** onto one disk.

   - If you complete all the exercises in some units, you might need to organize the files onto more than one floppy disk. These units are indicated by an asterisk in the Project Files List.

   - Make sure you label each disk clearly with the unit name (e.g., Windows XP Unit A).

   - When working through the unit, save all your files to this disk.

   ## Users storing files in other locations

   - If you are using a zip drive, network folder, hard drive, or other storage device, use the Project Files List to organize your files.

   - Create a subfolder for each unit in the location where you are storing your files, and name it according to the unit title (e.g., Windows XP Unit A).

   - For each unit you are assigned, copy the files listed in the **Project File Supplied column** into that unit's folder.

   - Store the files you modify or create in each unit in the unit folder.

3. **Find and keep track of your Project Files and completed files.**

   - Use the **Project File Supplied column** to make sure you have the files you need before starting the unit or exercise indicated in the **Unit and Location column**.

   - Use the **Student Saves File As column** to find out the filename you use when saving your changes to a Project File provided.

   - Use the **Student Creates File column** to find out the filename you use when saving your new file for the exercise.

Unit and Location	Project File Supplied	Student Saves File As	Student Creates File
Windows XP Unit A	No Files		
Windows XP Unit B*			
Lessons	Win B-1.rtf	Coffee Menu.rtf	
	Win B-2.bmp	Wired Coffee Logo.bmp	
	Coffee Cup.mpeg		
	AM Coffee.wav		
		Coffee Meltdown.wmv	
		Coffee Meltdown.mswmm	
Skills Review	Win B-3.rtf	Choose Coffee.rtf	
	Win B-2.bmp	Wired Coffee Logo 2.bmp	
	Better Coffee.wav		
	Coffee Cup.mpeg		
		Coffee Time.wmv	
		Coffee Time.mswmm	
Independent Challenge 1			Bestsellers List.rtf
Independent Challenge 2	Invitation Map.bmp	Invitation.rtf	
Independent Challenge 3			Stationery.rtf
			Stationery Logo.bmp
Visual Workshop	Win B-2.bmp	A Cup of Coffee.bmp	Good Time Coffee Club.rtf

*Because the files created in this unit may be large, you might need to organize the files onto two floppy disks if you are using floppies and completing all the exercises. Save the files on another disk, and label each disk clearly (e.g., Windows XP Unit B Disk 1).

Unit and Location	Project File Supplied	Student Saves File As	Student Creates File
Windows XP Unit C**			
Lessons	Wired Coffee folder	Wired Coffee folder	
Skills Review			
Independent Challenge 1			World Wide Books folder
			New Store Locations.rtf
			Employee App.rtf
			Employee D Quan.rtf
			Employee L Andersen.rtf
			Employee S Luoma.rtf
			Employee W Blair.rtf
Independent Challenge 2			Apex Cartons folder
			Suppliers Bid.rtf
			Manufacturing Bids.rtf

Unit and Location	Project File Supplied	Student Saves File As	Student Creates File
Independent Challenge 3			MO PC folder
			Customer Letter.rtf
			Business Plan.rtf
			MO Logo.bmp
			Shortcut to MO Logo.bmp
Independent Challenge 4			Sunrise Bakeries folder
			French Bread.rtf
			Torte.rtf
			7-Layer Chocolate.rtf
			Sweet Bread.rtf
			Shortcut to Torte.rtf

**Because the unit uses folders that contains several levels of folders with files, only the top-level folder and new files are listed.

Windows XP Unit D**

Unit and Location	Project File Supplied	Student Saves File As	Student Creates File
Lessons	Wired Coffee folder	Wired Coffee folder	
Skills Review	Wired Coffee folder	Wired Coffee folder	Disk Info.rtf
Independent Challenge 1			Sewing Works folder
			Wilson Letter.rtf
			Suppliers.rtf
			Bills.rtf
Independent Challenge 2			Day Camp folder
			Camper Data.rtf
			Activities Overview.rtf
Independent Challenge 3			Summer Program folder
			2 Weeks Art.rtf
			4 Weeks Art.rtf
Independent Challenge 4			Lines folder
			Shapes folder
			Ovals.bmp
			Lines.bmp
			Curves.bmp
			Clip Art.zip

**Because the unit uses folders that contains several levels of folders with files, only the top-level folder and new files are listed.

Unit and Location	Project File Supplied	Student Saves File As	Student Creates File
Windows XP Unit E			
Independent Challenge 4			Company Picnic Memo.rtf
Windows XP Unit F			
Independent Challenge 1	2003 Expense Budget.rtf		
	2003 Income Projections.rtf		
Independent Challenge 3			Win Tools Training.rtf
Windows XP Unit G	No files		
Windows XP Unit H	No files		

Windows XP

Glossary

Accessories Built-in programs that come with Windows.

Activation A process that is required by Microsoft and ensures that each Windows product is not installed on more than the limited number of computers allowed in the software's end user license agreement (EULA).

Active Refers to the window you are currently using.

Active desktop The screen that appears when you first start Windows, providing access to your computer's programs and files and to the Internet.

Active program The program that is open. The title bar changes from light blue to a darker blue.

Address bar Displays the address of the current Web page or the contents of a local or network computer drive.

Address Book Used to store mailing addresses, phone numbers, e-mail addresses, or Web sites, along with contact's title, street address, phone number, and personal Web page addresses.

Antivirus software A program that examines the files stored on a disk to determine whether they are infected with a virus, then destroys or disinfects them.

Applications *See* programs.

Argument A part of the command syntax that gives DOS more information about what you want it to do.

Articles Another name for newsgroup messages.

AutoComplete A feature that suggests possible matches with previous filename entries.

Auto-hide A feature that helps you automatically hide the taskbar.

Background The primary surface on which icons and windows appear; you can customize its appearance using the Display Properties dialog box.

Back up To save files to another location in case you have computer trouble and lose files.

Bad sector A portion of a disk that cannot be used because it is flawed.

Bitmapped characters Fonts that are created with small dots organized to form a letter.

Blind carbon copy (Bcc) An e-mail option to send a copy of your e-mail message to another person whose name will not appear in the e-mail message.

Briefcase A built-in accessory that synchronizes files between two different computers.

Broadband High speed connections to the Internet that are always active (continually turned on and connected).

Buddies A list of contacts with whom you interact regularly, transfer files, and share programs and whiteboard drawings.

Buffer A temporary memory storage area that transmits streaming media to play continuously.

Bullet mark An indicator that shows that an option is enabled, in a dialog box or menu for instance. *See also* Enable.

Burn *See* Write.

Burn in When the same display remains on the screen for extended periods of time and becomes part of the screen.

Byte A unit of storage capable of holding a single character or pixel.

Cable modems Cable television lines that provide a completely digital path from one computer to another.

Carbon copy (Cc) An e-mail option to send a copy of your e-mail message.

Cascading menu A list of commands from a menu item with an arrow next to it. Pointing to the arrow displays a submenu from which you can choose additional commands.

Case sensitive When a program makes a distinction between uppercase and lowercase letters.

CD or **CD-ROM** *See* Compact Disc-Read-Only Memory.

CD-R *See* Compact Disc-Recordable.

CD-RW *See* Compact Disc-Rewritable.

Center A paragraph alignment in which the lines of text are centered between the left and right margins.

Check Disk A program that comes with Windows and helps you find and repair damaged sections of a disk.

Check mark An indicator that shows a feature is enabled, in a dialog box or menu for instance. *See also* Enable.

Classic style Refers to the Windows user interface setting where you double-click icons to open them. *See also* Windows Classic.

Clean install To perform an entirely new installation.

ClearType A feature that smoothes out the edges of fonts on portable computers or flat screen monitors to look the same as fonts on the printed page.

Clicking The act of pressing a mouse button once and releasing it.

Clipboard A temporary storage space on a hard drive that contains information that has been cut or copied.

Cluster A group of sectors on a disk.

Collection A place to store and organize media clips in Movie Maker. *See also* Windows Movie Maker.

Command A directive that provides access to a program's features.

Command-line interface An interface in which you perform operations by typing commands at a command prompt.

Command prompt The place where you type DOS commands to run different tasks.

Command syntax A strict set of rules that you must follow when entering a DOS command.

Compact Disc (CD) *See* Compact Disc-Read-Only Memory.

Compact Disc-Read-Only Memory (CD-ROM) An optical disk on which you can stamp, or burn, up to 1 GB (typical size is 650 MB) of data in only one session (where the disc cannot be erased or burned again with additional new data).

Compact Disc-Recordable (CD-R) A type of CD-ROM on which you can burn up to 1 GB of data in multiple sessions (where the disc can be burned again with additional new data, but cannot be erased).

Compact Disc-Rewritable (CD-RW) A type of CD-ROM on which you can read, write, and erase data, just like a floppy or hard disk.

Compress Storing data in a format that requires less space than usual.

Computer virus A program that attaches itself to a file, reproduces itself, and spreads to other files, usually meant to cause harm to the infected computers.

Contact A person or company with whom you communicate.

Contact groups A group of contacts that you can organize together.

Contiguous Adjacent location on a disk.

Control Panel A central location for changing Windows Settings. A window containing various programs that allow you to specify how your computer looks and performs.

Conversation thread Consists of the original message on a particular topic along with any responses that include the original message.

Cookie A file created by a Web site that stores information on your computer, such as your preferences and history when visiting that site.

Copy A command that places a copy of a selected item in the Clipboard to be pasted in another location, but the text also remains in its original place in the document.

Cut A command that removes a selected item from a file and places it on the Clipboard, usually to be pasted in another location.

Default The standard way of displaying information or performing a task in Windows.

Defragmentation A process that allows you to rewrite the files on your disk to contiguous blocks rather than in random blocks.

Delete To remove a file or folder from a disk.

Desktop The screen that appears when you first start Windows, providing access to your computer's programs and files and to the Internet.

Destination disk The disk to which you want to copy.

Dialog box A window that opens when you choose a menu command that is followed by an ellipsis (. . .); many dialog boxes have options you must choose before Windows or a program can carry out a command.

Digital Video Disc (DVD) A type of CD-ROM that holds a minimum of 4.7 GB (gigabytes), enough for a full-length movie.

Disable To turn off a feature.

Disk defragmenter A Windows accessory that restores fragmented files in one location.

Disk label A name you assign to a hard or floppy disk using the Properties dialog box.

Display adapter A hardware device that allows a computer to communicate with its monitor.

Document A file created using a word-processing program such as WordPad.

Document window The work area of the WordPad window.

Double-clicking Clicking the mouse button twice.

Drag and drop A method that allows you to move text from one location to another using the mouse and without placing the information on the Clipboard.

Dragging Moving items or text to a new location using the mouse button.

DSL lines Wires that provide a completely digital path from one computer to another.

Download The process by which you access and display a Web page from the Internet.

DualView A feature that allows you to add a secondary monitor and expand the size of your desktop.

DVD *See* Digital Video Disc.

Electronic mail A system used to send and receive messages electronically.

Ellipses In a dialog box or on a menu, indicates that you must supply more information before the program can carry out the command you selected. *See also* Dialog box.

E-mail *See* Electronic mail.

E-mail servers An Internet location where your e-mail is stored before you access it.

Enable To turn a feature on.

Enable compression A formatting option supported only on NTFS drives that specifies whether to format the drive so that folders and files on it are compressed.

End User License Agreement (EULA) A contract that gives you permission regarding your use of the Windows software on your computer and imposes certain restrictions, such as against copying the software.

Extract To uncompress a file or folder.

File An electronic collection of information that has a unique name, distinguishing it from other files.

File Allocation Table (FAT) The standard file system. *See also* NT File System.

File extension A three letter extension at the end of a filename that refers to the program Windows uses to distinguish, create, and open files of that type.

File hierarchy A logical structure for files and folders that mimics how you would organize files and folders in a filing cabinet.

File management The process of organizing and keeping track of files and folders.

First-line indent marker The top triangle on the ruler in WordPad that controls where the first line of the paragraph begins.

Folder A collection of files and/or other folders that helps you organize your disks.

Folders Explorer Bar The pane on the left side of the screen that displays all drives and folders on the computer and connected networks.

Folder template A collection of folder task links and viewing options.

Font The design of letters, numbers, and other characters. For example, Times New Roman.

Format To change the appearance of information but not the actual content.

Format bar A toolbar in WordPad that contains formatting buttons.

Fragmented file A file that is broken up and stored on different parts of a disk.

Frame A separate window within a Web page.

Full format An option that removes all files from any floppy disk (previously formatted or not), and also scans the disk for bad sectors.

Gigabyte A file size measurement equal to 1,024 megabytes.

Graphical user interface (GUI) Pronounced "gooey." An environment made up of meaningful symbols, words, and windows in which you can control the basic operation of a computer and the programs that run on it.

Hanging indent marker The bottom triangle on the ruler in WordPad that controls where second and subsequent lines of the paragraph begin.

Help and Support A book stored on your computer with additional links to the Internet, complete with a search feature, an index, and a table of contents to make finding Windows-related information easier.

Hibernation A state in which your computer first saves everything in memory on your hard disk and then shuts down.

Highlighted When an item is shaded differently indicating it is selected. *See also* Select.

Hits The results of an Internet search that, when clicked, open a Web page or category.

Home page The page that opens every time you start Internet Explorer.

HTTP (Hypertext Transfer Protocol) A type of incoming e-mail server that is used for Web sites, such as Hotmail, and allows you to send and receive e-mail messages in Outlook Express or on a Web site.

Hyperlinks (links) Highlighted text or graphics in a Web page that open other Web pages when you click them.

Icons Graphical representations of computer elements, such as files and programs.

IMAP (Internet Message Access Protocol) A type of incoming e-mail server that allows you to access multiple folders.

Insertion point A blinking vertical line that appears in the work area of the WordPad window, indicating where the next text will appear when you type.

Internet A communications system that connects computers and computer networks located around the world using telephone lines, cables, satellites and other telecommunications media.

Internet account A set of connection information provided by an Internet Service Provider (ISP) or Local Area Network (LAN) administrator that allows you to access the Internet, and send and receive e-mail.

Internet Explorer A software program that helps you access the World Wide Web.

Internet Service Provider (ISP) A company that provides Internet access.

Internet (or Web) style The Windows user interface setting where you single-click icons to open them.

ISDN lines Wires that provide a completely digital path from one computer to another.

Keyword A word or phrase you submit to a search engine to find various Web sites on the Internet. *See also* Search engine.

Kilobyte A file size measurement equal to 1,024 bytes.

Left indent marker The small square under the bottom triangle on the ruler in WordPad that allows you to move the first-line indent marker and the left indent marker simultaneously, which indents the entire paragraph at once.

Loop An option that repeatedly plays a media clip until you stop it.

Maximize A button located in the upper-right corner of the window that enlarges a window so it fills the entire screen.

Megabyte A file size measurement equal to 1,048,576 bytes, which is equal to 1,024 kilobytes.

Menu A list of available commands in a program. *See also* Menu bar.

Menu bar A bar at the top of a window that organizes commands into groups of related operations. *See also* Menu.

Message flags An icon associated with an e-mail message that helps you determine the status or priority of the message.

Minimize A button located in the upper-right corner of the window that reduces the size of a window.

Monitor A hardware device that displays the computer screen.

Mouse A hand-held input device that you roll across a flat surface (such as a desk or a mouse pad). *See also* Mouse pointer.

Mouse buttons The two buttons (right and left) on the mouse used to make selections and commands.

Mouse pointer The arrow-shaped cursor on the screen that follows the movement of the mouse. The shape changes depending on the program and the task being executed. *See also* Mouse.

Multitasking Working with more than one Windows program at the same time.

My Computer A built-in file management accessory that uses a task pane to help you organize your files and folders.

Newsgroups Online discussion groups about a particular topic, usually in an e-mail format.

News server A computer located on the Internet that stores newsgroup messages.

Notification area Located on the right side of the taskbar and used to display the time and icons for current running programs and related processes.

Notepad A Windows text editing program that comes as a built-in accessory.

NT File System (NTFS) An advanced file system that provides additional performance, security, and reliability.

Open Type font A font type based on a mathematical equation that creates letters with smooth curves and sharp corners.

Operating system A computer program that controls the basic operation of your computer and the programs you run on it. Windows XP is an example of an operating system.

Optimization The procedure to rearrange fragmented files into one location on a disk.

Outlook Express Start Page Displays tools that you can use to read e-mail, set up a newsgroup account, read newsgroup messages, compose e-mail messages, enter and edit Address Book information, and find people on the Internet.

Output The results of a DOS command.

Owner The person who can make changes to a file in a shared or network environment.

Pane Refers to a part of a window that is divided into two or more sections.

Paste A command that copies the last item placed in the Clipboard and inserts it in the document.

Personal folders A storage area designed for managing business and personal files and folders, for example, My Documents.

Pinned Refers to putting items on the Start menu, where they will be easily accessed. Pinned items remain on the Start menu until they are unpinned, or removed.

Pixel A single point on your monitor's screen. *See also,* Screen resolution.

Places bar An area on the left side of the Open and Save dialog boxes that helps navigate to common locations or recently used files and folders on your computer or network.

Point A unit of measurement (1/72nd inch) used to specify the size of text.

Pointing Positioning the mouse pointer over an icon or over any specific item on the screen.

POP3 (Post Office Protocol) A type of incoming e-mail server that allows you to access e-mail messages from a single Inbox folder.

Power scheme A predefined collection of power usage settings.

Printing A process to create a printout. *See also* Printout.

Print Preview A feature that shows the layout and formatting of a document as it would appear when printed.

Printout A paper document that you can share with others or review as a work in progress.

Program button A button on the taskbar that represents an open program, program group, or file.

Programs Task-oriented software you use to accomplish specific tasks, such as word processing, managing files on your computer, and performing calculations. Also known as applications.

Properties The characteristics of a specific element (such as the mouse, keyboard, or desktop) that you can customize.

Quick Format The fastest way to format a previously formatted floppy disk by simply removing all of the files from it.

Quick Launch toolbar A toolbar located next to the Start button on the taskbar that contains buttons to start Internet-related programs and show the desktop.

Random Access Memory (RAM) A temporary storage space whose contents are erased when you turn off the computer.

Recycle Bin A temporary storage area for deleted files that is located on your desktop.

Registration The process of providing contact information that ensures you receive product updates and support information from Microsoft. Registration is not required.

Restore Down A button located in the upper-right corner of the window that returns a window to its previous size.

Restore point An earlier time before the changes were made to your computer to which System Restore returns your computer system.

Rich Text Format A standard text format that includes formatting information and provides flexibility when working with other programs.

Right-clicking Clicking the right mouse button to open a shortcut menu that lists task-specific commands.

Scheme A predefined combination of settings that assures visual coordination of all items.

Screen font A font that consists of bitmapped characters. *See also* Bitmapped characters.

ScreenTip A description of a toolbar button that appears on your screen when you position the mouse pointer over the button.

Screen resolution The number of pixels on the entire screen, which determines the amount of information your monitor displays.

Screen saver A moving pattern that fills your screen after your computer has not been used for a specified amount of time. *See also* Burn in.

Scroll bar A bar that appears at the bottom and/or right edge of a window whose contents are not entirely visible. Each scroll bar contains a scroll box and two scroll arrows. You click the arrows or drag the box in the scroll bar in the direction you want the window to move and display.

Scroll box A box located in the vertical and horizontal scroll bars that indicates your relative position in a window. *See also* Scroll bar.

Search engine A program you access through a Web site and use to search through a collection of information found on the Internet.

Sector The smallest unit that can be accessed on a disk.

Select To clicking an item, such as an icon, indicating that you want to perform some future operation on it.

Shortcut A link that you can place in any location that gives you instant access to a particular file, folder, or program on your hard disk or on a network.

Shortcut menu A menu that you display by right-clicking an item on the desktop. *See also* Right-clicking.

Shut down The action you perform when you are finished working with Windows to make it safe to turn off your computer.

Skin The Windows Media Player's appearance.

SMTP (Simple Mail Transfer Protocol) An outgoing e-mail server that is generally used to send messages between e-mail servers.

Source disk The disk from which you want to copy.

Standby A state in which your monitor and hard disks turn off after being idle for a set time.

Start button Located on the taskbar and used to start programs, find and open files, access the Windows Help and Support Center and more.

Start menu A list of commands that allows you to start a program, open a document, change a Windows setting, find a file, or display Help and support information.

Streaming media A technique for transferring media so that it can be processed as a steady and continuous stream. The Windows Media Player delivers streaming video, live broadcasts, sound, and music playback over the Internet.

Stretch A Display properties option that displays the wallpaper picture or pattern enlarged across the desktop screen.

Subfolder A folder within a folder.

Submenu A menu that opens when you select an item with an arrow next to it from another menu. *See also* Menu.

Synchronize To update a file or Web page stored on one computer with the latest version of the same file or Web page on another computer.

System restore A program installed with Windows XP Professional used to undo harmful changes to your computer and restore its settings. *See also* Restore point.

Tabs A user interface at the top of dialog boxes that organizes options into related categories. *See also* Dialog box.

Tab stop A predefined stopping point along the document's typing line.

Taskbar Located at the bottom of the screen, and may contain the Start button, the Quick Launch toolbar, the notification area, and program buttons, for example.

Task Scheduler A tool that enables you to schedule tasks to run at a time convenient for you.

Theme A set of visual elements, such as desktop background, screen saver, mouse pointers, sounds, icons, and fonts that provide a consistent look for Windows.

Thumbnails Miniature views or large icons.

Tile To display the background picture repeatedly in rows and columns across the desktop.

Title bar Located at the top of the window and displays the name of the program and the file name.

Toggle A button or option that acts as an on/off switch.

Toolbar Used in a program to display buttons for easy access to the most commonly used commands.

TrueType font A font type based on a mathematical equation that creates letters with smooth curves and sharp corners.

Uniform Resource Locator (URL) A Web page's address.

Web address A unique address on the Internet where you can locate a Web page. *See also* URL.

Web browser A software program that you use to "browse the Web," or access and display Web pages.

Web items Elements you can place on the desktop to access or display information from the Internet.

Web pages Documents that contain highlighted words, phrases, and graphics that open other Web pages when you click them.

Web site A location on the World Wide Web that contains Web pages linked together.

Windows Rectangular frame on your screen that can contain several icons, the contents of a file, or other usable data.

Windows Classic The look and feel of the Windows 95, 98, and Windows Me desktop display. Double-clicking icons to open them is an example of a Windows Classic option. *See also* Classic style.

Windows Explorer A built-in file management accessory that uses two panes to help you organize your files and folders.

Windows Media Player A built-in accessory that allows you to play video, sound, and mixed-media files.

Windows Movie Maker A built-in accessory that allows you to create your own movies from a variety of sources.

Windows program Software designed to run on computers using the Windows operating system.

WordPad A Windows word-processing program that comes as a built-in accessory.

Word wrap A feature that automatically places text that won't fit on one line onto the next line.

World Wide Web Part of the Internet that consists of Web sites located on computers around the world connected through the Internet.

Write The process of copying files and folders to a compact disc.

Index

Index

Index

Index